PRAIRIE
PEOPLE

BOOKS BY ROBERT COLLINS

NON-FICTION

East to Cathay (1968)
A Great Way To Go (1969)
The Medes and the Persians (1972)
The Age of Innocence: 1870-1880 (1977)
A Voice from Afar (1977)
Butter down the Well (1980)
One Thing for Tomorrow (with Joyce Brack, 1981)
The Holy War of Sally Ann (1984)
The Long and the Short and the Tall (1986)
The Kitchen Table Money Plan (with Barbara McNeill, 1992)
Who He?: Reflections on a Writing Life (1993)
*You Had To Be There: An Intimate Portrait of the Generation that
Survived the Depression, Won the War,
and Re-Invented Canada* (1997)
Prairie People: A Celebration of My Homeland (2003)

FICTION

Legend of the Devil's Lode (1962)
Rory's Wildcat (1965)

PRAIRIE PEOPLE

A Celebration of My Homeland

ROBERT COLLINS

M&S

National Library of Canada Cataloguing in Publication

Collins, Robert, 1924-
Prairie people : a celebration of my homeland / Robert Collins.

ISBN 0-7710-2257-3

1. Prairie Provinces – History. 2. Prairie Provinces – Social conditions. 3. Prairie
Provinces – Biography. I. Title.

FC3237.C55 2003   971.2   C2003-902056-8
F1060.C656 2003

We acknowledge the financial support of the Government of Canada through the
Book Publishing Industry Development Program and that of the Government of
Ontario through the Ontario Media Development Corporation's Ontario Book
Initiative. We further acknowledge the support of the Canada Council for the Arts
and the Ontario Arts Council for our publishing program.

Typeset in Bembo by M&S, Toronto
Printed and bound in Canada

This book is printed on acid-free paper that is
100% recycled ancient-forest friendly (100% post-consumer recycled).

McClelland & Stewart Ltd.
The Canadian Publishers
481 University Avenue
Toronto, Ontario
M5G 2E9
www.mcclelland.com

1   2   3   4   5   07 06 05 04 03

For Sadie

CONTENTS

PREFACE

This book has been a labour of love and a mountain of labour.

It aims to describe and define the 5.1 million people of the three prairie provinces: how they live, how they feel about themselves – their loves, hopes, hates, fears, values – and how they feel about the rest of Canada. In particular, it explores and explains the prairies' century-old distrust of and disenchantment with the Centre.

Most important, it is an homage to what the University of Regina's Dr. John Conway calls "a region hard to understand" and an effort to dispel some of the fallacies and misunderstandings of the West.

"West," for my purposes, refers to the prairies only. After settling on that definition, I discovered that the eminent Calgary-born historian G.F.G. Stanley took the same tack more than thirty years ago in his essay "The Western Canadian Mystique."

"Western Canada means that region lying between the Canadian shield on the east and the Rocky Mountains on the west," wrote Stanley (who died in 2002). "More specifically the area with which I am concerned includes the great plains, that vast expanse of treeless prairie, bright sunshine and relentless wind, split by dry water courses called coulees, and drained by the Saskatchewan and Red Rivers and their tributaries, both systems emptying into Hudson Bay. . . ."

This region is my original and spiritual home. I was born and raised on a Saskatchewan farm. After the Second World War, I attended the University of Saskatchewan. Further studies and jobs took me east, but for five years I lived in Calgary and Winnipeg, patrolling all three provinces as Western editor of *Maclean's* magazine. Since then I have returned more than a hundred times to write about, or simply be in, the prairie.

Calgary writer, editor, and critic George Melnyk says "prairie" is an outdated concept. "'Prairie' is such a geographic term, such an agricultural term, such a land-based term," he told me over a brew in the Second Cup. "It's a nostalgic idea, a romantic idea. It was a real idea a hundred years ago. But who's pioneering the land now?"

He has a point, but the prairie-province concept isn't going away. The physical nature of the land remains a powerful reality. Anyone driving between Saskatoon and Regina, or Edmonton and Medicine Hat, will find no finer display of prairie (from the Old French *praerie* for "meadowland") on earth. And even as Melnyk and I spoke, a gale-force west wind was whooping through Calgary, heading unimpeded over the flatland all the way to Saskatchewan.

As in any writing on contemporary times, change is a great hazard: people dying, people moving, statistics lagging. Toronto trendies may even have stopped wearing black before this is published. If change has caught up with any of my subjects when you read this, I can only say, "This is how they were."

For this task I travelled nineteen thousand miles over two and a half years, talked or corresponded with 280 men, women, and children, browsed 142 books and studies, drew on seventy years of memories, yet have barely scratched the tip of the subject or a fraction of the population. With these caveats, I hope you will find here an honest portrait of a distinct and durable people – and will come to know them better.

INTRODUCTION

"Who *Are* Those Guys?"

To the average Eastern infidel barrelling down the Trans-Canada Highway, the prairie is a region of stupefying monotony, best seen – or better not – from thirty-seven thousand feet. How could any sane person grow attached to a landscape so flat, so bleak, so bland, so parched and frigid by turns? Northrop Frye, destined to be Canada's most eminent scholar and critic, was posted to Saskatchewan for the summer of 1934 as a United Church student minister. "I would commit suicide without the slightest hesitation if I thought I should have to stay out here all my life," he wrote home to Toronto.

Probably, the visitor speculates, this hostile habitat accounts for Westerners' quirks; why, for instance, prairie people are continually griping about the iniquitous East when surely, deep down, they envy it. Who would not want to be an Easterner, given the chance?

Perhaps, outsiders theorize, the harsh prairie environment also spawns those loopy protest parties, always at the "wrong" end of the political spectrum. Perhaps it accounts for prairie "rednecks," famed in Eastern mythology: those whisky-guzzling, tobacco-spitting, racist, homophobic loogans in tractor-driver caps, rifles slung in the cabs of their pickups. Are they the mutant product of some noxious chemical riding the everlasting wind?

It is all too puzzling. As the baffled Butch Cassidy said to the Sundance Kid when the posse kept coming and coming, so do bemused Easterners gaze over their shoulders into the Western wilderness and wonder, "Who *are* those guys?"

A Region Hard to Understand

"The west is a region that is hard to understand, full of contradictions, politically uneasy, economically vulnerable, chronically unhappy," concedes Dr. John Conway, University of Regina professor of sociology and social studies. A big man with thick white hair, Conway knows his prairie as well as anyone, having been born in Moose Jaw and, after sampling other jurisdictions – earning his Ph.D. at Simon Fraser University, turning down an Ontario job offer – settling in Regina by choice. "I think because we're on the margins of the country, we've always been more open to contemplate social, political, economic experiments."

Contradictions indeed. If the three provinces and their people defy understanding it is partly because there is no one prairie, nor single definitive prairie person. Consider, first, the geography. Less than half the region is the legendary flatland so cherished by calendar artists, CanLit novelists, and CBC producers. Even the actual plains country is a medley of buttes, coulees, and gently rolling hills, full of subtle splendour for those who care to look.

The ability to see magnificence in the minuscule is a special trait of prairie people, and in their affection for the land they reveal themselves. "There's not a more beautiful landscape in the world," says university teacher Sigrid Eyre of Saskatoon. "My relatives from England say it's so boring. How can they not see it? The sky is always changing. The green and the long vistas of yellow wheat and hay . . . I just love it! One time when we came back from Vancouver and got to Calgary I just *ran* into the fields!"

My favourite English professor at the University of Saskatchewan was Edward A. McCourt, awesomely literate but with a saving wry humour. Much as we gauche undergraduates of 1947 admired him, we thought him rather a dry stick. True, he had published a novel, *Music at the Close*. But we didn't dream that this balding old fellow (he was forty) was just entering his creative prime, that he would write innumerable critiques, articles, contributions to anthologies, and more books, including *Saskatchewan*, possibly the best non-fiction account ever about the prairie.

With a passion that we never knew was in him, McCourt described his region: "Everywhere there are things to be seen and felt that exalt or soothe the sensitive spirit: crocuses spreading a mauve mist along railway embankments before the last patch of dirty grey snow has melted; wheatfields merging into a wave-surface green or golden ocean. . . . And the occasional vista – from the top of a ridge or butte or even a grain elevator – when a man sees all the kingdoms of the earth stretched out at his feet and feels himself a creature of utter insignificance in the sum of things or else the very centre of the universe."

Ken Mitchell of Regina, an English professor, author, and playwright, echoes McCourt's devotion. In his younger years Mitchell left Moose Jaw to live in London, Toronto, Beijing, Edinburgh, Cambridge, and the Greek islands, but wandering merely whetted his appetite for home. "If I retire, I won't be going much farther than Fort Qu'Appelle. The depopulation of Saskatchewan doesn't bother me at all – just creates more space for the rest of us. I love the open nature of the landscape and the people, the culture of risk taking, and the opportunity to ride horses across the grasslands."

Perhaps the most heartfelt tribute comes from a man one might assume to be pragmatic, former Alberta premier Peter Lougheed, who has dealt in hard facts and tough issues all his adult life. When I asked how he felt about the West, I didn't expect so fervent an answer.

"I love this part of the world so much," he said. "I love it because of the friendliness of the people. I love it because there is opportunity and everybody works hard. I love it because we care about our neighbour and help our neighbour. I love it because of the beauty of it. I would not want to live anywhere else."

Would that travellers hastening through could see McCourt's or Lougheed's prairie. Would that the doubters could understand that the three provinces together cover 758,000 square miles – more area than either of Quebec or Ontario – and that any one of them is bigger than Nova Scotia, New Brunswick, and Prince Edward Island combined.

Or realize that three-fifths of Manitoba is Precambrian Shield with treeless tundra and permafrost in its northern extremities; that half of Saskatchewan and Alberta are forested; that across the top of both provinces, the Athabasca sand dunes stand up to ten feet high.

Or know that 10 per cent of this virtually landlocked region is water: countless lakes and a dozen sizable rivers. (When Art Hopfner moved with his parents from parched Saskatchewan to Ste. Rose du Lac, Manitoba, in 1935, and laid eyes on his first lake, he thought they'd reached the ocean.)

Like the land, the people are wildly disparate. They are Canada's true melting pot.

"A lot of people came here escaping other places," says James Carr, president of the Business Council of Manitoba, whose parents fled the pogroms of the Ukraine. "In my speeches I often play this game with the audience. I say, 'Where were your parents in 1867 when Canada became a nation?' And in any group of a hundred, within twenty seconds I can get between ten and twenty countries."

"Toronto 'discovered' multiculturalism in the last thirty years," adds Alberta-born Preston Manning. "It was part of the West from the beginning."

And still is. A majority of Manitobans and Saskatchewanites have German, Ukrainian, French, Austrian, Scandinavian, aboriginal, or Filipino roots. Alberta has a strong contingent of American backgrounds, as well as some German, Ukrainian, French, Dutch, Scandinavian, and Polish. StatsCan figures released in January 2003 (with so many subcategories as to defy understanding) show a latter-day surge of immigrants into Ontario. This brought forth fresh boasts of ethnic diversity, yet Ontario still has more people originating from the British Isles than have any of the prairie provinces.

A Magical Hold

Agriculture is still a sentimental prairie favourite. The land exerts a magical hold on most of us. In 1912, seven years after Alberta and Saskatchewan were born, my father homesteaded on the prairie. Long after, when the farmhouse was abandoned and rotting, I retrieved from the tattered outbuildings an old ploughshare from the horse-drawn plough he used to break the sod. I keep it on a wall to remind me of where I began.

"There *is* a sentimental attachment to the land, even in the urban prairies," Preston Manning agrees. "It is very much a part of the prairie mentality."

Yet agriculture now accounts for only 3 to 7 per cent of the provincial domestic product. Farmers, ranchers, and villagers make up only 25 per cent of the population. More than 63 per cent of Saskatchewan residents, 72 per cent of Manitobans, and 80 per cent of Albertans are urban dwellers. Another myth destroyed.

It is a literate population. Public libraries in the major prairie cities, especially Saskatoon, Regina, Calgary, and Edmonton, consistently stand high, if not at the top, on lists of Canadian library users. Ottawa-based columnist Roy MacGregor, an Easterner of exquisite good taste, wrote in a paean to the middle prairie province, "Anyone who knows this country knows that . . . people from Saskatchewan are the very last Canadians able to recite poetry from memory."

So, prairie people are nothing like their well-worn image. They're different. But watch how you say that, pardner.

"A Different Type"

In November 2000, safe in the embrace of a friendly New Brunswick audience, Jean Chrétien indulged in a bit of Alberta baiting. People of that province, he said, "they are a different type."

Albertans rose up in high dudgeon. While Chrétien and his spin doctors tried to extract his foot from his mouth, everyone from Joe Clark to Ralph Klein stomped on him. Westerners *are* different, and proud of it, but not because a Liberal prime minister says so.

Looking West, a 2001 study by the Canada West Foundation, a Calgary-based public-policy research institute, asked respondents if they thought the West was "a distinct region, different in many ways from the rest of Canada." Nearly 87 per cent of Saskatchewan folk agreed, as did 84.2 per cent of Albertans. Even Manitobans, who tend to keep a toe in Eastern Canada, went along with it by 78.4 per cent.

"There's this political gap between the West and the rest of Canada," says Regina professor Dr. John Conway. "Central Canada sees the West as curious, outlandish, and redneck. And the West sees Central Canada as unfeeling, unreasonable, deaf."

There are common denominators across the country, of course. The prairies, for all their pastoral image, have crime. A recent survey placed Saskatchewan with the highest overall crime rate per capita among the provinces (some of the territories are higher).

They gamble. Clients of thirty-five prairie casinos pour millions into provincial coffers. Anti-gambling factions are deeply concerned about the resultant human misery. A study by the Pembina Institute of Drayton Valley, Alberta, found that Albertans wagered thirteen billion dollars on gambling of all kinds in a recent year. Nearly 90 per cent of the population gambles to some extent, but 112,000 of them wager close to twenty thousand dollars each.

Prairie families are enmeshed in the Internet. Albertans (tied with British Columbians) hold first place nationally in Net usage: 65 per cent of its households (most with children under eighteen) are glued to the monitor in a given year. Prairie youth also use drugs, hold raves, and gobble junk food, and they are as verbally challenged – "Like, I mean, y'know?" – as any in Vancouver or Toronto. In Regina a young woman in a sleek red car stops beside me at a light, eyes glazed as the familiar *thump, thump, thump* of mind-numbing music hammers her skull, my skull, and skulls in the next street. Just like back in Hogtown.

Maybe, a generation hence, when today's prairie youth grow up completely blended and blanded by television, the Internet, and video games, they will be part of one homogeneous Canadian mass.

But not yet.

The Differences Within

Beyond the common denominators, Saskatchewanites and Manitobans aren't much alike, and Albertans are different again. McCourt called Manitoba only "halfway plains country . . . her heart – so many truculent true-blue westerners affirm – yearns toward Ontario." In truth, Manitoba seems to hate Ottawa a little less; in 2000 it elected twice as many federal Liberals (six) as the other two combined.

"I think, to paraphrase Wilfrid Laurier, the twenty-first century belongs to the West," Preston Manning told me. "But you have to be careful about generalizing. We're going to have to work to ensure that Manitoba and Saskatchewan don't become a kind of have-not no man's land between Alberta and the East."

There is a calm and dignity in Manitoba, perhaps from its age, perhaps from its stability. Over and over Manitobans recite the mantra "We don't have booms, but we don't have busts either." Many of my interviewees called it a "comfortable" place to live. "We're more like the turtle than the hare," says Lieutenant Governor Peter Liba.

"Maybe," sums up David Friesen, president of a nationally known printing firm in Altona, "Manitoba is like a comfortable old shoe."

Alberta moves within a bubble of ebullience and well-being. According to the United Nations Human Development Index, the average life expectancy in Alberta is seventy-nine years, third after Prince Edward Island and first-place B.C. The Albertans are tied with (curses!) Ontario. It's the best place to have a heart attack. Across Canada 19.2 per cent of stroke patients and 12.6 per cent of heart-attack patients die within a month of admission to hospital, says the Canadian Institute for Health Information. In Alberta those rates drop by almost half.

Its population, around three million, is about nine hundred thousand more than the other two provinces combined – in part because large numbers of Saskatchewanites and lesser numbers of Manitobans migrate there.

"You drive back here into Saskatchewan from Alberta," Donna Beach of Morse says wistfully, "and suddenly lights in the country are no longer visible." Once, those hundreds of pin-point lights signified farms and villages, now dwindling or gone.

Albertans, with a big assist from oil, are wealthier. "The amount of money washing around this city is almost obscene," says Calgarian Jim Gray, co-founder and former chairman of Canadian Hunter Exploration. In 1998 Alberta families earned $52,388 after taxes, about $2,500 above the national average. Saskatchewan and Manitoba families earned $43,407 and $45,373 respectively. Single Albertans took home $22,318 after tax, again higher than the national average of $21,067. Saskatchewan singles earned $19,096; Manitobans, $19,064.

Alberta householders spend on average $62,090 a year, just a few hundred less than wealthy Ontarians and several hundred above the national average. (This does not necessarily mean they are better off: each Albertan on average carries a debt load of $21,172, and the cost of servicing that debt, $2,257, exceeds each of their single household expenditures except taxes.)

Albertans pay no sales tax, so their less fortunate neighbours often drop by to load up on tax-free appliances. Saskatchewanites add ruefully that they instantly know when they cross the border driving home: their tires go *brrrmp-brrrmp* over inferior roads.

Alberta's population is Canada's youngest. Only 10.1 per cent of its people are eligible for old-age pension, compared to the national 12.5 per cent. Next door, 14.5 per cent of Saskatchewan people and 13.5 per cent of Manitobans are sixty-five or older.

Probably because of their prosperity and American influence, Albertans tend to be flamboyant and aggressive. "Alberta will take a fling on a new idea," Manning says. "Sometimes it will be disastrous. Novelty seems to cut more ice with Albertans."

Americans came to the province in three main contingents: ranchers during the 1880s, dry-land farmers, notably Mormons, around the turn of the twentieth century, and oil workers and executives in the post-Leduc boom after 1947.

"When the oil industry got going there were more Americans in Calgary than any other city outside of the United States," says Jim Gray. "This industry was almost 100 per cent Americans when it got started. Now it's not, but to this day we have as much dialogue or discourse with Denver and Houston and Dallas as we do with Toronto and Montreal, because that's the oil-gas alley."

You'd expect Albertans to be brimming with optimism, and once they were. But in "Looking West 2003," the latest Canada West Foundation survey, only 37 per cent of Albertans – compared to 57 per cent in 2001 – expect their province to be better off within five years. They are now only slightly more hopeful than Manitobans. Meanwhile, Saskatchewan optimism, while still ranking third, jumped 10 per cent in two years.

Why? Loleen Berdahl, author of "Looking West 2003," guesses that Alberta's new caution may reflect uncertainty over the economy, including fears that the Kyoto Accord, if passed, would destroy the province's economy.

At the same time, she says, "I think there is growing recognition that the Saskatchewan economy is more than just agricultural." Even so, Saskatchewan still needs a dose of self-esteem.

"We have such a negative attitude in Saskatchewan," complains Mossbank farmer Warren Jolly. "It's a have-not attitude."

"Nobody wants to be better than the other guy," adds his wife, Paula.

"If you're a successful farmer you do your best to hide that," Warren says, warming to his theme. "You do not want to look successful. You don't want to brag. A farmer here who has more than one employee is not well-thought-of in the area."

"I notice huge differences between here and Alberta," agrees Cal Johnston, Regina's police chief, back in his home province after serving as chief in Calgary. "I had this very discussion on a planning committee for the 2003 Regina anniversary. I said we really can't expect other people to think well of us or hold us in high regard if we don't first know who we are and what we stand for."

There is reason for Saskatchewan's malaise. Population is declining at an alarming rate: fifteen thousand people left the province in 2001. "The loss is calamitous, the conclusion inescapable," wrote Saskatoon *StarPhoenix* columnist Les MacPherson. "Saskatchewan is dying."

But by no means dead. Calgary writers Don Braid and Sydney Sharpe described Saskatchewan as "the gentlest and perhaps the most civilized of the western provinces." *Globe and Mail* columnist Roy MacGregor has nominated it Canada's best place to live – based on its high ratio of volunteerism, charitable giving, and community involvement.

"This province has always been more humanitarian," agrees John Conway. "We're committed to culture. The humanitarian connection, the willingness to listen to arguments about how civil society ought to be better organized, to be fairer and more just – Saskatchewan's always been more open to that."

Saskatchewan, suggests Manning, is also "the province of sober second thought." But innovative, not boring, thought: it is Canada's cradle of socialism and of medicare, and spawned two of our most charismatic politicians – Tommy Douglas and John Diefenbaker.

Yet Alberta seems to get all the breaks. Which province bears the dubious honour of dandruff capital of the world? Manitoba – or so says a Cincinnati company that researches use of shampoo (we're still scratching our heads over that).

Who are the second-fattest people in the nation (after the corpulent citizens of St. Catharines, Ontario)? Reginans, says StatsCan. And the whole province is on the chubby side: a separate study – using the body mass index, which relates weight to height – found that 59.4 per cent of Saskatchewan folks are overweight or obese, a couple of points above Manitobans and roughly 10 per cent above the national average. And wouldn't you know: smug Albertans were just a nudge above the national average (thanks to their svelte women, only 40 per cent of whom are bursting out of their slacks).

Clean scalps and trim waistlines aren't everything. Albertans smash up their cars at the highest rate in Canada. (Many parts of the world ban the use of cellphones while driving – they cause accidents – but in Alberta a bill to ban them in 2002 was shot down in the legislature. M.L.A.s called it a violation of rights.)

Albertans are also the country's third-biggest polluters (after Quebec and Ontario, the major offender). Their "ecological footprint" – the amount of land and resources needed to satisfy their lifestyles – is 10.7 hectares (26.4 acres) per person, fourth-largest in the world (after the United Arab Emirates, Singapore, and the United States). The Canadian average is 7.7 hectares per person.

The gap in after-tax income between the richest 10 per cent in Alberta and the poorest 10 per cent is third-highest in Canada. Alberta's rich, after tax, are nearly seven times better off than its poor. Albertans are also the prairies' biggest boozers. Each inhabitant on average guzzles 111.5 litres of wine, beer, and hard liquor per year – a half-litre more than Quebecers, and second only to drinkers in Yukon. Manitobans drink ten litres less than the national average of 102.6, and Saskatchewan tipplers average a mere 85.5 litres per year, mostly beer, barely enough to chase the dust.

A Potent Formula for Survival

Thirty-odd years ago, historian G.F.G. Stanley stated: "History and environment have produced a distinct species of the genus *homo sapiens* in western Canada. . . . The fundamental fact is that the Westerner is different from the easterner. He acts differently, he thinks differently, he speaks differently." Stanley also said prairie people dislike titles, honours, and distinctions, are more politically radical and more democratic in outlook.

Sociologist John Conway and Paul Antrobus, professor of psychology at the University of Regina, single out a stronger work ethic. "People here through the generations, they're not afraid to work hard, they don't apologize for working hard, they don't have an expectation that they will do otherwise than work hard," Antrobus says. "They put their shoulders down and go to work."

"All the things you have to be to have settled a place like this and stayed," Conway agrees.

"There's a much better work ethic on the prairies than in Vancouver," confirms Earl Andrusiak, vice-president of HSBC Bank in Edmonton (he has worked in six prairie cities, as well as in Vancouver). "I have no trouble motivating my staff. They don't take time off if they have a hangnail."

Unemployment doesn't necessarily imply a lack of work ethic, but, for what it's worth, as of November 2002 the average unemployment rate in Canada was 7.5 per cent. The rate in British Columbia and all provinces east of Ontario (which had a rate of 6.7 per cent) ranged from 8.5 to 18.5 per cent. The three prairie provinces were all below the average: Alberta, 5.3 per cent; Manitoba, 5.4 per cent; Saskatchewan, 5.8 per cent.

Reverend Dwight Rutherford, United Church minister, serves two parishes around Foxwarren in west-central Manitoba. Rutherford was born in Winnipeg, spent fifteen years with the federal government before entering the ministry, and has lived and travelled in East and West. "Prairie folk have a very different outlook than people in Eastern Canada," he says. "Family values are far stronger here. The land is far more valued. Money is valued in a different way. A lot of folks out here say, 'If I don't have the money I won't spend it.' In the East you just spend it anyway."

Couple work and thrift with what Edmonton author Cora Taylor calls a "fatalistic pessimism ('if we had a good summer we'll have a rotten winter')," which somehow coexists with "the pigheaded optimism of Next Year country," and you have an odd but potent prairie formula for survival. These contrary qualities have helped prairie dwellers cope with a succession of hard times since the provinces were founded: Alberta and Saskatchewan in 1905, Manitoba in 1870.

The pioneer era is still close. Nearly every prairie-born person today has, or had, a parent, grandparent, or great-grandparent who pioneered. All that misery, hardship, determination, and plodding endurance has been passed on, vivid and real, by word of mouth, not in history books. Which is why, contends Max Macdonald of Regina, former vice-president of the *Leader-Post*, the average prairie dweller is doggedly self-reliant. "We are a bunch of fixers if people will just leave us alone."

"We were settled by independent people," Paul Antrobus concludes. "You had to be independent and very durable to come out here. A farmer had to be a particular kind of person to take on God, the weather, the international market, and a whole bunch of that other stuff and say, 'I'm gonna survive.'"

Although prairie people don't, by a long shot, agree on everything, they are almost unanimous in their mistrust of the East (meaning Ontario, Quebec, and especially Ottawa) and disenchantment with the West's place in Confederation. In essence, they expect the East to shaft them, and throughout history (see Chapter XIV) the East has regularly obliged.

In Search of the Great Western Redneck

In spring 1994 a bunch of the boys were whooping it up at a meeting of the Standing Committee on Indian Affairs and Northern Development in Ottawa. Ron Irwin, then the federal minister of Indian and Northern Affairs, fired a verbal rocket at David Chatters, Reform Party member for Athabasca. As Chatters recalls, Irwin said, "We have something in common and that's the colour red. Unfortunately, it's my book [the Liberal Red Book] and your neck."

Chatters was not amused. "Redneck" is the derogatory epithet aimed at Westerners, particularly Albertans, whose views do not coincide with those of enlightened Easterners. When the term first became common currency, Albertans were insulted but soon turned the slur to their advantage. If redneck was repugnant to the East, it couldn't be all bad.

Some began sporting lapel buttons: "Redneck and Proud Of It." A Medicine Hat man created and gave away bumper stickers that went one better: "Politically incorrect redneck and proud of it." Lists of social instructions for rednecks went the rounds: "Never go to a family reunion to pick up girls"; "Always clean your ears with your own truck keys." A brewer came up with Redneck Beer. Buzzard's, a Calgary eatery, has a jocular sign on the wall: "RED NECK PARKING. VIOLATORS WILL BE BEATEN."

The Edmonton-based national newsmagazine *The Report* (which, with its homophobic and anti-abortion stances, many Easterners regarded as the rednecks' house organ) pointed out that Albertans were simply mocking those people "whose narrow views and idiotic sensibilities they despise." Saskatchewan Reform Party member Lee Morrison, in his maiden speech in the Commons in 1993, described a typical redneck as "someone who does not belong to all the right clubs and who does not subscribe to trendy social and political doctrines."

Outsiders tend to confuse redneck with Alberta's individualism. In fact, says Barry Cooper, University of Calgary political-science professor, there's more tolerance for a wide range of voices in Alberta than in Ontario. "You shouldn't talk about abortion because everybody agrees? Well, everybody doesn't agree. You think everybody agrees about gay rights? No. So why not allow those who disagree to be heard?"

Writer Pauline Gedge offers the final word: "The prairie person knows that he is often called redneck. He knows that the epithet implies a certain ignorance, even bigotry, but he wears the term with pride. He knows that he is neither ignorant nor bigoted. He is merely detached from the furore of modern thought, the flavour-of-the-day. He will wait and see what endures, what is worth saving out of the chaos of social, political and religious flux, because he belongs to the sanity of slow time and gradual change."

There's no denying that Alberta has mean-minded, racist, homophobic individuals – some with a chaw of Red Man lodged in their cheeks and a rifle in the half-ton at the curb, some like the nice-looking man in a suit next door, but the Great Western Redneck may be an endangered species.

An Alberta survey in 2000 concluded that its citizens were pretty much in step with the rest of the country in attitudes towards social policies and individual rights, albeit by a slim majority on some questions: 67 per cent of Albertans put the good of the community ahead of the good of the individual, should the two conflict; 51 per cent agreed with permitting same-sex marriages (although the Alberta government stands against it); and 76 per cent approved of human-rights legislation being expanded to prohibit discrimination based on sexual orientation.

Lisa Young, a University of Calgary assistant political-science professor, thinks the survey showed that Alberta's redneck reputation is mostly myth, perpetuated by politicians and media. Politicians and editorial writers are, she suggests, "out of touch with the electorate."

It wouldn't be the first time.

I

WHEN THE PRAIRIE
CASTS ITS SPELL

*You must not be in the prairie; but the prairie must
be in you. . . . He who tells the prairie mystery
must wear the prairie in his heart.*

WILLIAM A. QUAYLE
"The Prairie and the Sea," 1905

The Transmogrification of Julie Bidwell

In the autumn of 1966 and the springtime of their lives, Paul and Julie Bidwell of Burlington, Ontario – earthly goods crammed into their white Volkswagen Beetle and the U-Haul behind it – set off to conquer the West.

Paul – dark, sturdy, and twenty-three – was just out of Queen's University with his M.A., soon to begin teaching English at the University of Saskatchewan for a princely seventy-two hundred dollars a year. Julie, twenty-two, was a slim brunette with a pixie haircut and, on good days, a smile that would light up the stars.

This was not a good day. She had never been west of Sarnia and didn't want to be. Mischievous friends had filled her head with prairie myths and half-truths. That she would have to take her lipstick into bed on wintry nights, else it turn to an icicle by morning (untrue). That the undersides of the Beetle's tires would freeze flat overnight and go *clunk-clunk-clunk* when they drove away in the morning (sometimes true).

Even Paul had qualms. His parents had fled Saskatchewan during the Dirty Thirties. They remembered miles of nothing running off to infinity. They remembered dust storms, grass-hoppers, poverty, and endless vistas of Russian thistle. They remembered one-, two-, and three-horse towns named after parts of people or animals (Antler, Elbow, Eyebrow, Moose Jaw). "Don't go!" they warned.

But as the Bug's bulbous nose pushed into Saskatchewan, Julie brightened. A CBC radio voice spoke of an "elite swine herd." An elite swineherd? Perhaps an elegant country gentle-man tending his flock in velvet jacket with lace cuffs – a verita-ble Beau Brummell of a swine minder. Maybe Saskatchewan was not such a godforsaken, windblown, dust-caked, culture-starved backwater after all. Then it registered: the announcer was describing a herd of exceptional pigs.

Julie dozed off as they drove north towards Saskatoon in suffocating heat, waking just as Paul stopped for gas in Davidson. "Well, hon, we're here," he said, as a little joke. She looked out at a dirt road and a clutch of grain elevators and burst into tears . . .

"We Cried a Lot"

Julie Bidwell is that most precious of prairie assets: a former out-lander who would come to truly appreciate the plains. There are many like her, and for them as with those of us who are prairie-born, this place for all its warts is a lifelong passion.

But the passion comes slowly – and only after learning to live with the warts.

"We cried a lot," Hedi Gossweiler says matter-of-factly, describing her first year in Saskatchewan. We are leaning on the counter at Hedi and husband Max's Lone Eagle Motel and Campground in Herbert, Saskatchewan. Their early years in Canada were an ordeal.

Max came to this country from Switzerland in 1968, and again in 1975, working on an Ontario dairy farm and dreaming of having his own place. He brought Hedi for a two-week honeymoon in 1980. She loved Canada too. A year later they immigrated, pursuing an advertisement from a Swiss investor who needed a tenant for a Saskatchewan farm. The dream turned to dust.

Their arrival in May was "really shocking." They had left behind lush Swiss meadows, spring flowers, forests, mountains. Saskatchewan "looked so plain and flat," Hedi remembers. "Just dirt, bare-naked fields; it was just before seeding." The wind always blew. "We had to make sure our mouths were closed or they were filled with flying dirt. We felt like turning around to go home, but we had an agreement, plus our pride."

The agreement took them to a dirty, badly insulated farm-house near Estlin. They had no car. They spoke little English. The telephone party line was a mystery: they answered at every ring until a neighbour explained the different rings that identified each subscriber. But it *was* kind-hearted Saskatchewan, so neighbour Marnie McQuoid welcomed them with a home-made cake, took Hedi shopping, and signed her up for pottery classes. Neighbour Roy Black sent his German-speaking wife to chat with them. Neighbour Betty Jefferson helped Max fill out income-tax forms. Hedi joined the Estlin choir and sang in English (rarely understanding the words).

The deal with the Swiss entrepreneur turned sour; Max ended up getting half the wage he expected. They looked for their own farm. It was the wrong time: 1983 land prices were too high for their savings. They'd just had their first child and the motel business seemed a decent environment for a family. They bought the Lone Eagle in 1983.

Why choose Herbert, population about eight hundred? Because the motel was close to the Trans-Canada Highway, and because the adjacent campground would fulfill Max's love of outdoor work. The town was named after Sir Michael Herbert, a British diplomat who had never set foot there. At times Max and Hedi wished they hadn't either.

"There was always train noise and a cliquey small-town atmosphere," she says. Six churches invited them to join their congregations. They declined. "By our not joining any churches a lot of local people started turning against us with gossip. They hurt us and the [four] children a lot over the years, but we learned to cope."

Their private religion helped. "Back home we only went to church for funerals and weddings," Hedi says. "It just didn't mean much to us." In Herbert they began listening to radio sermons, and started reading and studying the Bible. "That was when our life and focus started to change. Through the born-again experience we have peace in our hearts. Now we don't start a day before we read the Bible. It is truly our daily bread."

Even so, still longing for mountains, although having come to love "the big, blue, sunny sky, the impressive sunsets, and the open space," they planned to sell after a few years. The right offer never came. Max still had the farming bug, so in 1989 they bought land south of Regina. After ten years of operating farm and motel, the constant work and travel wore them down. They sold the land.

Now they raise alpacas, and that unquenchable prairie optimism seems to have seeped into their pores. Amid an unseasonable snow last April, Hedi e-mailed me, "The only plus with a snowstorm is we usually rent out our rooms in no time. Everybody is thankful for not being stranded on the side of the road!"

Not for the Faint-Hearted

Alberta author Pauline Gedge moved to Western Canada from England in 1959, when her father took up the Anglican parish in Virden, Manitoba. She was fourteen, fresh from the Cheney Grammar School for Girls in Oxford, and was "simply appalled" by everything around her: the harsh landscape, the fierce climate, and the Canadian standard of education.

"There was a class called Health, where we were taught the importance of brushing our teeth correctly," she recalls. "I'm not joking!" (Of course she isn't; I took the same course in school a generation before her.)

Gedge remembers being "a dreadful little snob," who thought Western men were too loud and the women too brassy. It took her ten years (during which time the family moved to Alberta) "to succumb to the curious allure of the prairies."

Now, from the small town of Edgerton, where she lives and writes hugely successful novels [see pages 213-15], Gedge is an ardent prairie advocate. Her literary flair helps express, eloquently, what many others may feel but cannot articulate.

"I have grown to love the prairies, or rather, the prairies have gradually insinuated themselves into my soul," she says. "The reasons seem trite, almost cliché, but behind each one is something profound. There's space here. The horizon is vast. The eye can travel unhindered. There is the utter silence of midwinter. There is a constant sense of timelessness, of the land itself being permanent and everything on it being ephemeral, which can frighten or strengthen the individual fortunate enough to experience it."

During her forty-four years in the West, thirty of them in Alberta, she has travelled much of the world. But after every foray abroad or elsewhere in Canada, she comes home "with a sense of great relief." She refers not merely to landscape but to the landscape's inhabitants, and the synergy between them.

"Prairie people differ from other Canadians, not because they were born and raised here but because the prairies draw a certain brand of human being," Gedge says. "They do not provide a home for the faint-hearted. They are not soft and sweet. But they offer the one thing that is the sum of space and silence, and that is freedom."

Many people have come to the Edgerton area from other parts of Canada or beyond, seeking that elusive peace and freedom, she says. "Prairie people prize their freedom. They are freethinkers in the correct sense of the phrase. No matter how far the government's tentacles reach, and these days they attempt to snake into every area of our lives, they come up against the prairie lover's obstinate refusal to surrender his mental freedom. He is suspicious of cant. He distrusts fads."

Waiting for the Tulips

And what of the Bidwells of Saskatoon? How did they fare in this multi-faceted, misunderstood, often-endearing, sometimes-perverse corner of Canada?

Saskatoon, when they got there, was an improvement on Davidson: trees, river, university with handsome greystone buildings, paved streets, people in suits.

Julie, who had a B.Sc. in nursing, landed a part-time job as an instructor in Saskatchewan's first two-year diploma nursing program. It grew into full-time.

"I can stick it out for a couple of years," she told Paul after a while. "Then I want to go back east."

After a three-year break in England, where Paul did graduate work at the University of Kent, it was back to the lone prairie, Julie kicking and screaming all the way. When they went for country drives she wanted to start out after dark so she wouldn't have to face the country. "That big sun up there like an intrusive eye really threatened me. The only place to picnic was in the shade of a building."

But after a few more years, she conceded, "Okay, I can live here but I'm not going to grow old here." They raised a son and daughter. Julie and three friends started a nursing agency that ran for sixteen years. The Bidwells took up canoeing and camping in northern Saskatchewan's idyllic Churchill River system, "learning that you can be gorgeously hot without being damp and exhausted the way you are in Ontario humidity" and "feeling like the only humans alive, on the still surface of Otter Lake early in the morning."

Finally she admitted, "Okay, I can see myself growing old here but I won't be buried here."

Now, at last, she *can* imagine going to her rest beside the South Saskatchewan or Churchill River.

Paul has become head of the English department at the University of Saskatchewan. Registered nurse Julie is with the rural health extension program, University of Saskatchewan Centre for Agricultural Medicine.

"In 1995, Paul and I bought property near Comox on Vancouver Island for our retirement," Julie says. "Now I've come to the strange pass of thinking, We'll have to sell our Saskatoon house to build there, but we'll buy a cottage in northern Saskatchewan we can come back to. Well, maybe we won't sell the house in case we want to come back permanently.

"Come to think of it, if our kids settle in Saskatchewan, maybe we just won't leave. I wonder how those new tulips will do next spring?"

Why the about-face? Julie becomes almost lyrical in the telling: "Just gradually learning to see beauty in ways I'd never realized it could exist. The eerie image of sun dogs on either side of a pale sun on a minus-forty Celsius day in January. The astonishing inversion of light and dark on a fall day when the sky is dark blue and all the light seems to come from the fields' white-gold stubble.

"I'm actually embarrassed it took me so long to love this place."

II

HOW NATURE SHAPES THEM

There is no Spring
although the satin crocus
shows purple on the faded prairie sod
unless you feel a tenderness within you
and know the miracles you see are God.

VESTA PICKEL
"Under the Prairie Sky"

An Obsession with Weather

Each fall, Fifth House Publishers in Calgary gears up with a song in its heart for its perennial best-seller. Not a book, a calendar. And not just any calendar with photos of grain elevators or children with white kittens. It is David Phillips's famous Canadian Weather Trivia Calendar, laden with facts, trivial or otherwise, about everybody's favourite subject. Fifth House sells about twenty-five thousand copies a year. A couple of autumns ago it sold out by October; they reprinted and sold out again in November.

Phillips, a senior climatologist with the federal Atmospheric Environment Service, started the calendar, which in 2003 was in its sixteenth year. Every season, two months before his promotion tour, the media begin clamouring for interviews (most authors would mortgage their mothers for such attention). He's an especially hot property in Saskatchewan, where weather groupies swarm the open-line shows, or wait outside TV or radio stations to touch the hem of his garment and tell him their favourite weather stories.

Everybody talks about the weather, but prairie people are obsessed. It totally governs their lives and economies. It helps make them what they are: adaptable, pragmatic, comfortable with solitude, hoping for the best but expecting the worst.

My interview subjects, when asked what they like about the prairie, often said, "We have four seasons." Well, doesn't everyone? Finally it dawned on me: they revel in the *change*, from fierce winter into gentle spring, from fiery summer into melancholy autumn, with all the accompanying joy and misery.

"Winter and summer and all points between, the prairies have some of the most changeable and exotic weather in the world," writes Saskatoon climatologist Elaine Wheaton in her lively book *But It's a Dry Cold!: Weathering the Canadian Prairies.* "We're captivated by it. We're sometimes *held captive* by it too. . . . We cannot ignore the weather. It entertains us. It humbles us. It can destroy our life's work, or make us rich."

It also sets them apart from sissies in softer climes. The prairie denizen, wrote Edward A. McCourt in *Saskatchewan*, is "toughened by climate, inside and out, to the texture of old cowhide. He is proud of his strength, confident of his cunning, and drunk on air all the year round."

"Winters give us our red badge of courage," says Brandon judge Rodney Mykle. "And it gives us something to tell the Americans in the summer when they come up. And, of course, exaggerate."

Naturally, prairie folks claim they are tougher than most others because they've suffered so much. "Scorched by sun and battered by wind three months of the year and confined to a deep freeze for six, the prairie dweller is soon afflicted by a kind of nervous irritability which impels him to flail out in all directions," McCourt continued. Such a person, he said, has "proved himself a man fit to whip his weight in wildcats."

"We're a bit like the ancient Spartans," says a Regina friend. "They used to put their kids out on the side of a hill. Only the strong survived."

At its best, prairie weather – and its supporting players: sky, earth, sun, stars – is a sensual pleasure. "Violets blooming in the pasture; skating on the creek in late February by moonlight with a bonfire on the bank; howling coyotes silhouetted against the setting sun. . . ." Those passionate words are from four elderly sisters – Ollie, Tillie, Marie, and Louise Muller (teachers, nurse, stenographer in their working years, not a poet among them) – in a 1990 history of my home community.

"I love how those green seedlings peek through the black soil," says Jocelyn Hainsworth of Redvers, Saskatchewan, farmer and occasional broadcaster. "For a day or two you can only see them at sunrise and sunset when the light is just right, but the colours are *so* green and *so* black. I know where the wild strawberries grow. Bullfrogs croaking their spring love songs I consider a lullaby."

"There's nothing like the spring of the year, the smell of the earth," farmer Wayne Willner of Davidson, Saskatchewan, says almost reverently.

Kelly Bonesky Green, who divides her time between a job in Winnipeg and the family farm in Morse, Saskatchewan, recalls a particularly magical winter night: "I went out to check the calves and the northern lights were dancing. It was like being in a domed stadium, with white lights scooting all over from horizon to horizon."

Prairie farmers "can't walk from the farmhouse to the barn without seeing a million stars," says Paul Antrobus, psychology professor at the University of Regina. Cities, even small ones, wash out this celestial wonder with artificial lighting, so Antrobus is urging city fathers to douse street lights for a designated hour each month "to afford people a possible return to infinity."

Steve Bown, a young writer in Canmore, Alberta, well remembers a mystical moment during a drive to Ontario years ago with some university buddies. "The way these things are always organized, we decided to leave at eleven at night. We drove and drove all night, and somewhere in Saskatchewan we could see the horizon, this orange glow. We were heading directly into it. Finally this orb burst over the crest of the earth, this giant huge orb, all fuzzy from being distorted on the distance of the horizon, and slowly rose in the sky. It was the most glorious thing!"

Even when the weather is bad, which is often, prairie people are surprisingly cheerful. Or at least pleased with their ability to endure anything nature doles out. They routinely come through the extremes, and with each telling and retelling, says Elaine Wheaton, "the hot spells become hotter, the cold spells longer, and the storms more magnificent."

The Depression-era drought of the 1930s – so often recounted that younger Canadians run screaming into the streets at yet another tale of dust and despair – remains vivid to us few remaining alumni. Today, we're better equipped to cope with the vagaries of the climate, but prairie people still cherish their weather records (and for many cited here I'm indebted to the indefatigable David Phillips). Where, you ask, did the biggest hailstone in this nation fall? In Cedoux, Saskatchewan, of course, when a 290-gram chunk of ice and snow (more than half a pound) crashed to earth in 1933. Fortunately, neither man nor beast was under it.

Year in, year out, Parliament Hill generates the greatest volume of hot air, but Midale and Yellow Grass, Saskatchewan, on July 5, 1937, set a record high for Canada with 45°C. (My hometown, about ninety-three miles from Midale, must have neared that record, but I only remember the adults saying, "Hot enough for yuh?") St. Albans, Manitoba, came close to the record with 44.4°C during Canada's worst heat wave, in July 1936. A hot day, as defined by climatologists, is when the maximum temperature hits 30°C or higher. In an average year there are ten to twenty of these in the southern prairies. Anything less is a mild annoyance.

Heat means sun, and the prairies have sunshine records to burn. Greatest average annual number of sunny hours: Estevan, Saskatchewan, with 2,500. Major city with greatest annual average number of sunny hours: Calgary, 2,395. Greatest annual average number of sunny days: Vauxhall, Alberta, with 330 (Calgary and Lethbridge place second with 326). Sunniest year on record: Manyberries, Alberta, with 2,785 hours in 1976. Greatest number of sunny days in one year: Medicine Hat in 1976 with 346. (Think of it – only twenty days *without* that sun glaring down.)

"Without a doubt," writes David Phillips, "the prairies are the sunniest region in Canada and the province with the most sunshine is Saskatchewan."

The prairies set no rainfall records – but just ask them about drought. The records for longest dry spells in Canada belong to

Medicine Hat (271 days) and Lethbridge (265 days). Overall, of the ten driest cities in Canada (meaning most days without measurable precipitation) compiled by David Phillips, eight are in the prairie provinces.

Weather is, as Wheaton says, both life and entertainment. A Calgary man on a business trip to Washington State was expecting his wife to join him. She was overdue. Worried, he phoned her father, a Saskatchewan farmer.

"Oh, she'll turn up," the farmer said casually. "How's the weather out there?" The son-in-law began to tell him. "Oh, got to go," the farmer cried before hanging up. "The weather's coming on TV."

"Mum, There's No Sky Here!"

Old joke: British Columbian says to Saskatchewan tourist, "How do you like our mountains? Spectacular, huh?"

"They're all right," the prairie guy says grudgingly, "but they sure get in the way of the view."

People out on the prairie cherish the view, meaning un-cluttered sky. Novelist Cora Taylor's son Sean moved from Edmonton to Toronto at age seventeen. It was not a happy choice. At first he lived under a picnic table in downtown Queen's Park. One night another homeless person was stabbed a few dozen feet from where Sean slumbered. Another night he slept, unaware until too late, on an anthill. "I managed to scrounge just enough money the next day to wash all my clothes and buy a cup of coffee."

He landed a job in a hosiery factory and found a basement flat "with a lovely view of the hookers practising their trade in the parking lot outside my kitchen window."

But worst of all he couldn't see the sky – except by looking straight up among skyscrapers at high noon. He took the subway to its western limits, rode buses farther still, ended up near

Pearson Airport trying to find uncluttered sky. "By the time I arrived the sun was setting."

He wrote home, "Mum, there's no sky here!" After six months Cora sent him a plane ticket and he moved back west.

His devotion to sky is probably genetic. Taylor, who often winters in the south, tells of driving north each April to "a wonderful expansion of spirits that I feel as I drive through Montana and hit Alberta. They [Montana] may call themselves Big Sky Country, but it's bigger in Alberta and Saskatchewan and it's food for my soul."

Prairie skies are close enough to touch, even in the cities. Saskatchewan's licence plates proclaim it "Land of Living Skies." From the upper floor of a Regina or Winnipeg hotel you can still see far into the distance, with spectacular sunsets or storms advancing. Which is why the first thing prairie people think about, in terms of their physical geography, is space.

To anyone living long in a city but remembering the prairie, its space is precious, a place for quiet contemplation, a chance for communion with the natural world. "The sense one has of prairie spaces is not of being crushed into insignificance in the face of the vastness but of being part of something huge and wonderful," says Taylor.

Such is my affection for the Alberta badlands, a two-hundred-mile stretch of steep lonely hills called buttes and hoodoos, weird pillars of hard-packed sandstone standing straight as sentinels beneath their rakish flat-stone hats. Sunset paints the rusty brown buttes orange and gold, and casts long eerie shadows from the hoodoos. Sitting high in this graveyard of the dinosaurs, taking care not to settle on a prickly-pear cactus, your imagination drifts back seventy-six million years to when parts of the badlands were born.

A drive through open plains southwest of Moose Jaw is equally exhilarating. The pastures and gentle hills sweep off to infinity under the bowl of sky. Your lungs and spirits expand.

This – without today's fragments of civilization, the huge cylindrical rolls of hay, the occasional faraway dot of a farmhouse – is
what the earliest pioneers saw. Were they frightened, lonely,
overwhelmed by the immensity? Or were they, too, the kind of
people who revelled in space?

Prairie sky is a cliché to outsiders and a permanent crutch
for beginners in CanLit. Yet there is no denying its power:
looming, embracing, dominating lives and moods and spirits. It
is a constant spectacle: sometimes soft cerulean mottled with
fluffy white clouds; sometimes sullen grey; sometimes a black
menace loaded with thunder, lightning, hail, blizzard. But rarely
boring, and sorely missed by its devotees, if they are forced to
visit blander climes.

"You come out of the bush driving back here from
Ontario," enthuses Bob Juby, a retired Mountie in Winnipeg,
"and hit the prairies and all of a sudden the whole sky just opens
up. It feels so good."

Jean Reinhardt of Courtenay, British Columbia, returns to
her former Saskatchewan farm home for almost half of every
year to watch for flocks of Canada geese feeding on stubble or
"the steady advance of a storm as black clouds build overhead."

A few years ago Marilyn Krislock Pomeroy moved with her
husband from Central Butte, Saskatchewan, to Aberystwyth,
Wales – a university city of fourteen thousand on the Irish Sea.
What could be more idyllic? Yet for Pomeroy something was
lacking. "The big sky, the flatness of the prairie, the open space,"
she told me on a visit back home. "Also the flat, straight roads.
Driving in Wales is always an adventure. Narrow roads, no shoulders. We were passing a car and got so close our mirrors clicked.
After a two-hour drive there you're practically in therapy.

"But mostly the space and the sky. I didn't think I would
miss it as much as I do. You can't explain that to people who have
never been here."

Wrestling With the Natural World

Prairie people, especially in rural areas, are ambivalent about creatures, wild or tame. Animals are livelihood, although some are pets. Every spring, ranchers castrate hundreds of calves – snip off their testicles and brand them with a sizzle of red-hot iron to hide. It has to hurt, but just for voicing that outlandish thought I will be banned for life from the Ranchmen's Club.

Farmers routinely shoot predators that threaten their livestock and, like hunters everywhere, also kill for sport. (No surprise that gun control hasn't won prairie hearts and minds.) Sometimes the line between sport and necessity is invisible. A Melville man, having heard that Kentville, Nova Scotia, had thousands of bothersome crows, told me cheerfully, "We don't have them here because we shoot the buggers. Blow them away!"

After farmers complained that gophers were eating them out of house and harvest, the Saskatoon Wildlife Federation in 2002 established a province-wide gopher derby. When the shooting, strangling, trapping, and drowning was done, 211 hunters turned in 63,610 tails. The winners were fêted at a chili and salad dinner.

Animal-rights activists called the contest barbaric. A Canadian Humane Society spokesperson said it sent a wrong message to children. An Alberta biologist told a wildlife conference, "We need to have people see hunters as leaders in conservation, caring for the land and the wildlife – not as rednecks . . . trying to rationalize and defend questionable practices." He suggested setting up nesting platforms for hawks to control gophers naturally. No matter: another derby was planned for 2003.

At the Calgary Stampede professional cowboys spur bucking broncos in eight-second rides for glory, bring roped calves tumbling to the ground, and send horse-drawn chuckwagons pell-mell around a circuit.

"Frankly, at the CHS we don't know how to feel during Stampede," says a Calgary Humane Society spokesperson. "It's fun to participate in the festivities. But when it comes to the rodeo and chuckwagon races, it's serious business for us."

Animals are regularly injured and sometimes must be euthanized. Stampede supporters say animals are tough, the cowboys care about them, and it's all just fun. The CHS knows that others more sensitive to the horses, bulls, and calves see only "pain, suffering, human arrogance."

The CHS monitors rodeo and chuckwagon events under the Animal Protection Act of Alberta, trying to ensure that "no person shall cause or permit an animal of which he is the owner, or the person ordinarily in charge of, to be or to continue to be in distress." The law recognizes only actual physical injuries as "distress."

The number of deaths and serious injuries has declined since eleven horses died in a chuckwagon race in 1986, largely due to stiffer rules and penalties and improved practices. Example: the twisting of calves' tails in the chutes is no longer permitted, nor is ear biting in the wild-horse race. But six animals died in 2002.

Amid this generally robust attitude towards other species – some of which, granted, are pests – there are exceptions: the many prairie people who exult in their natural world.

THE PIED PIPERS OF KLEIN COUNTRY

If you ever doubted Alberta's perfection, dwell on this: it has no rats. Well, none apart from (illegal) cuddly pets or laboratory helpers. Or an occasional stray from Saskatchewan, as good as dead the moment it tiptoes over the boundary.

*It is no accident. When rats were first sighted in 1950 in the village of Alsask (just a rodent's whisker across the border in that neighbouring province), Alberta set out with grim resolve to stop every Norway rat (*Rattus norvegicus, *if you care) that dared cross the line.*

Norway rats first reached the prairies from the United States and they're no laughing matter. Their tunnelling undermines the foundations of buildings. They gnaw through floors, walls, and insulation, eat large quantities of food and contaminate what they don't eat. Norway rats carried the flea that spread plague throughout Europe and Asia. Today they pass on organisms that cause food poisoning, hepatitis, and tularemia.

Manitoba and Saskatchewan grapple with them in varying ways and with moderate success, but nothing like Alberta's take-charge attitude.

"People here don't talk about doing something, they just do it," an Edmonton friend tells me (not specifically referring to rats, but you get the idea).

Early on, Alberta set up the RCZ (for Rat Control Zone) along its eastern border. It is 379 miles long and 18 miles wide. The province spends about $250,000 a year holding the pests at bay with a sophisticated array of poisons.

Geography and weather are on Alberta's side. The Rocky Mountains to the west, boreal mixed-wood forest in the north, and a great swatch of open, relatively unsettled short-grass prairie to the south (sometimes known as Montana) discourages the Norways. So does the climate. Unless a rat can find shelter (indoors or in a cozy haystack) from howling winds and numbing temperatures, it would just as soon stay in Ottawa.

Contrary to jeering reports from the East, Alberta does not have posses of gunmen guarding its borders, but at one time had some twenty-five municipal Pest Control Officers on rat control within the RCZ. Ordinary citizens are now encouraged to report sightings – ratting on the rats, as it were – or can even pull a gun on a Norway if they see one.

Trouble is – and this is embarrassing – Alberta is so rat-free that most folks don't know one when they see it. As the government Web site says, "most Albertans cannot identify rats or rat sign." Up to two hundred false sightings come in per year (they usually turn out to be gophers, muskrats, or voles).

With Ralph Klein country virtually rat-free, you'd think the campaign would die out. Not so.

"Personnel involved in rat control," the Web site warns, "must continually guard against complacency."

"I saw nineteen goldfinches at our feeder today – nineteen little shards of sunshine," says Michael Blanar, who was living in Elgin, Manitoba, at the time. "When I'm out driving, I carry a bird book and a wildflower book. There's always something interesting if you look."

Charlene Dobmeier, who lives near Calgary's Fish Creek Park, says her husband sometimes has to chase deer off their deck when the clatter of hooves wakes him up; he never considers "blowing them away." "I'll be lying in bed at night, and through one window hear distant traffic from the Macleod Trail and through the other hear coyotes howling," Charlene adds. "That's quintessential Alberta."

"Growing up in our area is a special thing," says Jennifer Strilchuk, the twenty-four-year-old schoolteacher daughter of a big farm family at Round Hill, Alberta. "Very few people of my age know most of the names of the wildflowers and where to find them at what time of year. Dad used to pick bull thistles for Mom."

The Boneskys of Morse, Saskatchewan, likewise find genuine pleasure in the wildlife around them. They routinely see moose, families of badgers, an occasional eagle. "This winter I went out to check the cows, shone the flashlight around. All of a sudden I see yellow eyes," Larry Bonesky says. "Coyote. As I got closer I shone the light right on him and I walked up and walked up. Finally I got so close I could have hit that coyote over the head with the flashlight." He didn't, because "it's kind of interesting to work with nature."

Karen, his wife and partner, doesn't prune their caragana hedge because, unkempt, it shelters prairie chicken and grouse. "And every spring a pair of geese flies to the roof of the barn. They are like messengers of spring for us."

Saving Birds and Chestnuts

A few years ago Laurence Beckie's wife gave him a plaque: "For Fifty Years of Loving and Observing Nature." He'd earned it. In 1943, when he was twelve, his grade-school teacher encouraged her students to keep spring migration records. Beckie, tall and mild-mannered with a kind, bespectacled face, has been at it ever since. Every June for seventeen years he has done the local survey for the Canadian Wildlife Service on numbers and distribution of breeding birds.

He starts out from his home near Bladworth, Saskatchewan, on a fifty-stop, twenty-five-mile route a half-hour before sunrise. At each stop he pauses for three minutes and records every bird he hears and sees. He spots around 120 species every spring and has seen 230 in his lifetime. But like so much else in the rural prairies, sad change is everywhere.

"A Baltimore oriole is a rarity now," he says. "Loggerhead shrikes and Swainson's hawks are depleted. The loggerheads eat grasshoppers and the pesticide gets them. The hawks were poisoned by farm pesticides in Argentina. We used to have one or two pairs of burrowing owls." Pesticides got them too.

Beckie does what he can to protect and welcome the remaining species. His property is strung with birdhouses, including one towering beside his farmhouse. Its regular tenants are sparrows, but his thirty other homemade birdhouses along the roadsides attract bluebirds and swallows.

"I'm lucky if I get bluebirds in three of them," says Beckie, adding a bird man's bit of exotica. "The bluebird is such a neat housekeeper while the tree swallow is a real pig. They don't take their feces out."

Their mothers should have taught them better.

He may have been the only man in Christendom to have a kind word for the lowly pigeon. Most city dwellers regard pigeons as dirty disease carriers, but to Ted Tatarynovich of Crooked River, Saskatchewan, they were God's gentle creatures. Ted, an immigrant from Byelorussia, who had nursed injured creatures since childhood, bought his first pair in 1934. From then until he died in 2001, at age ninety-eight, his flock grew to five hundred of all kinds. He kept them in assorted ramshackle buildings around his farm, fed and watered them daily, petted them, admired their many colours, talked to them, sometimes even fed their young from his mouth. He was always fetching home surplus or spoiled grain, such as the spill around elevators.

When Ted was in hospital, his son Mike back home noticed the birds were strangely subdued. "We really believe they could sense something was wrong." At Ted's funeral the family took a cage with four pigeons to the cemetery and released them during the graveside service. One stopped, walked around the grave, looked in, and flew home.

Mike still has about forty of the birds, in memory of his dad. The place wouldn't be the same without them.

The glorious horse chestnut, 115 feet tall, has stood in what is now downtown Edmonton for eighty-three years. Each spring its eight-inch clusters of blossoms burst out "like an explosion of white fireworks." Those evocative words come from Earl Andrusiak, vice-president of the city's main branch of the HSBC Bank. Andrusiak has tender feelings for the old tree, which grows outside his office. He saved its life.

Pioneer Sam Holowach brought it as a chestnut from Prague and planted it in his backyard in 1920. The tree and the old house remained long after the city grew up around them.

"I'd grown fond of it," Andrusiak says. He's originally from a Manitoba farm, and a tree lover, even though raised on "a quarter section of rock." The chestnut was directly in his line of vision as he drove out of the bank's underground parking lot each evening. "A beautiful sight at the end of a stressful day."

When Holowach died his heirs sold to a realtor. In 1998 the realtor came to HSBC for a loan to build a parking lot.

"On two conditions," Andrusiak said. "I want half the parking spaces [for bank clients]. And the tree stays." Quicker than he dared hope, the realtor agreed. Then a city arborist told them the chestnut tree was ailing. The realtor had paved too close to its base. It needed pruning, watering, and feeding.

The bank, meaning Andrusiak, organized a barbecue in the parking lot one August day. They hired a band. Donors provided burgers and soft drinks. "Go Nuts! Join Us for Lunch and Help Save Alberta's Largest Horse Chestnut Tree," the bank's flyers cried. Crowds came and donated thirty-five hundred dollars; HSBC matched it. The seven thousand dollars went into a trust fund to keep the tree healthy.

The paving's been cut back. The tree is regularly fed and watered. A wrought-iron fence protects it from cars. Beneath it, a bench donated in memory of garden lovers Hessie and Harry Bowen allows people to sit in the shade, contemplating the work of God – and of people who cared.

In 1976 Arnold Zabel decided to give back to birds and animals some of the life that farming and ranching had taken away from them. He and his wife, Ruby (my cousin), were born in Saskatchewan and loved it all their lives, as schoolteachers and as owners of the 1,280-acre Del Rio 4-Z ranch twenty miles southwest of Swift Current.

"Wouldn't it be wonderful," Arnold mused, "if a few spots on this old prairie could recover their natural dignity, with birds and beasts and plant life in harmony?" Arnold had the soul of a poet.

He set aside sixty-seven acres across a creek from the ranch house. Then through years of planting, weeding, nurturing, he and family and friends created a habitat called Four Seasons, with prairie grass, wild rose, sage, and willow, as well as brome grass, alfalfa, fall rye, crested wheat grass, caraganas, firs, choke-cherries, Siberian crab, Russian olive, dogwood, honeysuckle, and hawthorn, all native to the area or to climates similar to southern Saskatchewan's.

Birds and animals quickly took advantage of it: thrushes, meadowlarks, robins, kingbirds, pheasant, partridge, sharp-tailed grouse, teal, mallards, pintails, and Canada geese. Deer, antelope, rabbits, skunks, badgers, and a few coyotes dropped in.

Ruby and Arnold are gone now, but a Habitat Trust, under the auspices of the Saskatchewan Wildlife Federation, holds Four Seasons in perpetuity. Strangers are advised not to mess with the place.

"If anybody tries to change it," Arnold told me before he died, "I'll come back and haunt the bugger!"

Cold Enough For Yuh?

In our southern Saskatchewan rural school, eons ago, the standard conversation opener each winter morning was "Cold enough for yuh?" Cold – what agricultural scientist Don

Gayton calls "the prairie juggernaut, winter" – was the dominating factor in our young lives. Decades later, none of us was surprised when Hollywood chose the Brooks area of Alberta in which to film the bleak Siberian-style snowscape of *Dr. Zhivago*.

"I correspond frequently with a fellow aviation-history buff who is grimly fascinated by anybody who's able to live at minus-forty-three Celsius for long periods," says Will Chabun, Regina *Leader-Post* reporter-columnist. "That's the temperature at which Scott perished at the South Pole. But for those of us here, minus-forty-three is, well, a hardship, but one that is endurable and relatively brief. Also, it reduces life to its basics: if something really bad happens, you can die in it."

That so few people *do* die is a consequence of the strange and wonderful bonding that takes place in cold weather, Chabun contends. "People routinely help others whose batteries have frozen or whose cars have stopped completely. There is an element of the golden rule about it: you give your neighbour's car a boost because you might find yourself in the same situation some day."

These are the kind of people who, for fun, stand on ice heaving rocks at other rocks, with savage cries of "HARDER!" "NO, NO!" "YES, YES!" Curling, a prairies-wide winter religion, is now Saskatchewan's provincial sport.

Curlers, of course, mostly play indoors, swathed in finest spandex. Pioneer rancher Claude Gardiner recorded in his diary the required mode of dress for a lone rider tending cattle on the winter range of an Alberta foothills ranch around the start of the twentieth century. "I always wear 2 pair of trousers," Gardiner wrote. "When I ride and it is a cold day I put on 2 pair of the German socks, a pair of rubber overshoes, 2 overcoats, cap over my ears, woolen comforter, and a pair of woolen mitts with a pair of buckskin ones over them. You can only see my eyes."

Clothing is now high-tech, but winter is still winter. A bitter day can sear your lungs if you breathe deeply. Sooner or later frostbite seeps through all the goose down and layered nylon a person can muster. Climatologists, notes David Phillips in *The Climates of Canada*, define a very cold day as one in which the minimum temperature is below -20°C. In a typical year the prairies can expect sixty such days. In 1969 Edmonton shivered through twenty-six consecutive days of -18°C deep freeze. Fort Vermilion, Alberta, on January 11, 1911, gained some notoriety when its thermometers sank to -61.1°C. Only Snag in the Yukon and Fort Good Hope in the Territories have had it colder. Of ten Canadian cities listed by Phillips as having the coldest winters, seven were on the prairies: Thompson, Prince Albert, Fort McMurray, Brandon, Yorkton, Winnipeg, and Saskatoon. It's enough to make you proud.

As proud, though frostbitten, as prairie dwellers are of their records, sometimes enough is enough. Winnipeg – after enduring for generations the title of coldest, windiest corner in Canada for its Portage and Main intersection – no longer allows pedestrians to cross it in winter. They now wend their way through underground passages.

Moose Jaw, once capital of the dust bowl, has a spa. Some genius discovered that the town sits on a porous rock formation, laden with mineral water, forty-five hundred feet below. To this they added the Temple Gardens Resort Hotel with a hot pool on the roof. For six to thirteen dollars a day you can soak in the pool and look down on the snowbanks of Crescent Park.

Even Calgary, kissed regularly by warm chinook winds, buffers its normally fierce climate with its 2.5-acre Devonian Gardens, a green oasis in a downtown office building, and its sixteen-kilometre chain of fifty-seven glassed-in aerial skywalks between office towers. This Plus 15 system (most of the bridges are about fifteen feet above street level) is said to be the most extensive in North America. Thousands of pedestrians use it daily even in balmy weather (it's a neat way of dodging traffic).

Some critics pronounce it sterile; others say it robs the streets of vitality. Calgarians don't care. Plus 15 sure beats walking in the cold.

Music in the Grass

In his book *Tracks of the Wind*, Peter Steinhart wrote, "Wind is a plant's only chance to make music." If that be so, the trees, shrubs, crops, and grasses of the prairie provinces are a Mormon Tabernacle Choir.

There is always wind. It howls over hills and through gullies, driving sheets of snow before it. It scours the soil and spring seedlings, carrying off farmers' hopes (although dust storms of 1930s magnitude are less common now, thanks to zero tillage, meaning no summerfallow). In rare gentle moods, the wind sighs through planted tree belts, ruffles fields of golden canola, flips up the tail feathers of embarrassed hens, makes suntanned cheeks browner.

Many prairie people, while griping about the wind (griping is a regular and therapeutic prairie pastime), actually enjoy it. They need their daily fix, a shot of westerly breeze straight into the main vein. "You don't get out of the wind," wrote Wallace Stegner in *Wolf Willow*. "You learn to lean and squint against it."

For us smug expatriates, comfortably removed from the gritty pleasures of topsoil blown under the door and onto the butter dish, the wind's moan is strangely comforting, evoking a jumble of half-remembered childhood days. Even some of those still out on weather's front lines share that dubious pleasure. "My wife and I talk about this a lot," says Regina's Will Chabun. "Odd as it may sound to somebody from elsewhere in Canada, I *like* the sound of the wind in the eavestroughs, of a blizzard in winter."

"I do love blizzards, as long as I know that everyone I love is inside and safe," agrees Jocelyn Hainsworth. "There is nothing

cozier than to fall asleep to the howl of the prairie wind roaring
through the shelter belt and rattling the shingles."

A blizzard, by the way, says meteorologist Wheaton, is the
combination of temperature at minus-twelve Celsius or lower,
wind speed of forty kilometres per hour or higher, visibility of
less than one kilometre, and a duration of at least four hours. In
other words, a white and blinding hell. In late January 1947,
Regina put its head down and struggled through a ten-day blizzard. The CPR called it the worst storm in Canadian rail history;
one of its trains simply vanished into a snowdrift nearly a mile
long and about twenty-five feet deep.

Saskatchewan holds the silver medal for maximum hourly
wind speed: a touch over eighty-eight miles per hour at Melfort
in October 1976, exceeded only by a big blow in remote northern Quebec in 1931. No wonder Reginan Joyce Wells is a
wind-ophile. Once, she returned to Saskatchewan just in time
to step into a raging blizzard. Where less durable women would
have fled indoors and pulled the covers over their heads, Wells
stood out in it, joyfully, letting the wind hold her up. She and
her mother (a prairie farmer) were atop the Plains of Abraham
once on holiday when a splendid gust blew tourists away by the
dozen. The Wells women lingered, luxuriating in the breeze.

The phenomenon known as chinook, meaning "snow eater,"
is a warm, dry, westerly wind that blows through the Rocky
Mountains into the western prairies. It belongs to a worldwide
family of similar winds – the *foehn* in Europe, the *zonda* in
Argentina, the *berg* in South Africa – where long mountain chains
lie more or less at right angles to the prevailing air flow.

Chinooks are almost exclusive to southern and central
Alberta, and are most noticeable in winter. One in three winter
days is a chinook day, and can boost the temperature as much as
twenty-seven degrees Celsius in two minutes. Most people
appreciate the break from sub-zero temperatures, but for some

the chinook brings on headaches, earaches, depression, or even thoughts of suicide.

"Any hot, dry wind such as a chinook adds a lot of positive ionization to the air," explains the University of Regina's Paul Antrobus. "This contributes to depressed mood and slow reaction time. Just ask anybody how they feel after a thunderstorm: the air has been re-ionized, balanced out with negative ions, which we need. People feel different, almost semi-euphoric.

"So we have a very depressed kind of weather system in that sense. It keeps our people in a different psychological state than those in California or the B.C. coast, who get plenty of negative ions from the moist air."

Ah, but when a chinook is followed by rain, and the rain ends, and the sun comes out, that moment is more than special; for many it is spiritual.

"After a rain you just can't help but marvel at the beauty of this country," says Ann Brown of Central Butte. "There's no two ways about it: you know there's a God."

III

BEGINNINGS

Prairies let us out. . . . They aid to grow a roomy life.

WILLIAM A. QUAYLE
"The Prairie and the Sea," 1905

The Triumph of Ivan Pillipiw

In autumn 1891, Ivan Pillipiw, thirty-two, a peasant farmer of the village of Nebyliv in the province of Eastern Galicia, made a momentous decision. He would be a serf no more. He would crawl from under the iron heel of his Austro-Hungarian masters and go to a distant mystical place where, rumour said – it was almost beyond belief! – a man could have free fertile land and be his own boss. Canada West.

It took all the nerve he could muster. There would be long, arduous voyages by land and sea. There would be undreamed-of obstacles. But this life was not fit for a man. He was one of 3.3 million Ukrainian peasants in Galicia – most of them illiterate, all treated like the dirt they tilled.

A handful of feudal landlords ruled the country. Peasants were forced to doff their hats within three hundred feet of a mansion, couldn't marry without the lord's permission, and could be inducted into the army at age twelve. They could own a few acres if their average annual income of thirty-nine Austrian crowns (about $14.80) supported it, but brutal taxes dragged them down.

Pillipiw had an edge on most of his countrymen: he could read and write, which helped fuel his courage. He was one of the first Ukrainians to break away to join what would become a torrent of fellow immigrants to the Canadian prairie. His wife, like many others in their community, shrank from the dangers (not least of which would be the wrath of their masters) and fear of the unknown. Ivan left her behind with their three children. He would test Canada West – the romantic label for that part of what was then the North-West Territories – on his own. If it went well he would return for them.

He sold a team of horses, a yoke of oxen, and part of his land, paid off his debts, and set out with 156 Austrian crowns (about sixty dollars). Train fare to the border cost him $3.80; another $3.80 got him to the port of Hamburg. A shipping agent sold him boat and train fare all the way to Winnipeg for thirty-five dollars.

At Gretna, Manitoba, he found labouring jobs that paid him two dollars a day for two months. He saved enough to go back to Nebyliv. Neighbours crowded into his house. Where had he been? What was it like?

"Run, run from here!" Ivan cried. "Here you have nothing, but there you'll have free land and be your own master."

His tale raced through the village. One day the reeve, the priest, the village secretary, and the pharmacist – men of standing in the community – came to his house, spread a map on the table, and grilled him for an hour: "Show us where you went. Tell us what you did." Ivan answered each question forthrightly. Finally they accepted his word, but the reeve warned, "Watch yourself!"

Pillipiw ignored the warning. He began helping others negotiate the trip abroad. Sometimes they paid him. An agent in Hamburg gave him a commission for pointing new settlers his way.

Then Pillipiw was arrested and charged with inciting peasants to leave Galicia and embezzling their deposits (which was false). After two months cooling his heels in jail, he went to trial.

"Why do you need land?" the judge demanded. "Haven't you got enough?" And why did he want to leave the sheltering wing of their benevolent emperor? Ivan's answers did not please the court. He got another month in jail.

The moment he was released he sold his tiny acreage and moved his family to the Promised Land in 1893. Eventually he settled at Bruderheim – soon to be in Alberta but then part of the North-West Territories – and lived happily to seventy-seven. He died falling from an upstairs window at a relative's wedding.

Add to this the tales that follow here of Jacob Friesen, Peter Humeniuk, Ephraim Makemenko, Iwan and Wasylyna Mihaychuk, and Gus Romaniuk – eloquent testimony to the struggles and suffering of the earliest prairie settlers. They endured more hardship, discouragement, and sheer misery than any modern pampered Canadian could tolerate or even imagine.

Most of them survived. Their descendants today make up one of the largest, most-respected ethnic segments of the prairie population.

"They came here with guts, determination, and a lot of prayers, very deeply religious people who worked and lived for the church," says Elsie Anaka, a Reginan who married the son of a Ukrainian pioneer and lived among her husband's people at Stenen, Saskatchewan. "I picture them all, many different families, living in holes in the ground, then tents, then finally mud huts, working with oxen for a time and gradually building better homes and using horses for fieldwork and social life."

They, and others like them from other countries, became the indestructible building blocks of the West.

The Sweet Siren Song of Clifford Sifton

Ivan Pillipiw and his little family were mere drops in an astonishing human wave of settlement that poured into the prairies before and after the turn of the twentieth century. They came from all corners of the earth: the prairie was a mingling of nations long before the world ever heard of the U.N. In eastern Saskatchewan such villages as Dubuc, Bangor, Stockholm, Esterhazy, Langenburg, Thingvalla, and Churchbridge reflected their French, Welsh, Swedish, Hungarian, German, Icelandic, and British origins. Others came to the prairies from America, Austria-Hungary, the Balkans, Estonia, Holland, Ireland, Romania, China, Russia, Finland, and Norway. Because the three provinces are relatively new, those pioneers and their heritage are still bright in the memories of today's prairie people.

They came in sheepskin coats, fur leggings, Cossack boots, corduroy jackets, tweed caps, lambskin hats, babushkas, sashes, and shawls. They tumbled off their ships, hopeful, confused, with a babble of foreign tongues and fragmented English, hands fluttering in pantomime. They bestowed upon the prairie a legacy of new words, tastes, and traditions that make it now the most diverse and eclectic region of Canada.

And they were tempted, tricked, beguiled, and bowled along by gusts of rhetoric from governments, land companies, and railways in the biggest advertising campaign in history. Much of it was propaganda; some was outright deceit. "Men had been told that if they moved west they could not help but succeed," wrote Douglas Owram in *Promise of Eden*. "Such promises only served to obscure the very real difficulties involved in carving a livelihood out of a quarter section of land."

John Leech, for one, left England for Alberta after reading that prairie soil, merely "tickled with a hoe," would burst forth with crops and gardens, and the "mean temperature was a balmy 65 degrees." Later, Leech said he wished he'd known just how mean the temperature could get. In France, Georges Bugnet read that a strong, intelligent young man could make twenty-five thousand dollars in five or ten years on a prairie farm. Long afterwards he said ruefully, "We have still to see the twenty-five thousand dollars." German settler August Sorge was enticed to southern Alberta by an ad showing Johnny Canuck – that hackneyed symbol of Canada in Yogi Bear hat and high-laced boots – turning up gold coins in a furrow. Sorge's furrows turned up rocks.

The Canadian Pacific Railway surpassed itself in hype. It deluged Britain and the continent with pamphlets and posters proclaiming the glories of the Canadian West. Lecturers roamed about luring immigrants with the new magic lantern (precursor to the film projector), which cast magnified images from glass slides onto a screen. Rolling fields of wheat were a particular crowd-pleaser. The CPR sent horse-drawn vans laden with propaganda into rural England, its very own medicine show, selling not snake oil but an elixir called "prairie."

The federal government ran a poor second in the immigrant bounty hunt until, in 1896, the ministry of the interior hired a young Manitoba lawyer, Clifford Sifton. He tackled his task with zeal. Canada wanted immigrants as badly as they wanted Canada. In the ten years prior to 1900, its population had inched ahead by a mere half-million. Now the country was emerging from a depression. Urbanization and industrialization in Europe had created new markets, particularly for wheat. Choice farmland was becoming scarce and expensive in the United States: up to one hundred dollars an acre in Kansas, two hundred in Illinois. The Canadian prairie had free land, an early-maturing wheat, and a railway to haul people and grain. All it needed was people – but not just any people. "None but agriculturalists," ruled Sifton. "We do not recognize labourers at all."

Like many federal politicians after him, Sifton was concerned less with Western Canada's welfare than with a payoff for the East. He persuaded the railways to open up 22.5 million acres of valuable prairie land and simplified the process of acquiring homesteads: each settler could get one quarter section (160 acres) in any area declared open for settlement. For a ten-dollar fee he had three years to "prove up": live there at least six months of every year, cultivate, put up buildings and fences. If the settler kept his part of the bargain, the land was his, and he could buy a second quarter section, called a pre-emption.

Pamphlets, maps, atlases, and advertisements poured from the mighty publicity mill, singing their siren songs to eager ears abroad. Clever admen used the RCMP as a symbol of Canadian law, order, and historical romance. In one advertisement, a Mountie's horse had red-stained hooves from trotting through endless vistas of wild strawberries. Occasionally the literature was accurate. One ad guaranteed that Canada was "free of malaria"; nobody could argue with that.

The best-known propaganda piece was the Immigration Branch's first magazine-style brochure. Its cover cried out:

CANADA WEST

THE LAST BEST WEST

Homes for Millions

A garland of golden maple leaves embraced an idyllic scene: farmer driving a binder through wheat higher than a horse's belly, perfect stooks of grain, handsome farmstead with windmill and tree belt. And down in the corner the lyrical clincher: "Ranching, Dairying, Grain Raising, Fruit Raising, Mixed Farming."

Individual communities proclaimed their wonders. Wetaskiwin, Alberta, revealed itself in a brochure as "picturesque . . . [with] very rich soil . . . well-to-do and energetic settlers . . . hotel accommodation second to none. . . ." Was any place on earth a more congenial spot? Yes. Medicine Hat declared itself "city of eternal light . . . , best mixed farming district in the world . . . [and the] climate is the finest on the continent." Its natural gas ("finest, purest ever found in British North America") made it immune to "thunderstorms and other elements which interfere with electric light." A visiting newsman – perhaps fed, watered, and curried by local boosters – compared Medicine Hat favourably with Chicago.

Then, as now, the federal government knew the value of a docile press. It ran Western tours for international journalists with food and drink galore. Newsmen were urged to stress the fertile soil, fine crops, and laughing, prosperous settlers, which, as luck would have it, were paraded before them. The journalistic freeloaders, Sifton told Parliament, would "go back to their homes and give favourable reports about what they have seen. . . . It does not cost much and it is the very best kind of advertising we can get."

Newspapers came enthusiastically aboard, as in this *Toronto News* parody of Lewis Carroll:

"You are rich, Father William," the young man said.
"Yet in youth you had never a nickel.
"Since you came to the West Dame Fortune you've wed.
"Now how won you a woman so fickle?"
"In the bush in the East," the old man replied,
"I chopped out a homestead for Mary.
"But in the journey toward Wealth we've made better speed
"Since we took up a farm on the prairie. . . ."

Over six months in 1900 the government sent out more than one million pieces of literature. Initially, the heaviest concentration was on Britain, for political and sentimental reasons (Canada was, after all, still a "dominion"). The rugged farmers of Scotland produced good settlers, but England sent a disappointing mix of mostly inexperienced urban folk.

Sifton then turned his sights on America. "The first great demand," reported his 1901 *Atlas of Western Canada*, "is for persons with some capital." A five-hundred-dollar stake was good; five thousand was better. By 1902 advertisements ran in seven thousand American rural and agricultural newspapers. Part of the admen's art was persuading Americans that Canada was not one gigantic ice cube. So, the bitter prairie winter became "bracing"; the weather so salubrious that "the soft maple tree has been known to grow more than five feet in a single season." Western Canada was "the largest continuous wheat field in the world."

In 1905, as fifty-five thousand Yanks poured in, lovers of Empire began fretting over Americanization. Conversely, America was alarmed at the hemorrhage of its farmers. Montana opened large tracts of vacant land with irrigation, begging American farmers to try it first. New England advised its locals to stay home and turn those stony fields into profitable sheep farms. In South Dakota a booklet, *Saved from the Clutches of the King*, described a fictional American rescued from imperialist Canada before he lost his virtue. An anonymous poet in North Dakota furthered the U.S. impression of Canada as iceberg:

> If Medicine Hat were blown away,
> Clear down to the equator, say,
>   Then all the beastly cold would flit
> To some place where they've need of it.

None of this discouraged the American farmers: in a dozen years 785,137 came to Western Canada. And still the sprawling prairie needed more people, especially tough ones, who wouldn't balk at hard work or a cruel climate.

Sifton threw open provincial doors to farmers of northern Europe, particularly the yearning millions in the Austro-Hungarian Empire. To his critics – there were many among Canada's Anglo-Saxon majority – he uttered the lines to be quoted *ad nauseam* by generations of historians: "I think a stalwart peasant in a sheepskin coat, born of the soil, whose fore-fathers have been farmers for ten generations, with a stout wife and half a dozen children is good quality."

To avoid angering European governments with blatant poaching, he set up a network of steamship agents to do his work. They fanned out by the hundreds from German ports into Galicia and Bukovyna with handbills, posters, and speeches. The downtrodden serfs were a truly captive audience.

Beeda Meant Misery

The immigrants desperately wanted to believe. About 170,000 from the Russian Ukraine and from Galicia and Bukovyna joined the first wave into the prairie from the early 1890s to

1914. Anything was better than a life where an everyday exchange, as commonplace as "hello" or "goodbye," went:

"How is everything?"

"Beeda."

Beeda meant misery, or misfortune, distress, bad luck, calamity – take your pick.

The peasants couldn't envision the kinds of misery still ahead. Their preparations were simple, at times pitiful. When young Jacob Friesen and his parents left the Russian Ukraine, his mother dried months-long supplies of fruit and buns in the oven for the journey. In Galicia, Peter Humeniuk's father went from friend to friend borrowing enough money to get away. Then he built a big trunk and filled it with clothes, tools, candles, prayer book. At the last moment Peter's mother added a lump of Galician soil wrapped in a rag as a remembrance.

Getting out of their country was the first hurdle. The Austro-Hungarian landowners and their henchmen threw up every imaginable barrier. Mail with money or information about how to get to Canada might not reach the emigrants. District councillors or village elders might refuse to authenticate passports. Anyone showing interest in leaving was watched and often harassed by local police. Sometimes, at border points, passports and money were confiscated and the helpless emigrants turned back. The Friesens travelled to the Latvian border in a boxcar with four other families, all sleeping on straw. At the border, the entire train was searched and the guards stole the travellers' possessions on whim.

In time the peasants learned to pay off middlemen and agents with their meagre funds and escape the country in secret. Often they were nearly penniless when they reached Canada. The Friesens were financed by the Mennonite Central Committee along with some credit from the CPR for meals aboard ship and train. It took the father fifteen years to clear his debt. Emigrants needed certificates of health to get on a boat; if they had a sick child, they might have to bribe the doctor to get aboard. Doctors took wedding rings if a family had nothing else to offer.

The ocean trip could last nine to twenty-eight days. Longer trips meant worse food and service and sleeping in tiers of crude bunks with a mattress (if any) of straw or seaweed, amid fierce gales and vomiting passengers. In 1903, 2,684 men, women, and children were packed cheek by jowl into communal cabins and steerage aboard the ss *Lake Manitoba*, a converted Boer War troop ship. It was recorded as a peaceable journey: "Only 11 fights, seven incipient mutinies and three riots . . ."

Edward and John Roberts from Wales booked fifteen-dollar ocean passages to Canada on a harvest excursion. "I became so sick I thought I was going to die," John remembered. "Then I got worse and was afraid I wouldn't." Yet as Brits they were better off than Ukrainians, who were considered a "lower" race. On any ship shared with Ukrainians, the English got better food, better service, cleaner cabins.

Superior ships provided tea or coffee, bread or crackers for breakfast; more bread or crackers, soup, meat and potatoes or cabbage and rice, maybe pickled herring for lunch, and a vegetable snack for supper. Fresh drinking water was always scarce. Lesser ships, in those days before refrigeration, offered bad fish and worse pork. Thirty years after, one immigrant still couldn't "face the warm smell of pork without sweat starting on my forehead."

Eventually the dirty, bedraggled passengers reached Halifax. At the dock people laughed and pointed at the long sheepskin coats, men in white homespun trousers, women with kerchiefs. They entered the first of a series of immigration halls, often infested with lice and bedbugs. An immigration agent reported, "You can imagine the condition of the sheds when I tell you that I discovered greybacks crawling up my necktie after one of these trips. Of course with their big blankets and sheepskin coats coming off the vessel it can't be expected otherwise but certainly is not pleasant."

"Try to visualize this situation," wrote the Reverend Nestor Dmytriw in 1898. "A family arrives from Galicia – husband, wife and eight children. On the way here they spend all their money. The agents along the way extort the man's last penny. Ill clad, half naked, barefoot, dirty, destitute, they come to the immigration home like beggars.

"The administrators of the home wring their hands and are at a loss to know how to begin coping with these wretched people. Now and then some kindhearted person will give this family a few cents so that they can have food for the time being. Their children make nuisances of themselves in the stairway, crawling up and down and relieving themselves on the steps or beside the door.

"In desperation the administration curses and turns to the government for guidance in dealing with such people. But since the government has no other source of immigrants to bank on at this time, it tolerates our people as a necessary evil."

The train trip across Canada was another endurance test. There was no privacy. The seats were wooden slats. Travellers could boil tea or coffee, if they had any, on a coal-burning stove at one end of the car. The Humeniuks from Galicia – parents and two small boys – sat and slept on one seat because the coaches were so packed. The long, dreary trip through the Canadian Shield – days of blurring rocks and trees – never failed to depress the immigrants. On one train a voice wailed, "It would have been better to suffer in the Old Country than to come to this Siberia!"

"[The train] is very slow and tedious," wrote Reverend Dmytriw. "[It] is jampacked with passengers of different origins . . . the smoking car is extremely filthy due to the foul smoke from different sorts of tobacco and the disgusting spitting. It is enough to kill anyone who is not used to this kind of atmosphere."

At Winnipeg most newcomers moved into the immigration hall near the CPR station for a few days until they could buy supplies and disperse to homesteads. It was simple but relatively clean, and families could cook their own food on the premises. Calgary had a better hall, but even there new arrivals were advised to saturate their clothing with sabadilla powder (an insecticide) to ward off "American bedbugs."

BACK DOOR, FRONT DOOR

Ted Liba, twenty-three, came to the prairie from the Ukraine in 1926. He worked on farms, then on the railway, came to Winnipeg in 1928, got a job at the Fort Garry Hotel, and stayed.

When King George VI and Queen Elizabeth visited Canada in 1939, the lieutenant governor of Manitoba hosted them at lunch. The Fort Garry catered and Liba was one of the waiters chosen to serve at Government House. His admission pass, signed by the RCMP, allowed him entry by the back door.

Sixty years later Princess Anne visited Winnipeg. Lieutenant Governor Peter Liba greeted her at Government House. He thinks his father the waiter, who died in 1970, would have relished the sight of his son meeting royalty – at the front *door.*

The Promised Land

The one thing that sustained them was the thought that soon the journey would finally be over. Their dreams lay just over the horizon. The Humeniuks and their fellow travellers were kept locked in their train at Winnipeg because the powers that be said Manitoba's good land was gone; they must all go to Yorkton. But Ukrainians had already settled at Stuartburn, south of Winnipeg, and one of them was on the platform trying to spot friends from home. The Humeniuks and others recognized him, broke out of the train, and hitched a wagon ride over a rutted trail through clouds of mosquitoes to his rural cabin.

"Glory unto Jesus Christ," the wife greeted them.

"Glory forever," they replied.

That night twenty-nine people said their prayers and slept in one little cabin, stacked together like cordwood. In the morning their hosts cooked pancakes. Then the Humeniuks went out to build a new life.

Gus Romaniuk's father met his family at Winnipeg immigration. They took a train to Arborg about seventy-five miles north, then a horse-drawn sleigh thirteen more miles through a blizzard. Back home in the Ukraine they had lived in whitewashed buildings. Here the house was made of logs chinked with moss with a ceiling of hay and a bare earthen floor. The mother burst into tears. Gus announced he wanted to go home and live with his grandmother.

In summer they built a smudge to drive off the mosquito hordes; it burned the shack to the ground. They built another shack, then a house. They simply refused to give up. It was better than slavery.

But for Iwan Mihaychuk, another Galician refugee, the better times were long in coming. He was forty-three when he took his wife, Wasylyna, and their four sons to Stuartburn. It seemed worse than Galicia. Their first Canadian winter was a stunner, with temperatures as low as minus-forty. They had no clothes for such weather. At night the children slept on top of the homemade clay stove while the adults huddled around it.

Summer brought the inevitable mosquitoes, garter snakes, skunks, poison ivy. In 1903 they moved to a second homestead. They never hit it rich but at least no landlord was forever leaning over them. Iwan lived to seventy-three. Two of his sons became teachers, one became a newspaper editor, one studied dentistry.

As if the natural hazards of prairie life weren't enough, they were for years derided by their fellow Canadians. The *Edmonton Bulletin* jeered in 1898: "Several wagonloads of newly arrived Galicians passed through town on Saturday on their way from the railway station to their new home in the Limestone Lake country. They were the most grotesquely dressed party that has yet struck town."

The newcomers doggedly lowered their heads and pressed on. There were feats of endurance that seemed beyond normal men. Ephraim Makemenko, born in the Ukrainian village of Odaypil, shipped out to his uncle's farm in Alberta at sixteen. A recession was on and work was scarce. He and a cousin started walking through the bush towards Lac La Biche with a pot, a pan, and a bit of bread. They caught fish along the way. After three days of steady plodding they reached La Biche, couldn't find jobs, stayed overnight, then trudged farther north. Still no luck.

They struggled back to the uncle's farm, rested, and walked south to Edmonton, made the last lap by train, job-hunted until their money ran out, then walked back to the uncle's farm and worked for room and board. All told, in the course of that heart-breaking search they walked about 350 miles.

Finally Ephraim got a farm labouring job at fifty cents a day, then roadwork, earning eighteen cents per cubic yard of moss and twenty cents per cubic yard of earth excavated. There were no living quarters, so Ephraim and his mates built a shack and an outdoor oven. By working sun-up to sundown, he earned fifty dollars a month. He worked that way all his life. He was never wealthy or even well-to-do. It was a hard life, plain and simple.

The 285 Icelanders who reached Manitoba by train and lake steamer in October 1875 named their first settlement Gimli. It meant "abode of the gods," but it was a sorry substitute for paradise.

The entire contingent and its one hundred tons of freight went up the Red River in scows. There were no buildings and no hay, hence no livestock and no milk for the children. They slept in the scows until they could build crude log houses. Food was scarce. The boys learned to snare rabbits but the women shunned them: when skinned they looked too much like cats.

"Deaths were frequent among grownups and children," wrote Simon Simonarson, chronicler of that first winter. "It was a miracle that anyone survived."

When smallpox swept through Gimli in 1876-77, Winnipeg doctors placed the settlement under quarantine with a watch post at Nutley Creek, fifteen miles south. Gimli people couldn't leave; outsiders couldn't enter. That didn't stop Sigurdur Kristofferson and Carrie Taylor from being wed.

There was no minister in Gimli, so Sigurdur and Carrie had one meet them at Nutley Creek. One bright, bitter morning in February 1877 the lovers met the minister at a post marking the quarantine limits. He married them in the snow, the post becoming an improvised altar.

Everywhere, the pioneers prevailed and improvised. Hector Pinsonneault from Napierville, Quebec, homesteaded at Gravelbourg, Saskatchewan, in 1906. One year he grew a big oat crop and, lacking storage space, put it in his shack. He slept on oats all winter. There were few neighbours and no doctors. Pinsonneault treated his influenza with gin mixed with hot water and honey. Ninety-five years later his son Walter still used the remedy: "You start sweating and the bed starts turning under you and by morning you're all right!"

Charles Malcher, nineteen, left Sweden on a cattle boat in January 1903 and slept on sawdust in the hold. At Liverpool he boarded a steamer carrying six hundred passengers and slept with fourteen others in steerage. He ate standing up from tables slung from the ceiling by ropes. During the trip a four-day storm blew them four hundred miles off course.

Two months after he left home Malcher reached Wetaskiwin, Alberta, with twelve dollars in his pocket. He hitched a ride twenty-five miles east and walked the last mile and a half to his Uncle Hedlund's homestead in light clothing through three feet of snow at minus-thirty-two Celsius. Already he'd borne more discomfort than any contemporary young Canadian would see in a lifetime – and his ordeal was just beginning.

Marathon walks were common. In September 1887 a little Icelandic colony settled at Tantallon, Saskatchewan. As Christmas neared, Eivikur and Gudmundur Thorsteinson volunteered to fetch supplies from Moosomin, thirty-three miles away. They walked. On the way back they carried a hundred-pound sack of flour, ten pounds of sugar, ten pounds of coffee, eighty-five pounds of rolled oats, and some special Christmas treats.

Scottish-born Alexander McKerchar stretched his legs in the late 1870s, walking west from Winnipeg, sampling the soil in his fingers along the way, until after 175 miles he finally found land he liked. But on the same walk in 1881 he caught a chill in a rainstorm, developed pneumonia, and died at age fifty-four. That same year stout-legged A.D. Chisholm arrived in Winnipeg from the Ottawa Valley and walked one hundred miles to Griswold. He took out land, went back to Ontario, and returned with his bride (by oxcart on the last lap).

Around 1906 Alexander Jolly went from Wolseley, Saskatchewan, to take a labouring job near Edmonton. When he was finished, his employer couldn't pay him but offered him land. Jolly looked at the expanse of bush and decided he could do better back home. He walked back to Wolseley, roughly six hundred miles. Along the way he did odd jobs such as cutting wood to pay for a meal or a night's lodging in a barn. He later learned he'd turned down a chance to own the site of the University of Alberta.

If weather, disease, bugs, and bankers didn't bring a settler to his knees, fractious horses and cows with attitudes often did. Colin McKenzie of Elbridge, Alberta, won ten dollars from the *Edmonton Journal* in 1920 for an account of his first year of farming. The novice, a British navy veteran, started out in 1918 cutting hay. He fell into the mower, cut his hands, and went to hospital.

When he got out his neighbours helped him raise a log house. It burned down. They helped him rebuild. McKenzie put up a fence, stumped five acres of land, and ploughed three.

"I would have done more," he reported apologetically, "but a neighbour's horse kicked me in the face and sent me to the Royal Alexandra [hospital] for three weeks."

His cows were wild; one in particular "was a regular outlaw. It had injured three people." He and two neighbours built a massive stall for her. At milking time he looped a logging chain around her, tied her feet, and put a saucepan between the rails to catch the milk.

"Believe me, she sure was a peach!" McKenzie related cheerfully. "She kept me on top of the barn for an hour and a half one day."

The incredible tenacity of those pioneers, handed down through the generations by – what: genetics, example, family legend? – has distinguished prairie people ever since. Sadly, soft living and creature comforts are watering it down. In another generation it may be gone.

JOURNEY INTO HISTORY

At two a.m. on September 1, 1905, farmer Willet Orser and sons Orval and Hulbert (Hullie), got up and milked the cows, much to the cows' astonishment. Long before sun-up the trio was on the trail with horse and buggy to Ponoka, twenty miles west, to catch a special train to Edmonton. Alberta was becoming a province this day, and the Orsers, two years out of Ontario, wanted to share history in the making.

The train was crowded with Calgarians, miffed at Ottawa's decision to name Edmonton the capital and still hoping to influence the decision. Eighty miles farther, at the rail terminus on the south side of the Saskatchewan River, the travellers detrained to join twenty thousand others for the parade down Jasper Avenue. Governor General Earl Grey and Lady Grey led the way, Prime Minister Sir Wilfrid Laurier was next, then more dignitaries, three bands, dozens of floats, and a stream of citizens in wagons or on foot.

Lieutenant Governor George Bulyea was sworn in at noon. There were games, races, more music. The official party left for Regina to inaugurate Saskatchewan on September 4. The Orsers caught the train back south, claimed their team at the Ponoka livery stable, and reached home at midnight to milk the cows again — never begrudging a moment of the twenty-two-hour two-hundred-mile round trip.

Hullie grew up to fight for Canada at Vimy. He lived to tell in 1980, when Alberta and Saskatchewan were seventy-five, "I was there for the birth of the province. I remember it very well." In 2005, his daughter, Evelyn Orser de Mille, for decades the proprietor of a well-known Calgary bookstore, will help salute Alberta's centenary and her father's journey into history.

"No English Need Apply"

Nearly all the immigrants became valued members of the prairie community – all except the English. So bad was their reputation for arrogance and ineptitude that signs declaring "No English Need Apply" sprang up at hiring locations around the West. "Green Englishmen" became the stuff of laughter and legend.

One settler claimed his English neighbour sowed three bags of oatmeal in the fields so he could grow his own porridge. Another farmer hired a British cattle herder with "a positive talent for sleeping on the job." A Rocky Mountain guide remembered, "Wherever you went you found some damn-fool Englishman looking for the outer rim of beyond the beyond." He recalled four English ditchdiggers talking to each other in Latin. "The foreman thought they were plotting against the government!"

It was bad enough being the butt of jokes in a backwater colony, but in 1903 even the *Times of London*, editorial conscience of the Old Country, turned on them: "If one in four of these young Englishmen have any substantial balance of capital to show in half a dozen years it would surprise those who best know their type; and in too many cases it is their own fault. Drink, idleness and restlessness are the most fertile causes of failure...."

Clifford Sifton, patron saint of immigrants, who in the beginning had ardently courted all Brits, now admitted, "An Englishman out of a job in Canada generally, on examination, is discovered to be addicted to drink."

In part it was the fault of Canada's immigration department. Its recruiting literature downplayed prairie hardships. The original decree – "None but agriculturalists" – seemed forgotten (like so much federal government lip service, then and since). Experienced English farmers stayed home, and eager novices – shopkeepers, coal miners, druggists, ordinary labourers, at least one gymnast and one jockey – came wide-eyed to the Promised Land, utterly unprepared for prairie work or weather.

Among them were "remittance men," those ne'er-do-well sons of the rich and titled, so named for the money from home that kept them alive. Many came from the privileged sanctuary of public schools and comfortable estates. When elder brothers took over the family professions, the youngest were often shipped to Canada to make good, or at least get out of their parents' hair. An English magistrate reportedly scolded a young offender, "You have broken your mother's heart. You have brought down your father's grey hairs in sorrow to the grave. You are a disgrace to your country. Why don't you go to Canada?" (Thanks for that, Your Honour.)

They became symbols of English failure. Their cocksure attitude and veneration of all things British didn't help. A London journalist travelling among them in 1907 reported, "They talk of 'the flag' and 'the old country' with an effusive affection that startles the mere Englishman."

Many settled in the Alberta foothills from Priddis to Pincher Creek and played at ranching. To most settlers, dressing for dinner meant putting on a clean shirt. The young Brits donned dinner jackets. Some decked themselves out as cowboys. Alberta historian Hugh Dempsey quotes a report of the time: "The English fellows around Calgary have a way, doncherknow, of having their photographs taken *à la* broncho buster and sending it home to the old folks just to let them see how the son is doing in the wild and wooly west."

One posed in front of Calgary city hall. His family back home congratulated him on his smart appearance and "on the tidy and well-kept appearance of his horse stable."

All of this was a bitter pill for the Brits back home. The breed that built the Empire was being scorned in a mere dominion. When Canada tightened its immigration laws in 1906, providing in part for deportation of any who became a public charge, the English were the losers. In the first year of its enactment, 833 British and only forty-three Americans were deported. An aggrieved *Yorkshire Post* complained that the law might have been enacted in some quite alien country "instead of a part of the Empire." Canada had a right to bar undesirable aliens, the *Post* admitted, but how dare it bar people from the country "which bears the naval expenses of the Empire"?

Another amendment in 1910, requiring "aided" immigrants to get farm employment or go home, enraged London's immigration societies. They demanded, in vain, that the British parliament intervene.

In time the expatriate English regained esteem, particularly when they marched away to fight for King and Empire in the First World War. Many persevered to become fine farmers. If their temporary fall from grace taught them a modicum of humility it was perhaps a tiny step forward in Canada's ultimate growth from colony to nation.

IV

BAD OLD DAYS

Chinamen and white men do not mix
any better than glue and perfume.

CRAG AND CANYON (NEWSPAPER)
Banff, 1903

White Faces Preferred

The pioneers' prairie was indeed a land of opportunity – if your face was white. Prejudice was endemic in Canada going into the twentieth century and was nowhere more virulent than on the prairies. Today, pockets of bigotry and racism remain (fostered by a vocal few and, sometimes, by the media). They are not representative of the West, but it's instructive to examine their pioneer roots, which included the federal government of the time.

The original inhabitants of the region, people with noble ringing names – Cree, Blackfoot, Ojibway, Saulteaux, Assiniboine – had already been parcelled off by nineteenth-century treaties into government-designated reserves, reduced to pathetic second-class citizenship, and known by the all-embracing and usually derogatory label "Indians."

In the early West, even a white face did not guarantee acceptance. Immigrants from Central Europe were sneeringly called "Hunkys" or "Bohunks" (racist shorthand for Hungarians and Bohemians). Jews were castigated for being Jews. Author Jack Kates (formerly Katz) recalled in a memoir that a grade-school teacher in his Saskatchewan town singled him out in front of the class, "Let Jackie Katz stand in the corner. He's a Jew."

The patron saint of Canadian socialism, Reverend James S. Woodsworth, Methodist minister and first leader of the Co-operative Commonwealth Federation (now the NDP), lent his name to the book *Strangers Within Our Gates*, a pastiche of his own and other writers' views, ranging from politically incorrect to blatantly racist (by today's standards). It condemned blacks, Mormons, and Galicians among others.

Woodsworth, basically a decent and compassionate man, was a product of his time: if newcomers wanted to get ahead they should behave like white Anglo-Saxon Protestants. (Worse yet, Woodsworth later recommended a Western school of eugenics – improvement of the race by breeding those with desirable genes

– and ultimately favoured sterilization of "mental defectives.")

Blacks and Asians were treated as creatures from another planet. The Banff *Crag and Canyon* reflected a common view in a 1903 so-called news story. A local "Chinaman" had said something "objectionable" to a white man "who in his wrath struck the heathen in the face," giving him a black eye and a nosebleed. The assailant was fined five dollars and costs, but *Crag and Canyon* blamed the victim: "The young man who committed the assault cannot suffer much discredit in public opinion . . . whether or not the heathen was to blame for the breach of the peace it is a reasonable conclusion that had not the dozen or more Chinamen been imported here the court records would yet be clean. Chinamen and white men do not mix any better than glue and perfume."

The equally racist *Lethbridge Herald* in 1907 urged the Alberta government to deny Japanese or "a Chinaman" the vote: "Make these yellow men understand we are not going to allow them to secure any influence in our affairs. They have no right to compete with white labor and neither have they any right to compete with white votes." Later that year a mob attacked a Lethbridge Chinese restaurant because a "celestial" had allegedly killed someone with a hammer.

When black immigrants showed interest in Canada, authorities tried to persuade them the climate was too cold. In 1910 Alberta went berserk at the idea that Oklahoma's Creek-Negroes (blacks who had intermarried with Indians and were now fleeing racism at home) might immigrate. "Negroes Not Wanted in Province of Alberta," cried the Calgary *Albertan*. Around Edmonton, where blacks had already taken farms, boards of trade, women's organizations, press, and local trades and labour councils sounded the alarm. A petition with more than three thousand signatures warned the federal government of "the serious menace to the future welfare of a large portion of Western Canada, by reason of the alarming influx of negro settlers." The "menace" seemed to be fear of racial violence and, in a separate petition from the Imperial Order of Daughters of the Empire, that black men would ravish white women.

Racism spiralled out from the federal government itself, through a rigged Immigration Act. Medical problems, pauperism, and moral turpitude were grounds for exclusion. At border-crossing points, a medical and a character inspection was used as a pretext for excluding black American settlers. Frank Oliver, Clifford Sifton's successor as minister of the interior, encouraged an informal immigration program of foot-dragging and discouragement. By 1911 there were only 1,524 blacks in the Western provinces out of a 1.3 million population.

The Edmonton Board of Trade led the fight to slam Alberta's doors. In 1910 a board member named Powell said black settlers were "a serious menace" and Edmonton's one hundred black residents "had a demoralizing effect. . . . Even the best of negroes are not desirable as citizens since they are un-assimilable with whites." Powell urged a thousand-dollar head tax on all coloured immigrants.

The Board of Trade rejected the proposal (it had no authority to impose taxes anyway) but set up a three-man committee, including Powell, to study the issue. The board president remarked that some of the finest homestead land was being taken up by negroes, thus making it "worthless for white settlement."

Blacks were refused service in Calgary hotel bars; the attorney general said he couldn't force hoteliers to serve anyone. In Edmonton a black man – "well dressed, in fact stylishly and expensively garbed," said a news report – entered a busy restaurant with a companion and took the last remaining seats at a communal table occupied by a white family. The family stalked out in a rage. The proprietor offered to find the whites a private table elsewhere, but the father cried, "Eat in your place with cattle? No, I'll starve first!" Other diners glared, two more left, but the black couple stuck it out and finished their meal.

The Board of Trade circulated an anti-black petition in downtown banks, hotels, and realty offices; thirty-four hundred Edmontonians signed it. The board also pressured its Red Deer counterpart to take up the cause, which it did (its secretary, speaking to the anti-black resolution, said they were "an undesirable class of settler and would eventually become a trouble and a burden to the community").

In fact, many of the black settlers were well-heeled, averaging three hundred dollars each and, in some cases, bringing in as much as thirty-five hundred dollars. Many also brought their own tools and farm implements. "Canada gets only the best of the coloured immigrants," observed the *Edmonton Bulletin*, "for the railways refuse to give them reduced fares. Consequently, none except those that have considerable money make the venture."

There were a few encouraging signs. The Lethbridge Board of Trade refused to be bullied into joining Edmonton's crusade. "If a man has the ability, the honesty and industry to become a good citizen of this country, Canadian justice sees not the colour of his skin," wrote the *Lethbridge Herald*.

Meanwhile, Chinese immigrants suffered their own siege of persecution. Most worked in cities and towns, running restaurants, laundries, or market gardens. They tended to cluster in "Chinatowns" for friendship and because most of white society shunned them.

"The favourite whipping boys of the media . . . were the Chinese," wrote Western historian James Gray. "[They] were treated with contemptuous brutality. 'Cleaning out the Chinks' became a common phrase of the small town toughs and livery stable loafers. When they got sufficiently imbued with whisky courage they would gang up in an invasion of a Chinese restaurant or laundry and wreck the place, and in the riot that developed it was usually the Chinese who were arrested."

Saskatchewan passed an early law banning the employment of white women in "any establishment operated by a Chinaman." In Calgary the Chinese community, having been run out of its previous locale by Canadian Northern Railway expansion, pooled its money in 1910 to raise a twenty-thousand-dollar headquarters around Centre Street and Second Avenue. A deputation of angry property owners in the area demanded that city council segregate the Chinese. Their spokesman, James Short, K.C., said the Chinese "should be treated much the same as an infectious disease or an isolation hospital. They live like rabbits in a warren. Thirty of them crowd in where five white people would ordinarily reside."

The "celestials" or "sons of Confucius" were always good for a lurid story on opium or gambling. A trip to an "opium den" inspired news reports of "ten or twelve repulsive looking Chinamen lounging" or "two fearful looking Mongolians [lying] stupidly on one of the benches."

Little wonder that the populace at large applied the same damning clichés to all Chinese. One Sunday just before Christmas in 1913, a speaker in Red Deer addressed the Young Men's Club on "The Yellow Peril." To mark the season of brotherly love he stated that Asians were "a menace to law and order, to sanitation, to good morals and were hard to assimilate politically, forming a class far too easily bought by unscrupulous politicians."

As if white men's censure was not burden enough, law-abiding Chinese briefly contended with their own mafia. In 1911 Edmonton police clamped down on a "highbinders' society," a fifteen-man gang working a protection racket on Chinese businessmen. Or, as the *Journal* tastelessly described it, "a gang of lazy Chinks living a life of ease by tyrannizing hard working Celestials." (These particular thugs either had low expectations or were part-time laundrymen. According to testimony, Jim On and Mah Jim Gook threatened to kill storekeeper

Hong Tai if he didn't hand over one hundred dollars, a box of starch, and a case of laundry soap.)

Grudgingly, some facets of Alberta society accepted the Chinese. Chinese cooks became a fixture in homes and restaurants, usually with one-word names – Wong, Slim, Looie – like family pets. Chinese houseboys were prized by the well-to-do.

Today, many leading prairie citizens are of Asian background. Josephine Smart, born in Hong Kong and now a Ph.D. in anthropology teaching at the University of Calgary, points out that as immigration laws changed (in relatively recent times), newcomers with better education and economic standing were admitted to Canada, and "the children follow in the parents' footsteps. So overall there has been a very clear process of elevation of Chinese residents in Canada."

Boys in Their Hoods

That the Ku Klux Klan, of all organizations, should become entrenched in gentle Saskatchewan, of all places, now seems like a very bad joke. Yet entrenched it was, from 1927 to the beginning of the Depression.

The Klan, with its history in the United States of vicious racism, murder, and arson, and its ridiculous adolescent titles – King Kleagle, Exalted Cyclops, Grand Wizard, Grand Dragon – tapped into a prairie streak of racial prejudice and religious bigotry directed at Roman Catholics, Jews, and all "foreigners." More astonishing, it had an estimated twenty-five thousand members in scores of small Saskatchewan towns, most cities, and many Protestant churches. Even segments of the press, particularly small-town weeklies, endorsed the Klan, or at least failed to criticize it.

The Klan in its short Canadian life had locals from coast to coast. Its appeal in Saskatchewan dated back to the turn of the century, when waves of immigrants alarmed and angered the dominant Anglo-Saxon population. Veterans of the First World War felt that too few immigrants answered the call to arms, that many had stayed home making money and getting more land while patriots were out fighting. City labourers resented immigrants competing for jobs. A particular sore point was the teaching of languages other than English – especially French – in public schools, which in turn caused resentment against Roman Catholicism. This was fertile ground for the Klan.

Organizers from Indiana established the Canadian connection in Toronto in the mid-1920s. Next it tried the Maritimes, then started up in Calgary, and eventually spread to Red Deer, Drumheller, Vulcan, Taber, and Edmonton.

Three Klansmen reached Regina in late 1926: Lewis A. Scott (later King Kleagle, or chief recruiter, in the province, a self-styled godly man always with his nose in a Bible), Scott's son, and a shifty colleague, Hugh Emmons, who had a string of aliases. They littered city mailboxes with a pamphlet, "Why I Intend to Become a Klan Member," set up meetings, and established a local (members signed up for thirteen dollars a head) under the slogan "One Flag, One Language, One School, One Race, One Religion." A widely circulated letter urged the government to put the Union Jack in every Regina home and to hire only Protestants as teachers and civil servants.

Within a year there was a strong organization in Moose Jaw, where the Klan proposed to clean up River Street's bars and bawdy houses, and where on June 7, 1927, the biggest Klan Konclave in Canada drew close to ten thousand curious onlookers from all over the province. It ended with the burning of a sixty-foot fiery cross on Caribou Street.

Klan locals cropped up all over the province. There were no lynchings or house burnings, just an occasional flaming cross.

Early on, a few Klansmen wore their trademark white hoods, but the Klan quickly backed away from the bedsheets with the ugly American connotations. Mostly it relied on rhetoric, kindling people's innate fear and prejudice.

Things seemed to be going swimmingly for the Klan until September 1927, when Scott and Emmons disappeared with all the funds, an estimated hundred thousand dollars (a fortune in the 1920s). The Bible-thumping King Kleagle was never captured. The slippery Emmons was tried for embezzlement but acquitted. The money was never recovered.

That should have scuttled the Klan, but it still had momentum. By 1929 there were 125 locals and enthusiastic rallies across Saskatchewan. Its posture as a religious organization seduced the public. Ceremonies leaned heavily on Biblical quotations. Meetings opened and closed with prayer. Hymns were sung. Speeches had the sonorous ring of sermons. Protestant churchmen – particularly of the United Church – endorsed the Klan. Some were members.

Reverend William Surman, minister of Regina's Cameron Memorial Baptist Church, once told a Regina meeting, "As a minister of the Gospel, I see nothing contradictory in the principles which I teach and the principles of the Klan to which I belong." Surman was Exalted Cyclops (chief organizer) of the Regina Klan.

Fewer Anglican churchmen were suckered in. Their national publication, *The Canadian Churchman*, described Klan activities in the United States as "shocking folly" and "loathsome tyranny." But the Right Reverend Dr. G.E. Lloyd, Anglican bishop of Saskatchewan, played right into the organization's hands by labelling immigrants as "these dirty, ignorant, garlic-smelling non-preferred continentals."

The Klan became a hot political issue. Liberals, vigorously led by Premier James G. Gardiner, were mainly opposed, as were most of Saskatchewan's larger pro-Liberal dailies. But the Klan attracted followers from every party. Conservatives were the main supporters. There were hints – but no proof – that Conservative leader Dr. James T.M. Anderson was among them. Anderson publicly and strongly denied it. William Calderwood, author of the definitive study, *The Rise and Fall of the Ku Klux Klan in Saskatchewan*, put it well: "The Liberal party condemned the Klan as something alien and potentially dangerous to Saskatchewan – the only position it could take in order to placate the strong Catholic and immigrant segments of its support. The Conservative party . . . similarly adopted an attitude that was politically expedient by taking advantage of the emotionalism aroused by the Klan, by secretly obtaining the endorsation of Klan leaders regarding certain planks in its platform, and by publicly remaining silent on the Klan issue."

The Co-operatives (a coalition of Conservatives and others) won the 1929 provincial election, ousting the Liberals for the first time in twenty-four years. The Klan tried to gain a foothold in Winnipeg in 1928 with an avowed intention of cleaning up "rampant vice" and fighting the intermarriage of "Japs and whites, Chinese and whites" but soon died out.

By the early 1930s, the Depression, with its overwhelming despair and struggle for sheer existence, dispelled the Klan and its evil agenda. A female letter writer to the *Western Producer* aptly summarized the sentiment of that strange time: "The Ku Klux Klan is similar, I believe, to other organizations which have sprung up when people have lost confidence in constituted authority; when they feel that justice too often miscarries – that politics and patronage figure too largely in our courts; that the welfare of the state is made subservient to the interest of the party, permitting privileges to influential minorities – privileges detrimental to the best interest of society as a whole."

James G. Gardiner went into federal politics. The Co-operatives lost office in 1934, and the Conservatives were not elected in Saskatchewan again until forty-eight years later.

The only winner was Scott, the elusive King Kleagle, who perhaps lived happily ever after with the missing hundred thousand dollars.

Bad Girls and Worse Guys

When I was a lad, learning to be a ham-fisted mechanic in the RCAF Wartime Emergency Training Program (WETP), I was billeted with four other airmen in a boarding house on Moose Jaw's River Street. It seemed as though the Great God of Sex had smiled down upon us.

In that autumn of 1943, meeting girls – preferably bad ones – was high on our wish list, just behind an instant cure for acne. We could not afford to dance at Temple Gardens, to the music of Cal Temple's Tantalizing Toe Ticklers; anyway, only good girls went there. But our River Street, a nudge and a wink from the CPR tracks, was reputed to be the heart of a flourishing red-light district. Each morning as we marched to the WETP building (known to us as Wet Pee) we eagerly scanned the horizon for bad girls, whores even (pronounced *hoo-ers*).

We were, alas, twenty years too late. Still, a phantom red-light reputation lingered on, earning us River Street dwellers some respectful punches on the biceps from our fellows at Wet Pee. It was almost as gratifying as meeting an actual hoo-er.

The fact that slumberous little Moose Jaw was *ever* Sin City defies belief. Even before Saskatchewan became a province, the town had bootleggers and crooked cops but this was relatively small beer, so to speak, in a frontier society. Before the First World War, local citizens were more preoccupied with getting a better name for their respectable community. Critics of "Moose Jaw" called it "barbarous," "odious," and "the laughing stock of the travelling public," but it stuck.

Then came Prohibition. Finally Moose Jaw got some respect.

Prohibition reigned on the prairie from the late 1910s to the mid-1920s (it varied by province). Bootleggers in high-powered cars raced merrily across the flatland at night. The Studebaker Big Six, known as the Whiskey Six for its ability, with back seat removed, to carry fifty gallon-jugs of booze, was a favourite – especially when equipped with two spare tires, a thirty-foot chain dragged behind to kick up dirt in the faces of pursuing cops, and a spotlight to blind them if the dust failed.

Saskatchewan liquor-export houses, called "boozoriums," sprang up throughout the south. Some of these supplied rum-runners from the States. Some catered to Manitobans. Some just slaked the local thirst. By 1920 there were boozoriums in twenty-five Saskatchewan communities from Bienfait and Broadview to Swift Current and Senate. (Senate, as it happens, was the hometown of my maternal Aunt Ferne and Uncle Charlie Soderberg, but I am confident that not one drop of demon booze passed their lips. As evangelical Christians of the highest order, their drink was lemonade.)

Boozoriums were dealt a crippling blow in 1922 when the Saskatchewan government passed an Order-in-Council restricting liquor-export houses to cities of ten thousand or more. That narrowed them down to Regina, Moose Jaw, and Saskatoon.

Moose Jaw thrived in those times largely because it was the Canadian terminus of the Soo Line, a rail connection to Chicago and its gangsters. Speakeasies and blind pigs rose up all over Moose Jaw's south side, particularly on River Street near the railway. With the booze came gambling and prostitution. Moose Jaw was where Reginans went for a good time (which will send today's Reginans into fits of laughter).

The late James Gray, chronicler of the prairie's racy past, quoted an eyewitness to River Street's bad old days: "You came out of Moose Jaw station, turned left on River Street and you could have been in New Orleans. If it was early in the day you could see girls waving from the windows of the hotels across the street. If they caught your eye they'd call you up. . . .

"By night the streets were really filled with men roaming around, and the traffic down to the whore houses was something to see. There was nothing attractive about any of the houses or in fact about most of the girls. . . . How many women worked on River Street? A lot more in summer than in winter but I'd guess a year round minimum of at least 50 and perhaps more than 100 when things were really jumping."

Moose Jaw's police chief of twenty-two years, Walter P. Johnson, made many a flamboyant raid but never quite put the lid on local crime. Cynics said he didn't try, that he even tipped off proprietors before raids. They found it odd that Johnson could afford, on a cop's salary, a big home in town and a thousand-acre farm outside the city.

When American Prohibition went into force, the Moose Jaw–Chicago run carried booze the other way (it was legal to sell liquor to Americans as long as the Canadian government collected export duty). Al Capone – head of the Chicago-based American crime empire that reportedly took in a hundred million dollars a year from every known illegal activity – supposedly visited Moose Jaw himself.

Just why he would bother is difficult to fathom, but tales are still told of former citizens who met Scarface Al. One that I'd like to believe involves Carl Rud, who later farmed around my hometown and was a man of shining probity. Before his death he told his story to his granddaughter, Gina Knelsen Schall.

Carl moved to Regina from Minnesota in 1912 and worked for the Heinzmann piano company. Sometimes he tuned pianos in Moose Jaw and, to save hotel expenses, stayed with a friend who happened to be a gambler and bookie. (It's unlikely that straight-arrow Carl knew this at the start.) On one trip he walked into the friend's house unannounced. The bookie went into shock: "Carl, what the hell are you doing here?"

As Carl later told it, he saw three strangers. "One was sitting down at the kitchen table while the other two were standing behind and on each side of him. The men were wearing fancy suits and hats. One man had his hand inside his suit coat while the other was reaching into his coat."

The bookie hustled his surprise visitor out and Carl went to a hotel. Later the bookie told Carl he had blundered into the presence of Al Capone. The bookie had vouched for his friend, which perhaps saved Carl from being outfitted with cement overshoes. He never stayed at the bookie's house again.

Today River Street is tame, but the tourist industry is thriving. Part of it centres around underground tunnels, supposedly dug for and by hundreds of illegal Chinese immigrants of earlier decades who, it's said, lived in the dirt tunnels while trying to save enough money to pay the head tax that would enable Canadian citizenship. During rum-running days the passages were allegedly used to hustle liquor to various hotels and speakeasies. Today, the underground tunnels have been cemented, bricked, and prettied up for visitors from all over the world.

Trouble is, says Regina author Ken Mitchell, who heavily researched the subject for a CBC documentary, "It's all hogwash, a creation of the local chamber of commerce/city administration to promote tourism."

Mitchell says the tunnel legend seems to have originated in the 1960s, when the CPR main station was closed to passenger traffic and the underground walkway from the terminal to the trains was shut. "There is no newspaper or historical reference to any underground tunnels before that time. The fact is, not one secret tunnel has ever been located, excavated, or discovered. They're all recently constructed fakes."

The tunnels are reconstructions *and* originals, maintains Candis Kirkpatrick, spokesperson for Tunnels of Moose Jaw. "Many downtown buildings have evidence of passageways between them, long ago boarded or bricked up. We have seen a number of pictures, taken by city crews, of tunnels up to thirty feet long and four feet high. We tell stories combining what is known to be fact with what could have been. We do not claim to know who built the tunnel spaces or for what reason."

So year-round guided tours – with actors, animated figures, and youthful guides trying too hard to be witty – are based on the Chinese and on Capone. Moose Jaw is possibly the only city in Canada to use a dead gangster and debatable history as a tourist attraction.

"The Broncho's Lot Is Not a Happy One"

Popular recreational hangouts for Alberta ranch hands were, of course, bars, brothels, and dance halls. The women in such establishments, circa 1880s, were generally Métis or aboriginal. Some had never been to a white man's dance before. The cowboys treated them as beasts of burden: they were "bronchos" who had to be "broken" to perform the dances so foreign to them.

A compassionate onlooker at one such dance in Fort Macleod was disgusted by what he saw: "The broncho's lot is not a happy one, and she has not sufficient of her white sister's art to pretend that she in the least enjoys a dance. While her wild and woolly partner turns a hand spring in front of her, kicks over her head two or three times, and performs various other graceful feats, she hangs her head on one side, stands first on one foot and then on the other (her shoes hurt her), and looks on with stolid indifference."

The Last Great Train Robbery

The Canadian prairie never had the gunslingers, stagecoach robbers, or shootouts on Main Street claimed (not always accurately) by the American West. Much of our relative tranquillity was thanks to the RCMP, who kept the law from the time they arrived in 1884 as the North-West Mounted Police.

Even visiting gunmen turned into pussycats when they crossed the international border. The legendary Sundance Kid once worked in Alberta and was a model of propriety. While hiding out from U.S. lawmen, the Kid (real name Harry Longabough) took a job from 1890 to 1892 as a broncobuster at the Bar U ranch near Longview. The real Sundance, unlike Butch Cassidy's dour partner in the Hollywood movie, was rated a "thoroughly likeable fellow . . . a general favourite with everyone, a splendid rider and a top notch cow hand."

But in 1920 the West lucked into a pulp-fiction writer's dream: a bona fide train robbery with gunplay, killings, manhunt (wily bandit, dogged investigator), and a denouement that hinged on a single clue. Thirty-eight years later, as Western editor of *Maclean's*, I tracked down the surviving players to write the first complete account of the incident and its aftermath.

On the slumberous afternoon of Monday, August 2, CPR train No. 63 – two passenger cars, baggage and express, originating in Lethbridge and bound for Cranbrook – had just moseyed out of Coleman, Alberta. Beyond lay a whistle stop called Sentinel, then the Crowsnest Pass leading through the Rockies into British Columbia.

Conductor Sam Jones checked his pocket watch. Nearly five p.m. He admired the timepiece for a moment before slipping it back in his vest. It was gold, a twenty-three-jewel Elgin, only two weeks old. He'd paid ninety-six dollars for it, about a month's wages, and was inordinately proud of his purchase.

He strolled among the train's thirty or forty passengers – commercial travellers, housewives, a few campers heading for

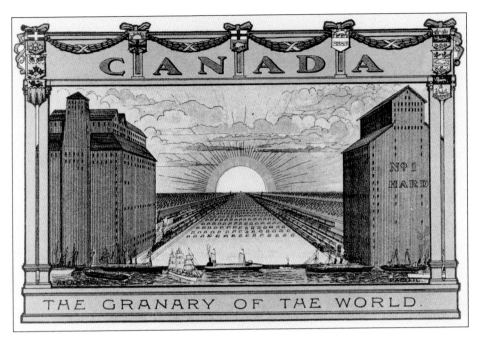

CANADA

THE GRANARY OF THE WORLD.

With gusts of rhetoric and outright obfuscation, the federal government lured settlers to the west. This 1903 pamphlet entices them to a romanticized landscape with towering grain elevator, huge benevolent sun, and fertile fields running off into infinity. (Glenbow Archives NA-789-161)

The reality was a little different, but
never more so than in the desperate
1930s, when incessant dust storms
blew away prairie farmers' crops and
hopes. In 1938 the familiar ugly black
cloud swirled into Parkland, Alberta.
(Glenbow Archives NA-2271-1)

From the late 1800s, hopeful immigrants swarmed in by the thousands, packed cheek-by-jowl into ocean liners (here, the *Empress of Ireland*, out of Liverpool in 1910). The trip could last up to twenty-eight days, with indifferent food, crude bunks, and seasick passengers. Some could never again face warm pork or pickled herring. (Glenbow Archives NA-1960-1)

Many Europeans, like these Doukhobors in Winnipeg's CPR station in 1899, arrived in their native dress – often to the derision of established Canadians. The newcomers endured the taunts, worked hard, and made the West a better place. (Glenbow Archives NA-2660-1)

The Grigg family sets out down
Edmonton's Jasper Avenue in 1910
for their homestead at Mayerthorpe,
Alberta. Today it would be an easy
one-and-a-half-hour drive. It took
the Griggs and their oxen twelve days.
(Glenbow Archives NA-477-1)

Before telephones, the chattering tele-graph was every small community's lifeline. John Thomson, tele-graph operator at Limerick, Saskatchewan, takes down a message from the outer world in 1909. (Glenbow Archives NA-3626-1)

When the phone became commonplace, linemen roamed the prairie raising poles and connecting wires. This southern Alberta crew outfitted its horses with burlap nose-guards to keep mosquitoes out of their nostrils. (Glenbow Archives NA-2581-5)

A bit of a dandy, this Milk River, Alberta, cowboy, with his chaps, necktie, clean hat, and fresh shave. Bring on the Saturday night dance. (Glenbow Archives NA-777-21)

The road to modern prairie cuisine was paved with cholesterol and acid indigestion. Pioneers, settlers and cowhands ate anything, as long as it was meat. Chances are this chuck wagon meal featured the ever-popular barely digestible beefsteak and beans. (Glenbow Archives NA-763-1)

How many Pincher Creek cowboys did it take to brand a calf in 1886? One to ride the horse, one to hold the rope, eight to hold down the top rail of the corral. (Glenbow Archives NA-936-39)

It still takes teamwork. The multi-talented Boneskys of Morse, Saskatchewan, all pull their weight: (left to right) son-in-law Jason Dean, daughters Kelly and Lori, mother Karen, father Larry. "Our strengths are awesome," beams Karen. (Robert Collins)

It doesn't look like Heaven-on-Earth, but for these barefoot mid–European immigrants, their 1903 sod shack near Yorkton, Saskatchewan, was infinitely better than the world they left behind. (Glenbow Archives NA-2878-63)

Scottish settlers James and Florence Aitkenhead, with daughters Florence, Lily, and Gladys, and sons Alexander, William, and Charles, all of Naseby, Saskatchewan. With their substantial sod house and Sunday best, they had the world by the tail in 1905. (Glenbow Archives NA-2384-1)

Never mind the washtub, hand-cranked wringer, and plain frame house, there's pride and a touch of elegance in this woman's dress and hairstyle on laundry day near Balzac, Alberta, in 1905. (Glenbow Archives NA-3731-8)

the Rockies, three labourers from Lethbridge. Train robberies were unimaginable by 1920. With faster trains, better express cars, fast telegraphy, and motorized police forces, robbers didn't stand a chance.

Which is why Jones's jaw dropped when he glanced into the lavatory and saw one of the "labourers" aiming a pistol at his stomach. At the other end of the car a second labourer arose waving a Mauser automatic.

"Put up your hands, everybody!" he shouted in a thick accent.

A third gunman – big, dark, square-faced, with a shaggy moustache – stood up with a Luger. Then, not bothering to put on masks, the trio began to rob the train.

Conductor Jones was more irked than frightened. He pulled the signal cord. One jerk meant to stop at the next point for detraining passengers. Two jerks would tell the engineer to stop immediately. Before he could yank it a second time, a bullet thudded into the woodwork beside his head. Jones sat down abruptly.

The shot discouraged other potential heroes. The bandits herded everyone into the first-class coach and began gathering money. They collected about three hundred dollars, grumbling, obviously expecting more. Suddenly the train jolted to a standstill. The engineer, responding to conductor Jones's single signal, had stopped at Sentinel.

"Why we stop?" one robber demanded. Jones refused to answer. As they jumped from the train one of them yanked Jones's new gold watch from his vest, breaking the chain. Another fired a shot. The startled engineer pulled away and the bandits disappeared over a hill.

By the next day the Crowsnest Pass was teeming with Alberta Provincial Police, RCMP, CPR police, reserve army, and civilians, including three aboriginal trackers. The bandits had vanished in a wilderness of bush and craggy rocks, but police had identified them from the descriptions. The moustached giant was Tom Basoff. His cohort with the Mauser was Alex Auloff. The third was George Akoff. Wags in the posse called them the "All-offs." They were believed to be Russian labourers in their twenties or thirties. Police suspected they had hoped for a bigger haul: the king of prairie bootleggers, Emilio "Emperor Pic" Picariello, often travelled this route with a wad of cash from his liquor profits.

The bandits were either too arrogant or too stupid to flee the country. On Friday, four days after the robbery, Basoff and Akoff visited a dance and a bawdy house in Bellevue, a coal-mining town in the Crowsnest. The next day they strolled boldly down the main street and sat down to lunch at the Bellevue Café. RCMP Corporal Ernest Usher and two Alberta Provincial Police, Frederick Bailey and James Frewin, went in after them.

Bystanders heard a volley of gunfire. Then the horrified residents of the little town witnessed a grim tableau: Usher stumbled from the café and fell bleeding on the step. Bailey backed out, fell over him, and lay temporarily stunned. Next came Akoff, bleeding and vomiting. He staggered a few feet and fell dead.

Finally Basoff emerged, limping from a bullet in his leg, and fired shot after shot into the two fallen policemen, killing them both. He limped away, oblivious to ineffectual sniping from the surviving constable, Frewin.

Now southern Alberta rose up in arms. Men poured in by car, train, and horse-drawn wagon. By Sunday at least two hundred were combing the Crowsnest. Still no Basoff – although word came down that he had appeared at a ranch only two miles from Bellevue, where a terrified housewife handed over bread, cheese, and water.

On Wednesday two deputy sheriffs from Seattle arrived with three highly touted bloodhounds: Dynamite, Lightning, and

Dan. The hounds were a flop. They bayed impressively, ran up and down hills, peed on bushes, but found nothing. It turned out Basoff had slipped through the police cordon, hobbled twenty miles east, got up on a railway trestle, and was close to freedom. Then he made a simple mistake in hobo etiquette.

That night a CPR engineer operating a pusher engine caught a man in his headlights. The man looked away. The engineer was instantly suspicious: even hobos routinely waved or at least looked up when a train passed. He called the police. Later that night they found Basoff huddled outside a shack in Pincher Creek. He was convicted of murder and hanged in December.

Still no sign of Alex Auloff and conductor Jones's gold watch. An Alberta Provincial Police assistant superintendent followed the escapee's trail through towns and lumber camps all over the American northwest. Auloff, with the help of friends (perhaps bought with robbery money), stayed a step ahead.

Calgary detective Ernest Schoeppe took over the manhunt. A patient, powerful, thick-shouldered man more than six feet tall, Schoeppe spoke seven languages. For three months, posing as a transient and friend of Auloff, he drifted through Oregon, Idaho, Montana, and Washington. Auloff eluded him.

Schoeppe went home, waited, and listened to his sources. In January 1924 a telegram from Oregon told him Sam Jones's watch had turned up in a pawnshop. Schoeppe grabbed a train to Portland, redeemed the watch, and learned it had been pawned by a miner from Butte, Montana. And there he caught up with Auloff, who was travelling under an alias and denying everything.

Schoeppe put him on a train for Canada. Along the way he silently dangled the watch under Auloff's nose. At last the bandit broke down.

"All right, I'm your man. That damned watch! I wish I'd thrown it away."

Sam Jones met their train in Alberta. As he entered the coach the cocky Auloff grinned at him. "Hello, conductor."

"Where's my watch?" Jones demanded.

Schoeppe handed it over. It later appeared as evidence at the trial, where Auloff was sentenced to seven years. Then Sam Jones tucked it back in his pocket. The last great train robbery was over.

HE GOT HIS MAN

It will never be a feature film starring Paul Gross, but this masterpiece of understatement — a RNWMP corporal's official report on his arrest of a minor badman — shows how Mounties in the Old West matter-of-factly did their duty:

"On the 17th inst. I, Corporal Hogg, was called to the hotel [in North Portal, Saskatchewan] to quiet a disturbance. I found the room full of cowboys and one Monoghan, or Cowboy Jack, was carrying a gun, and pointed it at me against sections 105 and 109 of the Criminal Code. We struggled. Finally I got him hand-cuffed behind and put him inside.

"His head being in bad shape we had to engage the services of a doctor who dressed his wound and pronounced it nothing serious."

V

A KINDER, GENTLER PLACE

*I need that enormous courtesy of people
who always seem to recognize a friend and a stranger.*

RALPH HEDLIN
upon returning to his native prairie from the East

The Helping Tradition

"The characteristic of the prairie person to me," celebrated Westerner Peter Lougheed told me, "the one that is most relevant, is the characteristic of helping one's neighbour in distress."

"When I read about Canadians being defined by their niceness, their modesty, their dedication to community," says former broadcaster Jeannine Locke of Toronto, "I always think that it is the people of Saskatchewan, my home and native land, that they're really describing."

Are prairie people friendlier, kinder, more generous? Statistics say yes. Overall, says a study by Paul B. Reed and Kevin Selbee, the prairies have the highest rate of volunteering – 39 per cent – and are Canada's biggest charitable donors: 85 per cent of them give, averaging $354 a year. Manitobans top the nation, giving $383 per adult person per year.

With those numbers goes a reputation for sunny dispositions. There are plenty of cranky Westerners, but most are kept locked up in root cellars when tourists pass by. In a Web site for Saskatchewan residents and expatriates you read, from Creston, British Columbia, "Nice here but I sure miss the people in FRIENDLY Saskatoon," and from Saskatoon, "It's so friendly here I can't leave the house without running into someone I know. That makes it tough to get up to no good."

Consider, too, the motorist's wave. It is mandatory on lesser roads – not on main highways, where all motorists, especially Albertans, are hell-bent on speed and destruction – to wave at an oncoming driver. The other must wave back. He may not know you, but then again he *might*, and dares not risk rudeness. It is fun to practise this in a village by waving at a motorist or some innocent on the sidewalk. You are moving slowly. The other can see your car and your face. Clearly you are a stranger, yet the prairie code compels him to wave back. And you leave him wondering, *Should I know that guy?*

The tradition of friendship, of helping, of working together for the good of all, is rooted in pioneer beginnings. Prairie co-operatives, credit unions, mutual telephone companies, and wheat pools were the homesteaders' defence against railroads, grain companies, banks, and the other monoliths ranged against them. The three provincial wheat pools arose from the conviction that farmer-owned co-operatives would give them a better deal than the established grain-company elevators which – with the railways' tacit approval – monopolized country shipping points and regularly bilked the farmers.

Alberta Wheat Pool organized first in 1923. Vincent Massey, one day to be governor general, called it "the greatest agricultural co-operative scheme in the world." Manitoba and Saskatchewan pools quickly followed. By the end of the 1920s the three had the largest cash turnover of any business in Canada: $323 million. (The pools are now vastly changed. Alberta Wheat Pool and Manitoba Pool Elevators merged to become Agricore, then melded with United Grain Growers as Agricore United.)

Other consumer co-operatives became an integral part of every community. In the late 1990s, writes Brett Fairbairn, of the University of Saskatchewan's Centre for the Study of Co-operatives, Saskatchewan alone had fifteen hundred co-ops with reported revenues of nearly seven million dollars and assets of more than nine million dollars. This in a province of (at the time) just one million people of which the gross domestic product was twenty-nine billion dollars. Two-thirds to three-quarters of the province's households have memberships in a co-op.

Co-operation has lost some of its original bent, thinks Roger Epp, associate professor of political studies at Augustana University College in Camrose, Alberta: "Even the nature of farm work today doesn't demand co-operation. If someone has a problem in the field, they don't call their neighbour, they call the factory."

He says young farmers in particular concentrate more on competing with each other than co-operating for general gain. "On the other hand, in these desperate times for farmers and for rural communities there is, in places, a renewed interest in co-operative enterprise." There is more informal talk of, say, machinery co-ops, and of joint marketing of grain by an entire neighbourhood, either to reduce capital costs or to regain some modest market power for producers in relation to agri-food processors.

Elsewhere, helping continues in the century-old tradition.

Unsung Heroines

The operative word is *caring*, wrote columnist Roy MacGregor in a hymn of praise to Saskatchewan. "Caring enough to give. Caring enough to help. Caring enough to become involved rather than simply sitting back and sniping from the edges, as most of the rest of us do."

The essence of caring is volunteerism and the prairie provinces excel at it. Saskatchewan leads the country: 42 per cent of its people do volunteer work, as do 39 per cent of Albertans and 36 per cent of Manitobans. Apart from Prince Edward Island (37 per cent) all other provinces fall behind.

Manitoba lieutenant governor Peter Liba says his province couldn't exist without volunteerism. It's a multi-billion dollar industry providing employment for as many as a hundred thousand Manitobans in various organizations. "It accounts for 15 per cent of our gross domestic product," Liba told me enthusiastically. "It represents more than seven thousand charities and non-profit organizations. Volunteers contribute some forty-four million hours of labour per year in Manitoba, which equates to about 23,500 full-time jobs. More than 340,000 Manitobans volunteer each year.

"It's time we recognize it as the third sector in society, with the public and private sectors," Liba sums up. "It is a huge part of life in our province."

The core of this prairie effort is women – a legion of unsung, unpaid heroines whose potluck suppers and unflagging energy help keep rural society alive. Gwen McEwan of Whitewood, Saskatchewan, is a consummate example. "I've never worked since I was married," says Gwen at her home of fifty-six years, brimming with bric-a-brac, figurines, and other precious clutter. "I like organization work, always did as a kid. They said if the dogs organized a group I'd be president."

She has been president of the local ladies' auxiliary for fifty-six years (she started it). She'll volunteer for any church that needs her. She's on the hospital committee, sings at seniors' homes with the local Harmony Choir, belongs to the museum association, helps dole out cookies and juice for vacation Bible schools every August. She is queen of the fowl supper, a mainstay of rural volunteerism. Nowadays these are often called "smorgs," as in smorgasbord, enabling donors to bring a variety of food, and earning as much as two thousand dollars a pop for worthy causes.

Usually there is a silent partner in the equation. Gwen has husband Al, one of those quiet retired gents who are the rock upon which volunteer wives stand. (When Whitewood was painting its famous wall mural – see pages 150-51 – Al lugged a sofa on site so the painters could rest.)

"We were *sick* one winter!" Gwen says, still exasperated at the memory. "Al and I had never been sick in our lives! I was like a caged lion. I'd get up in the morning and know it was a meeting day, or the Christmas party, everything that I'd never missed before. I said I'd get high blood pressure over it all and I *did*." Her blood pressure dropped to normal as soon as she was back organizing.

Gwen, Ann Brown of Central Butte, Anne Willner of Davidson, and Florence Widdicombe of Foxwarren, Manitoba, are sisters under the skin. Widdicombe calls volunteerism her "illness." "All my life in all my spare time I've been a volunteer. I taught folk ethnic dance for twenty-two years; sang with the Foxwarren Ladies Ensemble, now in its thirty-fourth year; was church-choir director for twenty-five years. I sat on all the church committees. I had piles of minute books behind the bedroom door."

Ann Brown, sixty-six, was secretary of the Central Butte homecoming that brought two thousand people back to celebrate their little town in 2001. Like Gwen McEwan, she has a stalwart husband, Fred, who says, "If you want to get something done in a small town, ask somebody who's busy."

Ann has served on the local Home Care board, played the church organ for twenty years, led two local choirs, was census commissioner, a Canadian Girls in Training (CGIT) leader, and a Brownie leader.

"I was thinking the other day of all I've done, and it's scary," she says.

"Every once in a while you were a mother," Fred retorts, with a weather-beaten grin.

"My house would be an absolute terror," Ann admits, "but Fred helps, washing dishes, cleaning up."

"If a guy's gonna eat he *has* to help," Fred says, but clearly he's proud of his perpetual-motion wife.

Anne Willner and husband Wayne, in their forties, have two daughters, Aleah and Chelsey, and farm twelve hundred acres of wheat, barley, mustard, peas, and lentils. That's full-time employment in itself, but they volunteer at the local rink a few hours every month. Anne is vice-president of the local Girl Guides Association, treasurer of the Davidson gymnastics club, and bookkeeper for the Sacred Heart church.

"I do volunteer work wherever I go," says Anne, a short, dark-haired dynamo, words tumbling out once she gets over her unease with my tape recorder. "Today I'm catering my neighbour's twenty-fifth anniversary, a roast beef supper. Just finished a reunion last week. It's all *very* much worth it. They said, 'What do we pay you for the catering?' I said, 'Just pay for the cost of the food.' To me, that's what a good neighbour would do."

Eighty per cent of their neighbours do volunteer work, she adds, "because that's the only way we can keep facilities in our small community. When Dad was in hospital dying, the neighbours pulled in five combines and helped us finish harvesting. They looked after my kids and cooked all the meals. In turn, someday we will go back and help them, and no payment is expected. What goes around, comes around."

The night before the Willners' own family reunion in 1999, they discovered the local campground had double-booked. At ten-thirty Anne began phoning. By eight-thirty the next morning she'd rounded up enough neighbours' trailers to accommodate fifty people in the Willners' yard. "We hadn't budgeted for that and trailer rental isn't cheap, so all we could do to repay them was host a supper."

Prairie people are big on impromptu suppers to keep spirits up in bad times. The summer I visited the Willners was perilously dry. To help take the curse off it, Anne said to Wayne, "We haven't had a barbecue for a while." They invited everybody to a wiener roast.

"I could tell you all the problems of the world," Anne said later, "but men hold it in. So when they get together like on that night, with other men, they talk. And it helps."

The vibrant spirit of prairie volunteerism is really an extension of the general civility of the people. Saskatchewan-born Ralph Hedlin, a Winnipeg freelance writer when I first met him in the 1950s, switched into entrepreneurism and followed the money east – but his heart wasn't there.

"After a good many years, I came back to the prairies," says Hedlin, now in Calgary. "I need that enormous courtesy of people who always seem to recognize a friend and a stranger."

The courtesy is genuine. One wet June afternoon, bound for friends near Coderre, I took a wrong turn off secondary highway 363 and sank to the hubcaps in southern Saskatchewan's famous gumbo. I started walking, it turned out, in the wrong direction (you really *can't* go home again, unless you know your right from your left) and trudged for forty minutes in rain without seeing so much as a gopher.

Then along came a vanload of people led by David and Pat Arnold. We'd never met, but they cheerfully alerted my hosts by cellphone, drove back to my stranded rental car, pushed me out (getting mud-caked in the process) and went merrily on their way. They never dreamed of asking for money.

In southeastern Saskatchewan Jim and Olive Hannah's daughter Margie had leukemia. Neighbours and acquaintances far beyond their town of Frobisher pitched sixteen thousand dollars into a fund to help send the girl to Vancouver for treatment. Her sister donated the necessary bone marrow. Margie recovered.

Would this have happened in any small community? Maybe, but the Hannahs think it is peculiar to the prairies, along with Jim's habit of ploughing snow for every sidewalk on his block in winter and mowing every lawn in summer.

Torontonians Ron Cole and Deborah Panko were stranded on a Saskatchewan back road one recent summer when their Volkswagen Golf gave up the ghost. Along came a party of roadworkers.

"How can we help?" they asked. ("Right away, that would never have happened down east," Cole says.) They siphoned gas from their truck into the Volks.

"Can I pay you?" Cole asked.

"It's free, courtesy of the premier!" the jolly highwaymen cried. The Volkswagen limped away, eventually to get a new fuel pump.

Cold weather seems to bring out goodwill in prairie people, which is lucky, since there is so much of it.

"In blizzards, strangers help to push out your car, expecting nothing more than a wave or a good-natured honk of the horn," says Will Chabun, Regina *Leader-Post* reporter-columnist. "Differences of class or race vanish in the rush to push out or dig out cars. When I was about eighteen, my buddy Don and I would drive around at night in blizzards – he had a powerful car so we never worried about getting stuck – and we roamed the city *looking* for people to help. It just seemed the natural thing to do."

As a volunteer with the Regina Open Door society, Joyce Wells took a newly arrived Bosnian family under her wing. The father, Sead Muhamedagic, forty-three, grew restless with the Canadian government's temporary support and English-language training. Sead wanted to be his family's breadwinner.

Wells spotted a job advertisement for a meat plant at Drake, about one hundred miles north, helped Sead write a resumé, then drove him to Drake for an interview. He got the job. Joyce found him a boarding place until he could rent a house. His wife, Hatiaza, got a job in the meat plant, as did their son, Almir. So did their son-in-law who, with their daughter, Almira, also lives in Drake. A happy ending. For Wells, now executive director of the Saskatchewan Book Awards, it was a reflex action. She was raised on a prairie farm; helping is in her genes.

"My mother was blind for her last twelve years and it was the kindness of her neighbours [in Saskatoon] that made independence possible," says Jeannine Locke. "They never made a fuss about being good to my mother. I think it's a Western trait not to make a fuss about your virtuousness or your success."

Her mother, Christena, had earned the kindnesses, Locke adds, through a lifetime of helping other people. Only once she overstepped: lending her husband's cardigan to the hired girl to wear at the local skating carnival. She didn't know that the girl was the town whore and the cardigan, emblazoned with a distinctive university crest, would be widely identified as her husband's.

A Humble Man

Some parliamentarians are seduced by their perceived importance. The late Gildas Molgat, speaker of the senate, was not one of them.

"He was a very humble man," says his friend Leonie Hopfner, of Ste. Rose du Lac, Manitoba, where he was born.

Molgat mingled, with equal ease and interest, with heads of state from around the world and the men who moved furniture in his office. At heart he was a small-town Manitoban, never failing to attend the annual high-school graduation in Ste. Rose. In Winnipeg, there's a disabled man whom Molgat knew long before he entered politics. Molgat subsequently found him a job and an apartment. On trips back to Winnipeg Molgat made a point of having coffee with the man (who, friends say, was enormously bucked by being seen with the distinguished Senator Molgat).

My own slight connection with Molgat was poignant. Although we had met during the writing of *You Had to Be There*, we were not intimates. Yet as soon as he heard I was writing this book, Molgat – ever considerate – voluntarily drew up for me a list of potential Manitoba interviewees. He left Winnipeg one day in February 2001, bound for Ottawa, with the list in his briefcase. He planned to present it to me in Toronto later that week. On the flight east he was felled by a fatal stroke.

When mourners queued up to pay their respects after his funeral in Ottawa, his widow, Allison, ruled that there would be no pecking order. Diplomats and members of cabinet lined up indiscriminately with constables and the woman who cleaned his office.

He is buried in Ste. Rose, where his headstone reads, "*Heureux qui comme Ulysse. . . .*" It is taken from the first line of a 1558 poem by Joachim du Bellay: "Happy is he who like Ulysses" travelled the world and finally returned to "the sweetness of home."

"I Like Happy People"

Her business card says it all:

Violet Mailman
Specialist in sewing of leather goods & vinyl
Barmaid at the Narrows Motel ★ Concrete consultant & landscaper
Jack-of-all-trades ★ Has more friends than anyone
Does not discriminate ★ Can figure out just about anything

"I should change that." Violet scribbles "ex" in front of "Barmaid." At eighty-seven she has given up slinging beer. Everything else on the card is accurate. She can fix anything, including your driveway. (There's a rumour that the base beneath her own driveway is composed of empty bottles from her barmaid days.) "I love work. I've got no talents. Just a workaholic. Icelanders are workaholics."

Mailman's home at Lake Manitoba Narrows – where the big lake pinches in at the middle, like a fat man tightening his belt – is a testament to her crowded life. You can't miss it: she has painted the walls in a black-and-white stones-and-mortar pattern. Inside, tables and walls are covered with photos, prints, a 1950 calendar permanently open to July (there's a story to that), souvenirs, knick-knacks, homilies ("Have You Hugged Your Mother-In-Law Today?") and heaps of leather gloves and mittens.

But first things first. "You've had nothing to eat!" Violet chides. While I was driving the forty miles from Ste. Rose du Lac, Violet's friend Leonie Hopfner, from whence I came, reported by phone that I had left her home unfed, despite her repeated invitations to dinner (lunch). That a man should miss a meal was beyond the ken of these hospitable women.

Violet – short, brisk, auburn hair, big smile – whips a home-made TV dinner from her microwave: meatballs, potatoes, corn. "I make up a lot of these and keep 'em on hand, the way you do when you live alone. Toast?"

"No, thanks, this is plenty." Violet pays no heed; a pile of hot toast appears in a flash.

"You'll want salad." Her knife hovers over a head of lettuce.

"No, really, this is fine."

Violet won't hear of it. "That might be enough for a woman but it's *not* enough for a man!" *Snick-snick-snick.* The salad is huge and good.

Violet is used to cooking for men: two husbands, before they died, and now as many as thirty goose and deer hunters and lake fishermen in season, mostly Americans, who have been coming for eight or nine years. "They're so happy to get here, they almost kiss the ground. They think they've met Mother Teresa."

They stay in bed-and-breakfast suites attached to her house, each with fridge, stove, microwave, TV. The hunters make their own dinners, but Violet cooks breakfasts. "I play hostess. I have fun. I like happy people."

Through her long life the indomitable Ms. Mailman has made hundreds happy, serving them, making them laugh. "That's what I thrive on, helping people. I don't want to be rich. I just want to live."

The living wasn't always easy. She was born to Icelandic parents at Beaver Dam Lake, about sixty miles from the Narrows, with a twin sister (now in Winnipeg) and four other siblings.

"Imagine the hardship," she muses. "We had to melt snow for washing clothes. There was no Pampers in those days. They bought ten yards of flannelette every time a baby was expected. Mama would be sewing flannelette diapers and it was hush-hush. We weren't supposed to know there was a baby coming."

The children survived whooping cough (a potential killer), bitter winters, and lean summers. "Now people talk about 'the good old days.' That's B.S.! Those were no good old days, they were survival."

Still, the family never wanted for necessities. Violet's mother knitted warm clothes. Her father sold cattle and each fall bought a year's supply of flour, sugar, salt, and oatmeal. In the summer they picked berries.

At twenty-two she married Marino Erlendson, a carpenter restless for change. In 1950 they bought the Alhambra Hotel in the nearby town of Eddystone (hence the permanent 1950 calendar). Eventually they sold, but Marino and Violet's brother Helgie itched for more enterprise. They bought another hotel (the town's second) in Gladstone. Violet, by then tending four children, was appalled.

"I thought, My God, how can you make a living with two hotels and a population of nine hundred?" When her husband fell sick Violet took over the business. Her mother and an aunt ran the restaurant.

"And I ran the men's beer parlour for four years. Women didn't do that in those days. I was about the first woman to do it. Everybody said, 'If you have a woman working in there you lose all your business.' Well, my business doubled! I could discipline the guys in the beer parlour better than I could discipline my own kids. I like happy people."

They stayed in Gladstone twenty-two years. After they sold the hotel Violet kept working, then tended bar another sixteen years at the Narrows. "I worked in a bar till I was seventy-five. I loved it. I had so much fun with the customers. I gave them good service. And I like happy people. . . . Had enough to eat?"

One winter in the 1960s, Violet, then forty-eight, worked as a commercial fisherman. It started, as before, with her menfolk getting into a situation and Violet taking over. Her son bought twenty fishnets to earn extra grocery money. Her husband bought twenty-two more. Then he was hospitalized and the son became bogged in farm work.

"Nobody had time to help me take those nets out. So I went by myself." Standing on glare ice, hauling up nets laden with fish is dangerous, gut-wrenching work. But Violet Mailman "can figure out just about anything."

She strapped ice fisherman's spurs to her boots and lifted five nets the first day. Within a week she had all forty-two nets up and stacked on the ice, brimming with fish. She hauled them home in a hay wagon. Her son sold the fish in town.

"I kind of enjoyed it," Violet says cheerfully. "I loved the fresh air. I done that all winter, and I'm telling you, I was in good shape in the spring! . . . Sure you don't want a banana?"

She couldn't haul fishnets today (although she claims she could still milk cows or pitch hay). She gets short of breath ("Maybe the old ticker's fading"), has a touch of gout and arthritis. It has not perceptibly slowed her. When her hunters and fishermen bid farewell to their Mother Teresa for another season, she buys two thousand dollars' worth of leather and makes piles of gloves and mittens from deerskin, sealskin, muskrat, elk, beaver, and a variety of furs. Beaver-fur hats with flaps that snuggle around the ears fly forth from her scissors and sewing machine. Great fur-lined gauntlets for snowmobilers; fancy white sealskin mitts for women; small mittens for children. They sell for around a hundred dollars a pair. A Minnesota hunter bought eight pair for his family. Sometimes Violet sews zipper pockets into the wrist, for car keys or cigarettes. Sometimes children's mitts get a pocket filled with candy.

"I like happy people," she reminds me. She has twelve grand-children and "sixteen or seventeen great-grandchildren. I love little kids. Some older people can't stand kids. But I just love the little beggars."

So, are prairie people friendlier? Violet considers. "I think maybe they are. Yeah, they are. I was roaming around this morning taking messages to people. And it's surprising how friendly all the campers are. They're glad when you talk to them."

Of course they are. Violet – did you know? – likes making people happy.

GrainLit

Something about wheat and co-operatives stirred the muse in a man. The profusion of wheat pools in the 1920s and 1930s brought forth an outpouring of doggerel from prairie farmers and elevator agents in rural journals. Let's call it GrainLit.

GrainLit rhymesters dealt mostly with grain-growers' fellow-ship and the bad things that would happen to a farmer if he didn't join a wheat pool. Their galloping meter was often pilfered from established poets. For instance, the 1930 rendition of "The Habitant (Pool Member)" by an Alberta elevator agent named McDougall was a dead ringer, in cadence and dialect, for W.H. Drummond's nineteenth-century poem "The Habitant" (when it was politically correct to make fun of accents):

> *I come from off the homestead place*
> *With my first load of wheat.*

> *I think I sell two, three, four load*
> *To grain company on street.*
> *I drive on the wes' side of town*
> *The road, she's full of tree*
> *The Pool man on the other side*
> *I think he no see me . . .*

But the Pool man does see him, and scolds him for selling to the other side. The habitant's wife, whose name is Evangeline (I'm not making this up), reprimands him. His priest is distressed. His neighbours are mortified. All because he doesn't market with the Pool. Finally the wretched habitant caves in:

> *My neighbour he don't break contract;*
> *He sells grain to the Pool*
> *And now he get two checks or three.*
> *I think me one big fool.*

The unofficial poet laureate of GrainLit was elevator agent Ferguson James of Roselynn, Alberta. When James was not weighing up loads or checking for weed seeds, verse sprang from his fertile brain. His poems, like those of his fellows, were pool morality tales, but they rhymed better than most. In his "Recollections of 1925 or 'Three Tough'" he reflected on the ills that befell men who shunned the Pool:

> *He drove into town with a load of wheat,*
> *With a three deck box and a high spring seat,*
> *And up the planks to old Jack he went*
> *Who told him the grade; and the air he rent,*
> *And yelled, "Open the doors; you can do your stuff,*
> *But you can't have my wheat for your old three tough.*

Number three tough was a poor grade. The stubborn farmer
tries many more elevators until, seven verses later, he sees the light:

It is three long years since these lines were penned.
He has joined the Pool and that put an end
To the worries he had. Now he hauls it in
And ships it out of his Special Bin,
His mind is at ease, for he knows well enough
It is "on the square" if it grades "three tough."

In other words: you could always trust your pool agent to tell
the truth. My father and his neighbours did not always share that
rosy-hued view.

The Electric Medicine Man

Empress, Alberta, in the late 1950s was a hideaway of five
hundred people, ninety miles north of Medicine Hat, nestled in
the crotch of the Red Deer and South Saskatchewan Rivers,
dwarfed by lofty bluffs. It had a twenty-bed hospital, a community hall, and one of the better hydro-electric systems in the
province, all largely due to the efforts of Dr. Archibald McNeill.

Dr. McNeill was, you see, a medical doctor *and* a qualified
electrician.

"When you see him going out on a call," a man told me,
"you never know if he's going to tape a sprained ankle or replace
a burnt-out coil."

In search of a magazine article (which never materialized), I
found him – big, brusque, cigar-smoking, in his late fifties – in the
cluttered little examining room in his home basement. He had an
M.D. and an M.Sc., had also taken a college course in electricity
and spent a summer holiday working with an electrical firm. He

went to Empress in 1926, planning to stay four or five years, then take post-graduate studies. The community needed him so much that he stayed.

The hospital at the time had six beds and an operating room that doubled as a kitchen. There wasn't enough power to run an X-ray machine. Doc, as everyone called him, got tired of sending X-ray patients to the city and converted the ancient lighting plant to 110 volts. The community was elated. Doc was immediately swamped with requests. He needed a bigger plant.

He found second-hand equipment. Local farmers and businessmen promised financial support, but it was 1932, the Depression was on, and the backers backed out. The doctor bought the equipment on credit and Empress Electric Light and Power was born.

"From then on I was tied down," Doc told me a little wistfully. "I never did get to do that post-grad work."

Within six months the plant was jammed to capacity. Over the next twenty-two years Doc upgraded the system six times. He wired the entire town, including the CPR roundhouse and the grain elevators. It took him two days every month just to read meters. For years he set aside Wednesdays for wiring; only a medical emergency could intervene. His daughters, serving as "electrician's mates," learned how to wire a house.

Finally the work became overwhelming. He sold out to Calgary Power but didn't leave town, because he had another crusade: a new community hall. It began as a volunteer effort, and sometimes only the druggist, a local farmer, and Doc were on the job – working mostly at night. It took seven years. Doc wired it, of course.

At the time of my visit, Doc was still dabbling in electricity the way some men play golf. The back seat of his Chev was heaped with electrical cord, light bulbs, wire, tools. He'd go to the hospital in the morning, his office in the afternoon, and sometimes at night would wire somebody's home "just to break the monotony."

He died in 1961 while, typically, wiring a friend's house. My lasting memory is of our final minutes together, four years before. The basement office grew quiet and Doc's cigar grew cold. Obviously, I said, the community had no regrets about his span of years in Empress, but what about the doctor: would he do it all over again? Doc McNeill's eyes lit up.

"If I was younger I'd go to the Peace River country," he said. "If I could get the electrical franchise."

Neighbourly Fred

In his eighty-plus years Fred McGuinness has worn many hats: associate editor and vice-president of the *Brandon Sun*, publisher of the *Medicine Hat News*, CBC correspondent, author, university teacher, proprietor of a Christmas-tree farm. But to an estimated 650,000 readers of sixty-five weekly newspapers in the prairie provinces, he will always be known as the author of a beloved weekly column, "Neighbourly News."

For twenty-three years McGuinness entertained, informed, and supported his audience with an inexhaustible flow of rural and small-town vignettes, stories of the quirks and good works that make small communities – declining though they are – the heart and soul of the prairies.

McGuinness, in person as affable as in his column, was born in Brandon. Apart from a Second World War stint in the Canadian navy, he has lived his life on the prairies and never wanted to be anywhere else. Sometimes, when employed by a major newspaper chain, he agonized over what he'd do if transferred to – ah, the horror! – Toronto or Montreal.

Early on, he recognized the power of anecdotes, those illustrative fragments of human behaviour, as a writer's tool. As a Cub Scout young McGuinness diligently sought good deeds. Once, he saw a woman in the post office stamping letters. The eager scout offered to help her lick the stamps.

"Sonny," the woman snapped, turning him down flat, "my spit's as good as yours." An anecdote for posterity.

He furthered his affection for vignettes as rural correspondent on CBC Radio's *Morningside* for a dozen or more years. Each Monday a box of 150 weekly newspapers from all over the prairies thumped into his home.

"It was gross overkill," McGuinness remembers. "But I gradually learned that a story I wanted was either on page one or on the editorial page, if they had an editorial page."

When the CBC dropped the series, weekly newspaper publishers urged Fred to keep it going in print. He remembered how DeWitt and Lila Wallace had founded *Reader's Digest* by excerpting articles from other magazines. "So I became a recirculator. I wanted to be the town crier who carried useful news from town to town. And I would make it as friendly as a letter from home."

The name "Neighbourly News" reflects his conviction that prairie people are innately amiable. "On the prairies, neighbourliness was built into the social structure," McGuinness says. "In homestead days your chances of survival without a neighbour's help were rare. Homesteaders built their new society on caring co-operation."

He claims that the column's only original material was the final paragraph, "when I would put in something maybe designed to make them smile and say good morning." It was much more. McGuinness has a rare instinct for spotting human interest and an uncommon skill for retelling a story with flair and humour.

McGuinness kept mining the weeklies for treasure. For years he laboriously typed the columns and mailed them to his clients. With the advent of computers and e-mail he served them with a flicker of the keyboard. Through it all, Christine, his wife of more than fifty years and "an artist with the articles of punctuation," proofread his copy.

Charlie Armstrong of Melfort, Saskatchewan, made the column because at seventy-five he was donating five and a half hours daily to seniors at the local Care Centre, helping feed them, cleaning up dishes, running errands. "Neighbourly News" told of tourist Edward Friedman from Washington who lost his dog to a hit-and-run driver in Rocanville, Saskatchewan. Bruce Dunsmore, the town Esso dealer, took Friedman home to his farm to bury the dog and invited the stranger for lunch. Friedman noticed the Star of David on a tablespoon and learned that some of the area's first settlers were Jewish. Subsequently Friedman had a tree planted in Israel to salute the Dunsmores' compassion.

Stories of community enterprise always excited McGuinness. McAuley, Manitoba, was a case in point. When the tiny community's school closed, the people transformed it. The Country Grocery Co-op (founded by seventy-eight families who each put up five hundred dollars) moved into one part of the school. A restaurant took over another. The library moved in. The municipality maintains playgrounds for local children. In a similar vein, "Neighbourly News" reported on Eston, Saskatchewan, where local activists stopped the uprooting of three hundred miles of rail line and organized grain-shipping groups to keep the line alive.

All of this, McGuinness maintains, is evidence of a rare community spirit. But, I once asked him, wouldn't you find it in any part of rural Canada? To a degree, yes, he acknowledged. "But it's stronger here. It goes back to the relative newness of the prairies." The helping tradition, so vital to pioneers, so essential because of the harshness of land and climate, was born and nurtured within living memory.

As an elderly gent himself – in years, not in spirit – McGuinness admires energetic seniors. Such as Audrey Snodgrass of Dauphin who, at eighty-six, felt she needed a new interest, so she went back to school to study business law. Likewise Jane

Flewitt of Minto, Manitoba, who asked for, and received, a one-hour ride in a hot-air balloon for her ninety-fifth birthday.

McGuinness spiced his columns with oddities. Readers loved the one about the RCMP officer near Biggar who drove into a farmyard desperately low on fuel. The farmer sent the Mountie away with a tank full of purple gas, which is sold strictly for on-farm consumption. Using it in highway vehicles could get you in trouble with . . . the Mounties.

But above all McGuinness was moved by tales of hospitality. When a couple from Headingly was caught in a blizzard at Shoal Lake, Manitoba, a "merry band of volunteers" bustled them into the school with "blankets, pillows, extra food and warm hugs." The hugs, wrote McGuinness, elevated caring to a new plateau.

With the rest of North America, "Neighbourly News" had a 9/11 story. When planes were called down from the sky on that awful day, Calgary was overloaded with stranded travellers. Calgary International Airport phoned the fire chief at nearby Rocky View: Could they take in two hundred passengers from a Frankfurt flight bound for San Francisco? Rocky View could. A Lutheran church had space in its gym. They laid out mattresses and blankets, opened computer rooms so travellers could send e-mails home, opened TV rooms for any who wanted to watch the breaking news, provided food.

Over twenty-three years, Fred's mail poured in, but it ended in the spring of 2002 when his eyesight failed. Macular degeneration made it impossible to scan the scores of newspapers every week.

"Now that the column's behind me," he told me, "I am astonished at the number of people who are talking about the utility of it."

It was more than utility. Fred McGuinness touched readers' hearts with his chronicle of what prairie people are all about. Shortly before he stepped down he was awarded the Order of Manitoba. Fred was pleased about that, but equally moved by a tribute from Neepawa newspaperman Jack Gibson, who wrote, "Wouldn't you agree that country dwellers on the prairies have lost their best voice, perhaps their only one, with the retirement of columnist Fred McGuinness?"

No argument there.

VI

PEOPLE OF THE SOIL

We have a relationship with the land that is different.
When you're on the land, walking barefoot on the land,
there's energy going on. It gets into your bones. It doesn't
make us unique, it gives us a perspective.

MARK ANIELSKI
Edmonton economist, forester, and gardener

"People Are Hurting"

Doug Armstrong of Whitewood deserves to be heard: he's made a special trip in from his fields to meet me in the local coffee shop when he should have been baling hay. But what more can he say that a dozen other Saskatchewan farmers have not?

Plenty. Over the next hour, Armstrong delivers a passionate *cri de coeur* on the plight of the prairie farmer. He is a fit-looking fifty-two, close-cropped grey hair, lean intelligent face behind glasses. His voice betrays the pain and frustration of one who has reached the end of his tether.

"It's not all roses out here," he says. "People are hurting."

Like so many others he is teetering on the knife-edge of failure. Incomes are declining. Costs are soaring.

"Equipment, you're looking at hundreds of thousands of dollars. Say a new combine right now: $225,000. Tractors are worth $100,000. Balers, over $40,000. Chemicals have gone sky-high. You can't spray any field under twenty dollars an acre."

Armstrong says he carries a $30,000 line of credit year-round. "I can't seem to get it paid off. Anybody who farms any amount of land, they'd be looking at $100,000 to $500,000 line of credit."

Like most of his contemporaries, he's disgusted with governments, and especially ministers of agriculture who recommend one impractical "solution" after another.

"Our governments won't get into the subsidy battle like they will in Europe. Europeans identify with being short of food; they've gone through war years and starved. In Canada nobody's ever starved and our governments won't take money from the public sector to support agriculture.

"Farmers don't want to get rich, they don't want to milk the system. They just want to survive, feed their families, carry on. I guess if governments would acknowledge there *was* a problem, that would be a start."

Young rural people are leaving Saskatchewan in droves. Most remaining farmers hold one or two extra jobs. Both of Armstrong's married daughters work off the farm. One son-in-law works in a nearby potash mine and drives a truck on the side. The other runs a crop-cleaning business as well as farming his quarter section. Armstrong himself does custom combining for others and, on days off, hauls buildings for money.

Non-farmers point to the pleasures of a rural lifestyle. Not so, says Armstrong. "It's a high-stress job. From the time you get up in the morning till you go to bed at night, you're looking at the sky, you're worrying about the weather, 365 days a year.

"Personally, I'm ready to give it up and just get a job and say, 'You pay me so many dollars per hour and I'll go home at night and rest.'"

His father-in-law died a couple of years back. He'd gone down fighting for the family farm, talking about it every day, lobbying governments, writing letters to senators – all to deaf ears.

"People in agriculture are very hard-working people on average. Honest, hard-working people. That's not enough any more. You can work from sun-up till sundown and still not [succeed]. It's a pretty gloomy picture, but that's the way I look at it."

He shakes his head and goes back to his hay field.

The Anguish of Change

> My farm to me is not just land
> Where bare, unpainted buildings stand.
> To me my farm is nothing less
> Than all created loveliness.
> My farm's a heaven – here dwell rest,

Security and happiness.
Whate'er befalls the world outside,
Here faith and hope and love abide.

These lines (author unknown) appeared in the 2002 obituary of an old neighbour from the rural community where I once lived. It says better than any government survey or TV documentary how farmers feel, or want to feel, about their piece of earth. Sadly, the prairie farm is no longer heaven or haven.

"The future is simply not bright for people who want to continue on as they have been," says Dr. Nikki Gerrard of Saskatoon, a community psychologist and author of a study on rural stress. "The future is change."

An unnamed farm woman summed up the anguish of change with great poignancy in another study compiled by the University of Regina's Wendee Kubik and Dr. Robert J. Moore. "I have been involved in farming for thirty-seven years, working alongside my husband as we farmed and raised a family of four," she wrote. "It has been such a wonderful life with many ups and downs, good times and bad, sacrifices and rewards. [But] we see our rural communities disappearing and a severe devaluation of our farm land and other farm assets we have worked a lifetime to attain.

"Our optimistic attitude toward 'next year' is dwindling. We can no longer control our own destiny and this is why we are witnessing increased depression, addictions (to drinking and gambling), suicides, divorce, family abuse. . . ."

Between 1998 and 2001, Saskatchewan's farm-worker population dropped 36 per cent, to 46,300. Alberta's fell 37 per cent to 57,000. Manitoba's fell 21 per cent to 30,400. Income in some cases is less than that of a junior office worker. In Saskatchewan the average net farm-operating income for 1999 was $14,529.

Some farmers blame the heavy hand of the Canadian Wheat Board. Pulse crops, such as peas and lentils, can be sold directly through brokers, but prairie farmers must, by law, sell their wheat and malt barley through the board. A few defied the law in 2002, and went to jail.

"If a guy didn't need to grow cereal grains to maintain crop rotation, there would be precious few grown any more," says Jocelyn Hainsworth of Redvers. "Board grains are not worth the money that it takes to plant and harvest them."

She and husband Glen have seen their original 1,920 acres of grain dwindle to 640, in addition to a pasture planted and fenced for cattle and their daughter's horses. "High debt and wheat prices dropping to less than half what they were when we took out our loans did us in, but we've survived and so has our marriage. Not everyone is so lucky."

Glen now works as a welder for a nearby machine shop; Jocelyn is postmaster in Redvers and contributes essays on rural life to the CBC. "Lots of people think we're crazy for not selling what we still have left and leave the worries of farming behind, but we love where we live."

As Doug Armstrong points out, equipment is another killer.

"A swather costs ninety-three thousand dollars," says Anne Willner of Davidson. "It can take twenty-five years to pay for the damn thing!" Husband Wayne farms sixteen hundred acres of wheat, durum, barley, mustard, peas, and lentils, using every trick to keep their debt load down. "We have old equipment, we repair a lot of it ourselves," Wayne says. "We go to salvage yards for spare parts." Or, he improvises with duct tape and tin. "Duct tape, the farmer's friend," Anne says wryly.

Above all, farmers feel they are alone in a world that is shifting beneath their feet: ignored by politicians, misunderstood by consumers. In the Kubik-Moore study, more than 90 per cent of respondents felt that "elected politicians soon lose touch with the people" and 77 per cent felt they "didn't have any say in what government does."

"City people don't have a clue about the farm," Anne Willner says. "They think when you're paying two bucks for a loaf of bread, the farmer's getting a dollar-fifty. Well the farmer's getting about three cents."

It's why so many couples take additional jobs. The Kubik-Moore study found that in 2001 for about 17 per cent of the respondents, off-farm work accounted for more than 70 per cent of farm-family income. For women it's most often clerical work, nursing, and teaching. For the Willners, extra income derives from antique-wood refinishing. It started when Wayne refinished two battered bedroom suites. Neighbours admired the work, so Anne took courses and they went into business part-time. It earns about seventy-five hundred dollars a year.

Moore and Kubik's study produced a staggering inventory of rural worries: low prices, high costs, scanty rural health care, chemicals in food and water, rural depopulation, and debt. All are tied to the grandfather of all worries: Will we lose the farm? Nineteen per cent of respondents said their debt was unmanageable; 24 per cent said they were going backward financially and the future looked bad; 43 per cent expected to "pull through in the long run." One woman said grimly, "The only thing you've got to look forward to in life is bouncing back."

Easier said than done. "I worry," one respondent told Dr. Gerrard. "I never shut down. I wake up in the morning, it's there: 2:30 or 3:30 or 4:20, you're awake. It's just too much."

All three provinces have rural helplines, serviced by trained volunteers, often other farm people. They receive hundreds of calls per year, some from people who just need a sympathetic but anonymous ear. Baring one's soul to the neighbours in the goldfish bowl of a small community is not necessarily helpful.

"Living in a close-knit rural community, it's nice in one sense that people look out for one another and people help one another," one respondent told Gerrard. "But the down side is everyone knows your business and there's not a lot of privacy."

A 2001 Canadian Farm Safety and Rural Health conference heard that Canadian farmers are less likely to commit suicide than the general population: their suicide rate is 24 per 100,000 compared to the general population's 26.5. But how many farm accidents are actually suicides?

Between 1990 and 1996 a total of twenty-four hundred men and women were killed or seriously injured in farm accidents in Saskatchewan alone. Some of the survivors are movingly recorded in words and photographs in *OffGuard: Farmers and Machinery Injuries*, an art-gallery catalogue produced by Julie Bidwell and Brenda Pilkey, both of the University of Saskatchewan.

Is stress a cause of accidents? Ask Don Zimmer of Handel, Saskatchewan, whose left hand was caught in a baler. After surgery and three years of rehabilitation he regained partial use of the hand.

"Stress was definitely a factor – of trying to get the job done, trying to make a living farming," he told *OffGuard*. "If the stress was not there, I would have shut things down and done things properly. So, I don't know whether you'd call it stress or stupidity."

Fifty-five per cent of farm women – whom Kubik and Moore call "the invisible partners" in farm work and their families' "anchors" – said their lives are "somewhat stressful." Another 29 per cent said "very stressful." They cited everything from sleeplessness and backaches to upset stomachs and allergies. About 21 per cent said they were having more arguments with their spouse or partner and 12 per cent admitted to serious marital problems.

Little wonder. On average they work ninety-six hours a week (nineteen hours of farm labour, thirty hours of housework, eight hours of gardening and canning, twenty-six hours of child care, nine hours work off the farm, and four hours of community service). "I write papers, do laundry, bath a kid, cook supper and I'm doing all that farm stuff at the same time," one wife told Gerrard. "It has a lot to do with gender . . . because I'm female those are my jobs. . . . I question if [my husband] even realizes it."

They also help their families to cope. "These women are still expected to 'stand by their man,'" reported Moore and Kubik, "in spite of how much it may adversely affect their own well-being."

Despite the incessant strain, farmers insist repeatedly, they never wanted to do anything else. The country is still a good place to raise children, says Anne Willner, although "there's mega-drugs in our area, and there's mega-alcohol. We have to teach our children the right thing to do and hope they'll listen to us."

The Willners share with other survivors that extraordinary rural resilience. They were nervous about my visit, Anne confided to me. (How would *you* feel if an old guy in sneakers and tractor-driver's cap, from Toronto of all places, came probing the most intimate recesses of *your* life?) But as we established rapport, she opened up: witty, warm, full of stories, such as how in 1990 their second-hand tractor broke down and the new one took money they had saved for land.

"We had quite a fair amount set aside for the kids' education – every baby bonus, every gift they received," Anne continues. "When we didn't have enough money for the land, we had to take the education fund. I spent a couple of days crying over that. That was the children's future."

They're good parents. Anne helps out in the fields as late as four-thirty in the afternoon. If Aleah and Chelsey get home from school at four they're on their own for a half-hour. "But I have a phone on the tractor and I call in and say, 'What are you doing, what are you eating?' That's another way of economizing, because you can't get a babysitter for less than $3.50 an hour."

Home for the Willners is like the farm in my old neighbour's obituary: a place where faith and hope and love reside. "The longest I've lived away from this house is April to October, the year we got married, in 1990," Wayne remembers. "We were in Kenaston, but I drove back here every day."

"We'll stay as long as we can afford to pay for the land," Anne adds. "We're in our forties. Where could we go to have as nice a home and as nice a life as we have? If we went to the city he'd have to pump gas and I'd have to be a store clerk."

Anne did work in Saskatoon from 1978 to 1990. She hated it so much her hair all fell out, a bad case of nerves.

"I wouldn't change my life again," Anne Willner says. "I don't want to go bald!"

For beleaguered prairie farmers, one safety valve is sardonic humour that pokes fun at governments, city folk, themselves, and the fickle finger of Fate.

Stranger: *Congratulations, sir, you've just won the lottery! A million bucks! How're you going to spend it?*

Farmer: *Guess I'll just keep farming till it's all gone.*

"It's a Wonderful Life"

Warren Jolly is not a punch-your-biceps, joke-cracking kind of guy. He's agreeable, articulate, even makes a little joke about his stature, maybe five-seven or five-eight ("My grandfather was a little over six feet, my dad was five-eleven: I don't know what happened to me"). But his mind is focused every waking hour on the all-consuming business of farming.

Sitting at his office computer – early fifties, serious face behind horn-rims, university-educated, equipped with the necessary tools of the electronic age – he could pass for any city businessman. His wife, Paula – slim, attractive, outgoing, very much a working partner – could similarly pass for any city businesswoman. They are farmers of the future.

"Technology *is* the future," Paula says. "Warren spends more time in the office than he does on the land. The record-keeping is just phenomenal and it's always been his baby."

"Record-keeping's the part of this farm that's growing fastest," he agrees. "When the consumer's ready to have that process we want this farm to be ready. We already have a few years' data to back it up."

He means a time, maybe not far off, when Saskatchewan farmers will stop shipping raw products, and jobs, out of province. A time when they'll sell, say, their own chickpeas in cellophane bags in the supermarket, with a guarantee from Jolly Farms of every step that product has taken along the way, including what chemicals were applied.

"We're already hearing that consumers are asking for this in Europe. I think it's coming here. We're setting it up on our farm."

"Urban people still classify us as the 'dumb farmer,'" Paula says. "But if you had the same amount of money invested in a city business you would have maybe a board of directors, a president, a secretary, and an accountant. We have an accountant, but Warren makes all the decisions."

Both were born here near Mossbank, Saskatchewan. Warren is a third-generation farmer, but with the eight thousand acres that he, their son, and a brother-in-law operate, he is light-years ahead of his father's and grandfather's small acreages.

"I call it a family-farm business," Paula says. "To outsiders that means a little farm where you have pigs and chickens and cows. But that's just not gonna make it any more."

Everything is carefully calculated. Warren has a part interest in a small aircraft; he checks their crops from the air and notes variations in growth and chemical effectiveness. Given that their annual bill for chemicals and fertilizer runs about six hundred thousand dollars, it's important to know if the stuff is doing its job.

He buys fertilizers and fuel when the prices are lowest and stores them. No more summerfallowing; he ruffles the soil only once, during spring planting. "Every time you disturb it you lose moisture."

Jolly Farms grows mainly durum wheat (for pasta) and pulse crops such as chickpeas. They rotate crops to take advantage of nutrients and moisture. They don't stint on technological tools: fax, scanner, two telephone lines into the house, and two computers, including a laptop they take on winter vacations to Mexico. Like many other farmers, they are hooked into the Global Positioning System (GPS). "It's date- and time-fixed. When that tractor's in the field, it's recording it and we can prove it." GPS is a space-based triangulation system using a thirteen-billion-dollar system of satellites in sun-synchronous orbit above the earth. It can pinpoint a position anywhere on earth twenty-four hours a day, in any kind of weather.

GPS helped them win a dispute with the chemical giant Monsanto. As Jolly tells it, he applied a herbicide that normally takes two or three months to break down slowly. Weather conditions caused it to activate in about ten days and damaged their wheat crop, cutting the yield by half. The chemical company fought the claim. "Their lawyer was from Toronto," Paula says. "He treated us like country bumpkins."

But the bumpkins had documented everything. "They still weren't gonna settle until they saw our GPS yield maps and time-dated stuff and then they settled immediately," Warren says evenly, no sense of gloating. "There was a two-year gag order. If we talked about it to anybody for two years there was no money coming." Smaller farmers might have folded under the long wait and legal fees.

Being big does not necessarily win friends among neighbours. Is Jolly one of the most successful in his area?

"Well, we'd like to think so, but that isn't all our fault," he says defensively. "My grandfather and father had a huge amount to do with that." Where else would a man apologize for making good?

Jolly takes a contrarian view of farm subsidies. With them, he says, "fertilizer prices and chemical prices and machine prices went up way more than the subsidy amounted to, and when the subsidies are scaled back machinery and fertilizers and chemicals don't come back as far. So I would personally prefer to see subsidies gone everywhere, right to zero. If you can make it on your own, you make it. If you can't, you go broke and do something else."

He and Paula don't intend to grow old and weary on the land. "I told my son and brother-in-law that five years from now I'll still be around a bit, helping with seeding and harvest and doing the planning, but I'm not gonna be making the major decisions."

The Jollys enjoy Mexico, and Warren thinks baby boomers are ready to travel there en masse. He wants to be the one, perhaps with a partner, to offer them a retirement-community alternative to Florida or Arizona. But he'd always keep a toe in the farm.

"People are still gonna eat," Warren says. "We need to get closer to our customers. Right now the government's between us and our customers. But I don't think that'll be there for much longer. I like agriculture. It's got a tremendous future."

"It has its ups and downs, everything has," Paula sums up. "But it's a wonderful way of life."

A city guy accosts a farmer with a flock of sheep: "Sir, I'll bet you a hundred dollars against one of your sheep that I can tell you the exact size of your flock."

The farmer says: "You're on."

"Nine hundred and seventy three."

"Sonofagun! You win, take an animal."

The city guy picks one, starts to walk away.

The farmer stops him: "Wait. Double or nothing, I can guess your exact occupation."

Laughing a city guy's laugh: "You can try!"

"You're an economist for a government think-tank."

"Amazing! How did you know?"

"Put down my dog and I'll tell you."

The Politics of Poison

When Glen Willner died of prostate cancer in 2000, his son Wayne swore off farm chemicals forever. He's convinced the poison killed his father.

"In the old days when you were filling the sprayer, maybe you wore rubber gloves, maybe not," says the tall, balding Willner. "If nature calls, you're not going to run two miles home, so you just relieve yourself out there. So how clean are your hands? A lot of neighbours used to mix the stuff with their bare arms. It was supposed to be safe, but it *was* not and *is* not."

Pesticides, herbicides, and fertilizers were also pushing him into the poorhouse. Chemicals cost him the equivalent of ten bushels of wheat per acre. He had to borrow from the bank to pay his annual twenty-eight-thousand-dollar bill, for minimum usage on sixteen hundred acres. So, in 2001 he and his wife, Anne, began the transition to organic farming – the non-chemical technique now employed by more than a thousand farmers across the prairie provinces.

Could organic farming be the prairie's salvation? Some farmers dream of using it to promote a revitalized Saskatchewan – a pristine environment with pure products branded "Saskatchewan-Grown" for all the world to see. But they doubt that their government cares enough about farmers to promote it, given the dwindling rural population and farming's small percentage of the prairie GDP.

Regardless, they feel they're doing right by themselves and the environment. Every year a blizzard of poison falls on prairie fields as farmers spray for pests and disease. Around the Davidson area alone, organic-farming pioneer Elmer Laird counts sixty-four different chemicals for sale, although he hasn't used them for thirty-four years. With many others, he believes they harm the soil, wildlife, and human health.

The use of chemicals is a contentious issue. Organic farmers, still a minority, are used to skepticism or even derision from their non-organic neighbours and from the agricultural establishment. "Most of them aren't gonna be here very long," Warren Jolly says of organic growers. "They'll find in about two or three years the weeds and the insects will have taken over completely. A lot of that isn't necessarily their fault. Like, there's probably still 95 to 98 per cent of this area that isn't organic. So we keep that stuff under control on our farms, but it builds up in the area, so it's gonna take over theirs."

Dr. C.M. "Red" Williams, professor emeritus, University of Saskatchewan, does not believe in totally eliminating "chemical assists"; he favours setting "achievable limits" on the use of pesticides. He thinks organic farming will carry on "until the market is oversupplied, as happens in almost all such instances. If that bubble bursts on them, they could lose whatever they put into it."

Organic farmers disagree. "Sure, our yields will be lower," Wayne Willner admits. "It's a gamble, but not that big of a gamble. If we only get twenty bushels an acre instead of thirty, we still don't have that expense of chemicals." And he's insistent about the threat to human health. "Some of those chemicals are deadly. We had a little bug called a wheat midge come through here. One guy was spraying a field for it. He turned around, saw a deer get up where he'd just sprayed. It ran about a hundred yards and dropped dead."

Epidemiological studies indicate that, compared to the general population, farmers are at a higher risk of developing lip cancer, non-Hodgkin's lymphoma, leukemia, multiple myeloma, soft-tissue sarcoma, brain cancer, prostate cancer, gastric or stomach cancer, testicular cancer, and skin (squamous-cell) cancer.

"There *is* an association between pesticides and cancer," Dr. James Gomes, director of environmental health for the University of Regina, says flatly. "However, cancer is not the only major cause for concern." Agricultural poisons can lead to "adverse reproductive health (infertility, sterility, loss of libido, decreasing sperm counts), birth defects in offspring (undescended testes, undeveloped penis) and others such as neurological disorders possibly leading to Alzheimer's and dementia. Hormonal pesticides cause a whole spectrum of hormonal disorders and adverse health effects."

This checks with farmers' experience and gut instinct. "I just didn't feel that herbicides and pesticides were doing us or the consumer or the land any good," says Kevin Beach of Morse. "Whenever I handled them I didn't feel right afterward." He and his brother farm 7,840 acres and have been organic since 1989.

The Prince and the Pea Farmers

Six weeks before the scheduled visit of Prince Charles to Assiniboia in 2001, Kevin Beach got a phone call.

"Prince Charles wants to meet some organic farmers," the voice said. "Do you and your family want to meet him?"

"Well, yeah, I guess," Beach said. It wasn't high on his wish list. His wife, Donna, and daughters, Abbie and Alishia, were

less blasé. As the media hype heightened, and after the RCMP *cleared them to hobnob with royalty, even Kevin perked up.*

They drove a hundred miles to Assiniboia one April day, gathered with three other families in the town office, drank tea, ate saskatoon-berry pie, and waited. Finally the prince arrived. Everyone stood up. A host farmer introduced them. The Beaches were nervous, but Charles put them at ease.

"It was a conversation, like talking to you," Kevin says. "He has big thick hands, strong and kind of callused. Had a Band-Aid on one finger. About like a farmer."

For fifteen minutes Charles quizzed them about their farming practices. Kevin was surprised: "He's as knowledgeable as I am."

"He really did know about organic," Donna says. "It wasn't, 'Oh, that's nice.' He would respond with a comment or question that proved he knew. And I thought 'Wow!'"

While Charles met other families, Kevin made small talk with a royal aide. "Prince Charles likes being home on his farm," the aide said. "That's where he is most content, out in the country."

Another escort glanced at his watch and muttered, "Five more minutes."

"No," said his partner, "this is the high point of the prince's day. We let him take as much time as he wants."

Beach regarded the visit as a boost for organic farmers. "We are 1 per cent of the farm population. You can hardly talk to your neighbours 'cause they're all talking chemicals. But when Prince Charles came to see us, just for a moment it raised our profile right to the top."

There was only one glitch in the perfect day. Charles was wearing a business suit, not the sweet white stockings of his counterpart in Cinderella. Alishia, four, was disappointed.

"Is that *him?*" she asked her mother. "That's the prince!?"

Organic farming requires stringent practices to retain its integrity. Land must be proven free of chemicals for three years before being certifiable for organic. Summerfallowing is not permitted and is enforced with annual inspections and meticulous record-keeping. It's paying off in richer soil with better moisture-holding properties.

Each organic-grain shipment, carrying a lot number, can be traced back to the original farm. All organic equipment must be pressure-washed to banish any chemical residue from conventional farming. Organic farmers keep a twenty-five-foot barrier strip around their fields that, theoretically, protects them from neighbours' spraying. The Beach brothers use natural phosphate, sulphur, and calcium compounds instead of commercial fertilizer.

What about grasshoppers, the bane of prairie agriculture? One defence is to plant crops they don't like. Fall rye qualifies because it is well established before the hoppers hatch. A crop called "serious peas" secretes an enzyme that repels grasshoppers. Plant it around a field's perimeter and only a highly motivated grasshopper will pass through it.

"Seeding when moisture and temperature are optimum and the seedbed is firm to promote rapid germination, and seeding at a higher rate may help to get ahead of the little devils," Beach says. "But, no, it's not easy for us to control the pests."

Nor is there an easy way to keep down weeds. But on the other hand, says Donna Beach, "if you *don't* have a lot of weeds, you're suspect."

"When we have weeds we like to say we have good biodiversity!" Kevin grins.

Beach also raises organic cattle, feeding them a natural-based mineral supplement and giving antibiotics only in an emergency (in which case the animal is removed from the organic program). "In six years we've given about three animals a shot of penicillin.

Before, if we had an animal with a sore hoof, we'd have given them a shot. But unless they have an infection, or something's wrapped around the foot, if you just leave them, in about four days they're fine. It's amazing."

Beach thinks his organically fed cattle are more content, a little less skittish. "They don't get sick very often, touch wood."

Overall, his yields are lower than his neighbours' by 10 to 18 per cent. "But when you factor our lower yield against our higher per-bushel return plus lower input costs, our net income is still a little better. We're not making a really good living, but it's still better than conventional farming."

There is another fringe benefit: feedback from grateful consumers. A Regina woman gets severe allergic reactions from supermarket meat but can eat meat from Beach's cattle. He shipped wheat via their Swift Current outlet to Vancouver customers. Back came an enthusiastic response: "Where did you get that wheat? It's the best we've ever tasted."

The ebullience of organic converts is akin to sinners discovering God. Monique Sundlie of Wandering River, Alberta, used to help her father raise market vegetables on a three-acre plot.

"We began noticing we were making the same amount of money as some of my uncles who farmed a thousand acres each using anhydrous ammonia and every other little thing. One year one of my uncles netted three thousand dollars after expenses on a bumper crop. That same year, gardening organically, we netted a little more than four thousand. So more chemicals did not equal more money. That same year one of my uncles was severely burned by anhydrous ammonia and couldn't work for a couple of years."

Monique persuaded her husband, Warren — who worked in the gas fields and swore he would never farm — to buy a bigger garden. The 160 acres had been leased to a farmer "who sprayed for every bug that flew or jumped or even thought about it." The

Sundlies planted alfalfa and timothy to give the land time to heal. Now they have fruit trees, strawberries, potatoes, and carrots, and have ten cows and several beehives.

Warren is happy, Monique says, "So I am happy, too. We are raising our children the way I was raised, organically."

Kevin Beach finds the same enthusiasm throughout the organic community. "If you go to a coffee shop in town you have to cut through the air with a machete, it's so negative." That's with conventional farmers; organic growers, he says, tend to be more optimistic — "Let's try this next year" — and their families tend to be more involved.

Anything that puts heart back into farm families must have something going for it.

Government man (to farmer in Lloydminster, which straddles a provincial boundary): *Sir, we've just finished a new survey of your land. Your place is actually in Alberta, not Saskatchewan.*

Farmer: *Thank God! I couldn't stand another Saskatchewan winter!*

Team Bonesky

If there is ever an Olympic event for rural teamwork, the Boneskys of Morse, Saskatchewan, will win the gold, hands down. They love their life, work in tandem, and have fun (at a time when few prairie farmers find much to laugh about). "Sitting around the dinner table here, it's hilarious," says son-in-law Jason Dean.

"I love being a part of this family and this farm," says Karen Bonesky, co-head of the five-person clan with her husband, Larry. "We do what we do with passion and zest."

Their energy seems infinite. Karen – short, dark, and bursting with ideas – has been a school librarian, taught business education, was an accountant, worked in a bank and in a credit union, and is learning to be a reiki master. With a partner she runs a "facilitation service" to help people "define what they want and develop it." She's planning an eco-agritourism venture for their farm.

Oldest daughter Lori, in her mid-thirties, is a sociologist, a qualified reflexologist, a volunteer 4H leader, and is studying reiki, aromatherapy, and quilting. She farms too, doing anything from welding to treating a sick calf. She seems gentle and soft-spoken, but claims, "I like to entertain and annoy people."

Her tall, bearded husband, Jason, has a degree in agricultural economics, is a board member for the Saskatchewan cattle feeders, participates in the Canadian Agricultural Lifetime Leadership program (it seeks badly needed leaders for all aspects of agribusiness) and volunteers for 4H. He's a planner. "I'll be on the tractor or combine, working on this year's crop and thinking about next year. That night I'll go to the computer and start putting down plans."

Youngest daughter, Kelly, slim and athletic, has a degree in business administration and does volunteer work with disabled people who aspire to the Special Olympics. She and husband Denis Green live in Winnipeg – he's with Agriculture Canada, she works for Saskatchewan's information service – but she comes back often to her own share of the land.

"I live in both worlds," she says. "This will always be home, no matter where I am. I sleep the best of anywhere in my room upstairs. I just like *being* here."

And there's Larry, handsome, dark-haired, in his late fifties, with deliberate speech and a reputation as the family wit. He's their man for all seasons.

"Dad is the only one with a title," Kelly says. "He's a Farmer at Large. He can find anything and knows everybody, 'cause he's out there talking to people."

During a recent parched spring Larry predicted, "It won't rain until the week of July 10." It rained *on* July 10. "Just part of my FAL role," he says with a little smile. He flies a Cessna 150, partly for relaxation, partly to see which crops need attention.

Sometimes Team Bonesky's outlook on life seems too perfectly formed, too good to be true. They aren't the stereotypical tongue-tied farm folks. That image was never entirely accurate, but the Boneskys are far beyond it.

"We're here in life to learn lessons," Karen says. "When we learn the lessons we move on to other ones. We have some real strengths. Jason has a systematic approach. He's analytical and will figure it out and knows it will be the right way. Larry is intuitive and creative. Lori can be *really* to the point, so she jolts us sometimes and makes us think. Kelly finds the dollars; it has to make business sense. So we're a team. We look at our strengths and it's awesome."

Federal agricultural ministers occasionally descend from the East, telling prairie farmers how to do their jobs. One recent edict from on high was "Diversify." The Boneskys grow mustard, canola, rye, hay, clover, lentils, and chickpeas on forty-five hundred acres of cultivated land and pasture. In a typical year they have 200 to 250 calving cows. They also do custom harvesting.

"I don't know what we could do to diversify more," Larry Bonesky says in a measured way, pausing like a good stand-up comedian to deliver the zinger. "I guess the next thing left is if we figure how to market gophers." The Team hoots with appreciation.

Amid their diversity there is little room for wheat, once *the* crop in this one-time breadbasket of Canada. The Boneskys raise wheat primarily to get bedding straw for the cattle. "We sell the grain but we don't make money at it," Karen says. "The CPR makes more from it than we do."

They live by choice on Larry's Ukrainian father's home-stead, circa 1910, in an upgraded version of the house his dad built in 1926. He chose the site for its good water, a valley for shelter, and a knoll for the house to stand clear of spring runoff. Until he dug a well, his oxen drank out of one side of the slough and he drank out of the other.

Larry, one of nine children, began driving trucks at age seven and was farming at fourteen. His future wife, Karen, was born nearby to Mennonites who survived decades of turmoil in the Ukraine and got out after the Second World War. The Friesen parents and daughter learned English together. By age six Karen knew she wanted to be a farmer; at nineteen she married one. First child, Lori, was "our 1967 Centennial project."

Lori and Jason live four miles away. Jason, too, has soil in his blood. He began work at age nine and is their resident agrono-mist. He can actually make the life and times of a chickpea sound interesting. Nutritionists prize chickpeas for their high protein, calcium, and fibre content, as well as iron, vitamins, and minerals. There's a chickpea called Desi and another called Kabuli. The Boneskys opted for Kabuli after Jason analyzed them fore and aft. "He ran it all through the computer, printed out the costs and the pros and the cons," Larry says. "Then the whole family sat down and decided as a group what to do."

Everything is plotted. Their cropping decisions are gov-erned in part by respect for the land. If it is best suited to grass, they will leave it in grass, never mind whether they could make extra money by ploughing it up. On cultivated fields they rotate crops to maintain a soil balance.

"Different crops have different root structures, get their moisture from different places, draw different nutrients," Lori explains. "An oilseed likes sulphur. Lentils and chickpeas like phosphorus. Chickpeas make nitrogen."

All the planning, computerization, and expensive machin-ery aside, farming still comes down to plain hard work, such as getting up in the night every three hours to check the cows at calving time.

"If it's cold you have to be out there or calves will be dead, or froze so bad they might as well be dead," the Farmer at Large explains. "Or the cows may be having a difficult birth. Or they calve and then walk away. Or two cows calve at the same time and they mix 'em up." Mothers and newborns are quickly ear-tagged to avoid mix-ups. Even in this grinding labour Karen finds pleasure: "You wouldn't believe how beautiful the night sky is at that time of year!"

Their annual fuel, chemical, and repair bills easily reach a hundred thousand dollars and they're irked at officialdom's casual attitudes towards farmers and farming. "We feed everybody," Larry points out. "Everything that's eaten by people, some farmer somewhere has produced it. So we believe we should have a fair shake in getting paid to do this." Like most other farmers, he thinks Canadian consumers are spoiled, demanding (and getting) some of the lowest-cost food in the world and not acknowledging that farmers should be suitably rewarded.

Team Bonesky emissaries have seen first-hand how the other half of the world lives. In 1995 Lori and Jason spent two months in an exchange program on a co-operative farm in Zimbabwe. The food was plain, living conditions were spartan, and most farm work was done by hand. Jason and Lori lived in a tiny guest house with no running water, showered from a solar-heated water bag, worked side by side with local people, and showed that Canadians knew how to haul rocks and scrabble in the dirt.

Karen would like to travel too some day, but like Dorothy in the *Wizard of Oz*, she knows there's no place like home. "For three winters we were in a house in the city, and I couldn't wait to be back out here on weekends. I'm here because I *want* to be, not because I *have* to be."

She is the most passionate of her family in voicing her love of the farm. "Some people choose to be in agriculture to use the land. It's important that we think about sustainability. About what we're doing here." Her voice chokes a little. "We're just here for now. Others before us have made an impact. All of us make a contribution. It's really important to think about the future."

City guy: *"That's a fantastic crop of barley you have there, sir. Best I've ever seen!"*

Farmer: *"Yeah. But it sure takes a lot outa the soil."*

Happily Home on the Range

"You go west of Sundre on Number 22," the woman's voice said long-distance, "then north up to the James River crossing. Follow the river west about twelve miles, you'll go over three cattle crossings, and a mile after that there'll be a log post sort of falling down, and a driveway to the right, but it's not mine. When you think you're in the middle of nowhere, you are!"

Not exactly nowhere – although I met only one other vehicle the whole way – but on Patti Scott's ranch, nestled among spruce, pine, aspen, and poplar, with an honour guard of round-eyed Red Angus cattle checking me out along the last stretch of dirt road. Some twenty miles west beyond the foothills lay the Rocky Mountains.

Scott is a slim thirty-eight-year-old single mother with long dark hair tied back and a Pepsodent smile flashing through her suntan. When she's decked out in her dress-up white hat, red kerchief, chaps, boots, and silver-buckle belt, she could pass for Queen of the Stampede. But as certain macho cattle buyers and patronizing male bankers have discovered, she's not just another purty little thing in a Stetson.

She rides and ropes, vaccinates and herds cattle as expertly as any other cowhand. She's a fourth-generation rancher and university graduate who runs 150 Red Angus on six thousand acres. She and her ex-husband bought the place fourteen years ago and she has operated it alone for seven years. She and her neighbours pool their labour for big jobs such as branding and castration; for the rest, she manages without hired help.

"When you like the life it's not too much work," she says. She lived in Saskatoon for seven years, long enough to know that "ranching is in my blood."

Ranching is an old and honourable Alberta tradition, but the "ranch" as we know it from history or Hollywood is increasingly rare. Beef is Alberta's number-one agricultural commodity, accounting for about four billion dollars a year in farm receipts, and the province has thirty-five thousand cattle "farmers" raising six million animals in total. But 90 per cent of those operators keep only 122 cows or fewer. Of the remainder only a fraction are the legendary big ranches.

Patti Scott grew up on what is now the Glenbow Ranch, originally part-owned by her great-grandfather. Oil-rich Albertan Eric Harvey bought him out, after which Scott's great-grandfather, grandfather, and father each managed the ranch in turn. Young Patti learned her trade there.

The hardest part when she went on her own was selling her purebred bulls to cattle buyers ("They'd say, 'Can you get your husband on the phone?'") and negotiating mortgages with bankers. "Bankers think women will get pregnant or too tired for hard work. I had a lot of convincing to do, but I overcame it."

She handles the work as well as any man, including getting up every four hours for forty-five to sixty days during spring calving, more often if it is very cold. "Like last spring, it was thirty below. I thought I was gonna die! But if they are born in that snow they're dead instantly, so you're out every two hours."

She also weathered the devastating drought of 2002. Scott does her own books with a very sharp pencil, and reckoned she'd be better off keeping most of her land in pasture, rather than raising hay, which would require astronomically expensive machinery. Her range – four thousand feet above sea level, close to the Rockies, and well treed – got enough moisture, but her feed costs were the highest ever: for baled hay it ran about $150 a ton plus delivery.

"It takes about four tons to feed a cow over the winter. You have to wait it out until you sell your calves in the spring." Some ranchers couldn't hang on in 2002 and had to sell. Patti stayed. "Right now is probably one of the toughest times."

Her daughters Casie, eleven, and Birch, eight, are her joy: sunny girls who board the school bus at seven-thirty, ride nearly nineteen miles to and from school, get home at four-thirty, help with the chores, and get top marks. She is burstingly proud of them and they of her. Summer, when the cows are at pasture, mother and daughters have holiday trips.

Their nearest neighbour is ten miles away, but Patti and the girls are never lonely. They have each other and enjoy a rare oasis in a frenetic world. How long will it last? More and more make-believe ranchers from the city are buying weekend places in cattle country, but Patti Scott, the genuine article, will stay as long as she can make a living.

"I love it," she says. "I love being where there's no one else."

SIXTY CROPS

Most men would say, "I farmed for sixty years." Retiree Frank Quigley of Central Butte, face reddened from a lifetime of wind and sun, told me simply, "I raised sixty crops." Not a bad measure of a life.

"Best Sight I've Ever Seen"

"About three years ago a fellow from Quebec came out [to Saskatoon] just to see the cattle show and stuff," Marvin Evans of Kenaston is saying. "We had talked to him on the phone once or twice, so he wanted to come out and visit."

Evans, in his late sixties, farms forty-seven quarters "whatever that adds up to" (7,520 acres) with his sons, some of it land his father farmed a generation before. His affection for his Charolais cattle is palpable. Not many men, or women like Marvin's wife, Marilyn, would stop off on their way home from their honeymoon in Banff to check out a ranch that had some of the earliest Charolais-cross breeds.

And, if you prod him, Marvin will tell diffidently but proudly how his bull calf won the Breeders Classic in 1995 and a year later was Grand Champion Charolais, sort of the Academy Award of cattle. Probably the Quebec visitor picked up on that.

"The cattle were out west of here a couple of miles. I drove him out through them in the morning."

It was a pretty sight: maybe three hundred cows and calves with their creamy wheat-coloured coats; the macho young bulls butting heads, jockeying for seniority; the softly rolling fields reaching to the horizon.

"He was to fly back the next morning about ten. Well, that night, late, he telephoned from Saskatoon. 'Could I come out in the morning,' he said, 'and have one more look at those cows?' I said, 'What time?' 'Oh I'll be there by six or six-thirty,' he said. I forget when the sun come up, probably seven-thirty then. So we go back out soon as it was light enough to see. When we're coming back, the sun was going up. He said, 'That's the best sight I've ever seen. You don't see that at home.' He got more out of that, how great that was. I guess out here we just take that for granted."

The Summer of 2002

It was one of the worst years on record. By late autumn the farm periodical the *Western Producer* reported that grains, oilseeds, and special crops were down 26 per cent from 2001 and 40 per cent below the ten-year average. Much of the surviving crop was expected to be poor because of a wet, snowy harvest.

For Marvin Evans, it was the craziest year in memory: first the searing drought, then too much rain, poor germination, feeble crops, some still unharvested at year's end. He managed to salvage feed for his beloved Charolais cattle, which won prizes at both the Saskatoon and Regina agricultural fairs.

The Boneskys of Morse likewise can't recall another year as bad. Some of their stunted crops had to be turned into fodder. "It breaks your heart," Karen said.

They're not quitting, but they're disillusioned. "Do we believe we produce food for citizens that care about us or the quality of their food? No. Do we believe that the federal or provincial governments have the wisdom and understanding to care about agriculture and the West? No."

Doug Armstrong of Whitewood scaled back from seven quarters (1,120 acres) to four, sold most of his machinery, and is down to seventy cows. He drives a truck and a bus, off-farm, for extra income. His wife teaches school and works part-time at a local auction barn. Neighbouring farmers are still deep in debt. "Some have operating loans of five hundred thousand dollars. It's scary."

For organic farmer Kevin Beach it was the *annus horribilis*. The very dry spring, followed by the unusually wet June, followed by a simmering July drained the subsoil moisture and brought a late hatch of grasshoppers, "an organic farmer's worst nightmare. Their ravenous appetite ruined the lentils and quite a lot of spring wheat."

Hail pounded his wheat in late July. Heavy rains came in August, bringing "billions of mosquitoes that drove us and the animals nuts," and flooding formerly bare sloughs, including some Kevin had seeded in the spring.

"Then, guess what? It froze lightly on August 1!" September and October brought below-normal temperatures, rain and snow.

"I could go on, but I might become vulgar," Kevin said. Instead he ended with the prairie farmers' mantra of hope, the steadfastness that has made these people special for generations. "The bright spot is that moisture conditions now are very good, so everyone is trying to forget the immediate past and look forward to a better future."

Then came 2003 – and Mad Cow Disease.

VII

THE PRAIRIE TOWN

What is nice here is you can get in the car and stop
wherever you want . . . and just be alone with
God and nature whenever you feel like it.

MARGARET BOYD
Kinistino, Saskatchewan

Requiem for an Old Friend

It was a wet, windy September day in 2002 and Daniel Murphy looked small, vulnerable, and miserable atop the High River, Alberta, grain elevator. He was in the second-last day of his week-long sit-in, on a recliner chair anchored to a temporary platform on the cupola, the very peak of the weather-worn red-and-green building. The fifty-year-old Murphy, president of the High River Historical Preservation Society, dislikes heights. The cupola is about seventy-four feet up.

"The scariest part was the damn wind," he told me later. "I could feel the old building shaking and shuddering." But the platform held, and Murphy earned nineteen thousand dollars in pledges (to be matched by a government grant) to refurbish the working elevator and perhaps allow for revenue-building annexes, such as a restaurant.

And in a way he struck a blow for the survival of prairie towns.

You can hardly find the little towns any more. The grain elevators that identified them on every horizon are going-going-gone. Once the elevator was a prairie icon, the stuff of a million postcards, calendars, and Easterners' jokes. Its cupola, like a small head on big sloping shoulders, rose above every town and hamlet. From miles away those landmarks signified life, warmth, and community, long before the low huddle of buildings around them came into view.

To small boys riding wagonloads of grain with their fathers, as once I did, the elevator was a holy place – cool, mysterious, redolent with the tantalizing aroma of wheat. We drove the horse-drawn wagon onto weigh scales in a shed attached to the elevator. The agent, his every movement bespeaking High Authority, sampled the load for weed seeds, moisture, firmness. He weighed the wagon loaded, tilted its contents into a hopper, weighed it again. The difference between full and empty wagon was the weight of our delivery. Depending on the outcome, my father drove away smiling or cursing the price, the grade, the agent's ancestry, and, on principle, the Canadian Pacific Railway.

The elevator was the focal point of our financial year, but its romantic and emotional roles were equally important. It was a status symbol: a five-elevator town considered itself a cut above a three-elevator town, and a ten-elevator town wouldn't speak to either of them.

No more. Now, along the country roads, fewer and fewer towering pointy heads signal "Shamrock is over here" or "There lies Mossbank." In the 1933-34 crop year, the prairies had 5,485 grain elevators. Now there are 418 (as listed by the Canadian Grain Commission; the grand total is well under 500). After enduring decades of wind, sun, sleet, and hail they have been vanquished.

When railways began closing their branch lines after the Second World War, the elevators were doomed. Many were scrapped. A few are used for organic farming. Some have become museums or heritage parks. Boissevain, Manitoba, has a mural depicting the inner workings of an elevator on the wall of an actual pool building. Sangudo, Alberta, has a giant sundial made of boulders surrounding a twenty-one-foot stylized grain elevator. Inglis, Manitoba, keeps all five of its elevators, designated as National Historic Sites, in near-original condition, to be used for a craft shop, maybe a microbrewery, mill, and bakery.

Those are rare. And 25 to 30 per cent of the aforementioned 418 elevators are ugly, efficient cement boxes called "high throughput." Typically, they can hold twenty thousand metric tonnes – about twenty-eight times the capacity of their wooden ancestors – and can load 50 to 110 railcars within eight to twelve hours. Mammoth grain trucks, ranging dozens of miles to feed these monsters, are pounding the life out of prairie roads that were never designed for such traffic.

And the romance is gone. The prairie skyline has lost its distinctive face. Little towns, struggling for existence, no longer raise those homely wooden heads to announce "Over here, it's us!"

Small Town Blues

Vanishing elevators are only one manifestation of small-town malaise. A Saskatchewan woman described the methodical decay of her town to Dr. Nikki Gerrard, community psychologist with Saskatchewan District Health. Gerrard was studying rural people's resiliency, and turning up painful truths.

"First the courthouse went," the woman said. "The hospital went. The doctor will go. The rail line will go. We used to have two schools, now we have one. Our SaskTel man is retiring, will he be replaced? We used to have a CN crew here. The town is going down and it's being done to people without their input, without their knowledge until it happens."

The root cause is the loss of farm people, and it's a vicious circle. Fewer people means the schools consolidate. The hospital, if any, goes to a larger community. Local businesses wither, and as their services shrink their customers reject them; it's worth driving the extra distance to a big town for more choice or better prices.

It's happening everywhere, but Saskatchewan, the province of small agricultural communities, is hardest hit. The latest census reported 362 Saskatchewan villages and 147 towns, but half of the villages and two-thirds of the towns had lost hundreds of people in the preceding five years.

"We go to the city more every year," says farmer Warren Jolly. "You can get bread and milk here in Mossbank, but that's about it." Mossbank, as we spoke, had 350 people. "We used to have eight machinery dealers and six elevators. Now there's one machinery dealer and no elevators. The biggest problem is going to be trying to raise a family out here." With schools amalgamating, students will have to travel ever farther for an education.

As communities shrink, some are less safe. One early summer morning, I went for coffee at the Esso café in Herbert (between Moose Jaw and Swift Current on the Trans-Canada Highway). A dozen men in tractor-driver caps surrounded two long communal tables.

Every prairie town has at least one such hangout, where the guys meet daily for gossip and commiseration over crops, weather, machinery costs, and the goddam government. The fierce black coffee is incidental. This is their place to let off steam, a lot cheaper and more manly than a psychiatrist's couch.

On this day there was a new topic. The proprietor, tall, lean, with slicked-down black hair, said his car was broken into the other night.

"So was mine," someone else said. Heads shook in disgust. A few mild cuss words.

At the cash register, trying to show I was not just another callow tourist, I said, "I grew up south of here. Used to be safe. Never locked our doors."

"Not any more," the proprietor said. "We got so much shit happening here, coming off the highway."

Later, in Yorkton, RCMP Corporal Iain McLean, big, red-headed, outgoing, confirmed that crime is up. His staff, he said, is run off its feet every day and some of it was "pretty serious stuff. There was a time when you could go camping and leave everything out. Not any more; it'll get stolen."

Not just in his town, but across the board, there are more assaults and more drugs. "The big fear for me is marijuana," McLean said. "The marijuana we're seizing now is 23 per cent tetrahydrocannabinol [THC]. It smells so bad it makes some of our members physically ill when they make seizures. And it's addictive."

McLean fears that people of his generation (late forties) now in government, who used a milder marijuana socially when they were young, think pot is okay.

"It's not. They call it 'skunk.' They've hauled literally tons of it off Number 1 Highway. And if you're catching that much, you know how much is getting away. It should be scary for everybody."

A Picture on the Wall

Community still endures in some towns. Often it just needs a kick-start. Artist Janet Blackstock, the moving spirit behind a wall mural in Whitewood, Saskatchewan, says it succeeded "by being the antithesis of a productive project. We need to find a way of reversing how we've been doing things."

The tourists from all over Canada, the United States, even Europe, peel off the Trans-Canada in their lumbering buses, turn down Lalonde Street, cross the CPR tracks, pull up at Third Avenue, and climb out with a chatter of camera shutters to view Whitewood's pride and joy. It's a man-woman-and-child-made mural, covering an entire wall, depicting market day on this spot a century ago.

"It doesn't *do* anything," says Blackstock. "It doesn't earn any money. It just sits there. And that's why the mural is so important. It did a whole lot of things in not doing anything. It did *so* much for the morale of the town."

Whitewood, a well-groomed place of a thousand, is feeling the pinch of a shrinking rural population. Rather than give up, its citizens put their wits to work.

"Some people say, 'What's the point? We're dying,'" says Barbara Vennard, retired teacher and Janet's sister. "But we *are* valuable, and we *do* have some power, and you *can* do something."

A mural had been idly discussed for years. They are wildly popular throughout the West as both outdoor historical galleries and tourist attractions. Whitewood initially thought it would be too difficult and too expensive. Town administrator John Billington thought otherwise. Billington had already demonstrated his smarts by updating the insurance on the town rink, just before it burned down. The rink was replaced, hockey was saved, and Billington was a local hero. He saw the mural as a Millennium project. The town got a modest federal grant.

Blackstock browsed through old photos at the local museum and settled on a black-and-white print of market day in Whitewood, circa 1895: a mélange of horses, riders, cows, sheep, and a sprinkling of frame buildings. She made a line drawing. Helpers projected an enlargement of the image on the wall. Blackstock climbed up in a blizzard of mosquitoes, traced the lines with a black marker, and plotted colour locations.

On the first day, volunteers turned out in droves. Seniors from the nursing home, some in wheelchairs, and small children painted as high as they could reach, meaning they did the grass. As summer heat increased, and the mural rose higher, Janet and a few others did most of the work on scaffolds. Tourists, hearing of it on radio, drove in to watch. One night a local wedding party wandered down. The job was finished in three weeks. At the end Janet painted a little joke into a corner: a woman chasing an errant cow (not part of the photo).

Most of Whitewood attended the dedication party. During the first Halloween, volunteers stood guard against vandals, but, says Blackstock (who is now local economic-development director), "If something happens to it, well, that's life. You've got to try."

Whitewood keeps trying. Another mural (a harvest theme) is finished, and more are planned. Flowerpots adorn the main street. A flag garden flies at the edge of town, representing the British, French, Germans, Hungarians, Finns, and Swedes who settled the surrounding area. There's a walking tour, brainchild of local history buff Blaine Coleman, with thirty points of historical interest, and more to come.

Joe Ashfield, who ran the town newspaper for twenty years, contributes in his own way: his Whitewood Trading Company ("We Buy and Sell Old Stuff of All Kinds"), a mad array of knick-knacks, bric-a-brac, and treasures from estate sales, flea markets, and garage sales, draws tourists from England, Finland, even Saudi Arabia. "It brings people into town and they eat. In adversity, small-town people band together."

Whitewood has one more ace in the hole: a gaggle of phantom noblemen. In the 1880s fourteen French counts, their families, and servants chose Whitewood as the site of their New World dream. They built fancy homes and ambitious businesses – sugar-beet plantation, cheese factory, distillery. The businesses faltered, the counts moved on, but Whitewood clings to the memory. A museum, with letters, photos, coats of arms, and other memorabilia, is dedicated to the de Pradal de Farquettes, the de la Forest de Divonnes, and the other noble families. Naturally, Whitewood bills itself as the French Count Capital of North America.

"I'm hoping all this works," says Mayor Malcolm Green, a transplanted Brit who runs the local meat market. "Small towns on the prairie today, it's an uphill battle to stay alive."

Staying Alive
Why keep them alive? For Whitewood's Barbara Vennard the answer is simple: it's a better way of life.

"Will I move to the city when I retire? Why would I do that? I can walk down the street, people know who I am. If I'm not at church on Sunday, people will check to see if I'm okay. I love knowing that my neighbours know who I am."

Trudy Bosch, fresh out of university, moved from Halifax to Grenfell, Saskatchewan, to write for the local *Sun*. At first she missed fast-food outlets on every other corner and pizza deliveries at midnight. These minor inconveniences were soon outweighed by Grenfell's trust, friendliness, and cleanliness. People returned her phone calls. Clerks smiled. Bosch is a small-town convert.

Shaunavon, Saskatchewan, doctor Martin Vogel, from South Africa, says when his two daughters were small they could pull their wagon to the store and come home with groceries and a piece of candy. "There's nowhere else on this planet where you can send three-year-old children to do your shopping for you."

Maintaining this precious lifestyle puts town and country people on their mettle. How can a town of 250 gain attention? Pierson, Manitoba, does it yearly with a Carnival of Crafts that attracts two thousand visitors from as far away as Winnipeg, Regina, and Saskatoon. Profits run around eight thousand dollars, which helps keep the Pierson arena going. Where the arena lives, a community lives.

Author Al Scholz lists in his book *Don't Turn Out the Lights* eighteen thriving small industries in Saskatchewan alone, including a mineral spa, a winery (fruit wines from chokecherries, crabapples, strawberries, and raspberries), a company that makes textiles, and another that makes organic soaps and essences.

Andrew Strempler had a dream. He was twenty-five, not long out of college, managing a pharmacy in Rossburn, Manitoba, but already tired of being an employee. He wanted his own business, but how could he afford it? He and his bride, Catherine, twenty, drove through Minnedosa, a pretty valley town of twenty-six hundred, 125 miles northwest of Winnipeg.

A two-storey building was for sale. The Stremplers bit the bullet, drew up a business plan for a new pharmacy, borrowed to the hilt, and went out on their own. It was tough for two young-sters from Winnipeg to penetrate small-town caution. Minnedosa already had a pharmacy, run by a man with long-established family connections. Catherine, pretty and fair-haired, spares a half-hour to tell me their story (Andrew, boyish-looking in a T-shirt, is too busy to talk).

"The elderly customers were scared," she says. "They thought if they went to a different pharmacy they'd be given different pills. Andrew, not being one to accept failure, spent his free time – which he had lots of – looking for ways to find business." How, he wondered, could he overcome the limitations of the small local market?

He prowled the Internet and discovered Americans were buying products at prices he could beat: such simple items as Nicorette chewing gum (to discourage smoking) and blood-sugar monitors for diabetics. He sold his first Nicorettes on the Internet auction site e-Bay in 2000, developed a Web site, and modest sales kept the Stremplers afloat.

Finally, they were able to take out-of-country drug prescriptions by fax or regular mail. When a prescription comes in, they interview the client by phone to check on other medications being taken. A pharmacist approves the dosage; a Canadian doctor approves the prescription.

It caught on. Former classmate and pharmacist Mark Rzepka and his wife joined the firm. Within two years Mediplan Pharmacy had 120 employees, and clients all over the United States, as well as in China, Japan, Australia, Iraq, and Germany. Mediplan operates fourteen hours a day, Monday to Friday. Prices and service are competitive. In 2002, for example, a thirty-day supply of Tamoxifen, used by patients with breast cancer, could cost $500 U.S. in some states. With government controls keeping prices low in Canada, Mediplan could sell Tamoxifen for about $30 U.S.

"A lot of our customers have the choice of either eating or taking their medication," Catherine says. "They are saving thousands of dollars a year and they're very grateful. We try to keep a personal touch to what can be an impersonal business." Every customer gets a phone call and receives a handwritten thank-you note in their parcel.

How long can it last? The Stremplers are optimistic.

"Pharmacists in the U.S. are not crying about three to four hundred prescriptions coming up to Canada," Catherine says. "Many people are crossing the border in busloads to Ontario pharmacies, doing a lot more business than we can do. With any new business, especially within the health profession, you're going to have detractors who are afraid of change. We have had our battles. But we're trying to work with our associations and with the health profession to establish guidelines for our type of business. Overall, a lot more people are rooting for us than against us."

That includes former doubters in Minnedosa. "I guess when you go from employing one person to 120," Catherine smiles, "you're more accepted in the community."

It was a lucky day for Altona, Manitoba, when David W. Friesen bought a little confectionery store early in the 1900s. He seemed to be just another industrious Mennonite, common in those parts. (Of the roughly 130,000 Mennonites in Canada today, nearly 60 per cent are in Manitoba.)

But D.W. was an uncommon go-getter. He became postmaster, agent for Manitoba Government Telephones, and deacon of his church. He bought a local bookstore and made it a distribution centre for texts and other school supplies. The next generation moved it up a notch. Son David (D.K.) bought a second-hand press, ran it from his father's basement, parlayed it into a full-fledged printing plant, and launched the biweekly *Altona Echo*. In 1950 three of the four sons incorporated as D.W. Friesen and Sons (now simply Friesens).

Gradually the word seeped through the Canadian book industry: some outfit in the Manitoba boondocks was printing high-quality books. In particular, it was cornering yearbook and community-history markets. Community histories took off with Alberta and Saskatchewan's golden jubilees (1955), centennials in Manitoba (1970) and British Columbia (1971), and Canada's own centennial (1967). D.K.'s son, David G., fresh from the University of Manitoba, recognized the potential. Since then thousands of histories and yearbooks have poured out of Friesens at One Memory Lane.

The company doesn't shout or beckon when you enter tidy Altona. No sign proclaims it to be Book Capital of Manitoba. Head office is tucked down a side street. Friesens doesn't throw its weight around, but it *is* Altona. The population is thirty-five hundred; the company employs five hundred, most of them from in or around town.

"What we have here is almost a community at work," says now-president and CEO David G. Friesen, a young-looking fifty-five in shirt sleeves. "We know each other. We went to school together. Our kids go to school together. We golf at the same single golf course. We eat at the same one restaurant in town, go to the same churches. And as long as it doesn't get *too* close, it can work out."

Employees are shareholders in the firm. Friesens' own accredited graphics-arts college trains six students per year with eight hundred hours of theory and practical training in the latest hi-tech printing procedures. About 60 per cent of the graduates join the company, a steady supply of young professionals.

The plant is airy and immaculate. David G. is an unapologetic neat freak: no eating outside the cafeteria, no junk hanging on walls, no cluttered aisles. The ceilings are vacuumed every year. Friesen, president since 1986, believes a clean shop helps foster pride in the product.

That, along with excellent colour reproduction and a guarantee of on-time delivery, puts it in printing's big leagues. "I hired a woman from New York and picked her up at Winnipeg airport," Friesen says with mild amusement. "As we were driving through the city to come here, she wanted to know if Winnipeg was a suburb of Altona."

Strangers who have difficulty equating the magnitude of the company with its one-horse-town environment don't realize how big the horse is. All the major Canadian book publishers use Friesens, as well as many in the United States. From Altona has come *Natural Worlds*, the first Robert Bateman book to be printed in Canada; hundreds of thousands of Harry Potter books; 370,000 copies of the best-seller *Boom, Bust & Echo*; 600,000 *Titanic* books; 400,000 copies of just *one* edition of Albertan Jean Paré's fabulously successful cookbooks (Friesens has printed all fifty-five of her books so far, totalling many millions). The Altona company has printed more than fifteen million copies of Robert Munsch's *Love You Forever*, rated best-selling children's book of the nineties by the *New York Times*.

Friesens developed its own courier service long before professional couriers came to Altona. "We can get something out of here and to New York City before ten-thirty tomorrow morning. We're only ten miles from the U.S., right on the Interstate highway. We can ship anywhere in the U.S. or Canada over a weekend. They can't get much better service in Toronto."

To make life sweeter for clients, Friesens keeps two apartments in town for their exclusive use. They're occupied almost full-time. "We know we have the newest, cleanest, most modern printing book manufacturing plant in North America," David G. says. "We don't want our clients to walk out of that and think they're in a two-bit town."

The Friesen dynasty will eventually end. David's two sons are doing other things. "In 1983 we, primarily my father and his brothers, decided this should be an employee-held company."

Friesen has hired a young successor. "Ironically and coincidentally his name is Friesen, but we're not related. So the company will continue."

Which is good news for the book industry and better news for Altona.

WHERE EVERYBODY KNOWS YOUR NAME

In 1982 Michael Blanar, Ph.D., English professor at Brandon University, and his future wife, Shirley, went looking for an inexpensive home. They found a one-hundred-year-old, one-and-a-half-storey house with a sixty-by-sixty-foot lot in Elgin, forty-two miles south of Brandon, for twelve thousand dollars.

They knew their city backgrounds would be under the microscope in a community of sixty-five people. They vowed to be models of fellowship and propriety. Soon they were invited to bonspiels and community suppers.

"Shirley could always cook pie. But what were they going to do with me? They let me pour coffee and sweep floors." Blanar knew it was a test — would the Ph.D. guy deign to dirty his hands? He willingly did, and was promoted to cashier.

A neighbour invited them for coffee and diffidently mentioned the previous owner's seventy-five-foot wire clothesline tied to Blanar's tree. "The wire is cutting the bark and killing the tree," the neighbour said. "Mind if I take it down?"

"I'll do it," Michael said.

A week later the Blanars returned from a walk to find a mighty clothes-post (cut-down telephone pole, actually) standing in their yard — a thank-you for saving the tree.

Blanar learned small-town etiquette: "You walk into the coffee place, pour yourself a cup, and say, 'Anybody want some more coffee?'" There were unwritten rules. "You kept your eyes open and your mouth shut, because the person you might be criticizing could be your listener's brother or sister."

Blanar, now retired, is still a teacher at heart. His plump face and keen eyes are alive with interest in everything. Presumably, the locals found it irresistible. In time he was elected to the three-person town council. Shirley also served on council. Michael ended up as chairman, equivalent to mayor.

By 2002 Michael and Shirley, sixty-nine and sixty-eight respectively, could no longer manage a big garden or flights of stairs. They moved to Winnipeg. Elgin gave them parties and affectionate farewell speeches. A prized going-away gift was a painted cream can portraying their Elgin home on one side and their northern Manitoba summer log house on the other.

The Blanars carried their small-town wisdom to Winnipeg. When a next-door neighbour went on holiday, Michael said, "We'll keep an eye on your place while you're gone."

"Why, that's so nice of you!" said the neighbour. "The man who lived here before never did that."

Obviously, the previous resident had not been schooled by the neighbourly people of Elgin.

World's Largest Everything

It's a rare town that has a Friesens or a Mediplan to hike its economy, but anybody can raise an oddball statue. Welcome to the World's Largest monuments to vegetables, birds, bugs, beasts, wheat stalks, and a monster sausage. These weird icons, mostly of fibreglass or metal, are meant to drag tourists off the road into town and, above all, to establish an identity for the town. "Hey, look, we're *here!*"

They can have, as does Vegreville, Alberta, the World's Largest Ukrainian Easter Egg, or, as at Vonda, Saskatchewan, the World's Largest Bootlegger's Still, a replica of the real thing from Prohibition, when Vonda called itself the Moonshine Capital.

Andrew, Alberta, displays the World's Largest Mallard Duck: a five-thousand-pound B52 of a bird with a twenty-four-foot wingspan, marking a nearby resting area for wildlife.

Most communities feel compelled to attach cute names to their statues. Squirt the skunk looms thirteen feet high over Beiseker, Alberta. Porcupine Plain, Saskatchewan, has thirteen-foot Quilly Willy as its standard-bearer. Castor, Alberta, features a beaver (*Castor canadensis* in Latin) named Paddy, gnawing a pseudo-stump in front of the local post office. Eston, Saskatchewan, shows off an eight-foot Tyndall-stone gopher, reminding us that Eston is home to the World Gopher Derby (an event the gophers would rather forget).

Sara, a camel as big as a bungalow, stands in Glenboro, her nose pointing north towards Spirit Sands (locally called the Manitoba Desert). Inwood, Manitoba, has memorialized garter snakes, which hole up for the winter in the surrounding limestone.

No need to ask why Turtleford, Saskatchewan, has a twenty-eight-foot turtle, but what about the mighty one – surely World's Largest – towering over Boissevain, Manitoba? Seems that turtle trainers from around the continent bring their fleet-footed reptiles here for the World Turtle Derby. How fast do turtles race? Not very.

Wilkie, Saskatchewan, has a grasshopper statue eighteen feet long (almost as big as the real ones in the Depression; remind me to tell you how bad it was). But why would Komarno, Manitoba, have a mosquito with a fifteen-foot wingspan? It's a functional weather vane, and *komarno* means "mosquito" in Ukrainian.

Three of the World's Largest Non-edible Mushrooms rise twenty feet above Vilna, Mushroom Capital of Alberta. Twenty-seven feet above Glendon, Alberta, soars the World's Largest Perogy on a fork; good enough to eat if it weren't made of steel and fibreglass. Mundare, same province, is proud of its World's

Largest Kielbasa Sausage – forty-two feet high, six tons, can withstand 160-kilometre-per-hour winds. This Ukrainian sausage is doubled into a mighty oval. It looks a bit obscene, but maybe that's just me.

Roland, Manitoba, declares itself World Pumpkin Capital with a twelve-foot sixteen-hundred-pound pumpkin. Regrettably, Smoky Lake, Alberta, (home to the Great White North Pumpkin Fair and Weigh-Off) seems to have trumped Roland's ace with a gargantuan pumpkin weighing in at six tons.

Long ago, St. Paul, Alberta, welcomed little green men from afar with the world's first UFO landing pad. Then Vulcan elbowed in with its Vulcan Starship FX6-1995A. It is thirty-one feet long, resembles *Star Trek's* USS *Enterprise*, and has plaques welcoming visitors in English, Vulcan, and Klingon.

For the ultimate in kitsch, see the Gopher Hole Museum at Torrington, Alberta. Its display cases feature scores of stuffed gophers dressed up for everything from a wedding to a fashion show. It's how Torrington would look if the gophers took over.

A Touch of Europe

"It's a good town," Gerald Legault was saying from Legault Hardware in Gravelbourg, Saskatchewan. A large man of sixty-eight, greeting all who crossed his threshold with innate courtesy, Legault was about to sell his store. He will retire here, though, because the town is his life.

He was born here in simpler times (being two months premature, his mother tucked him in the oven in lieu of an incubator). French is his first language but like many he is fluently bilingual.

"In commerce here, it is mostly English. A few still want to deal in French, which is good. French is a very beautiful language, I think an awful lot of it." A playful smile. "In the old days we used to say it was a beautiful language to cuss with!" But the language is struggling and therein lies Gravelbourg's dilemma.

When I was a child, Gravelbourg was our cherished destination, but not for its "foreign" charms. We drove fifteen miles, over gumbo roads that would have sucked the shoes off Arnold Schwarzenegger, for the joys of a movie (in English) plus sausage and mashed in the Chinese café. We never dreamed of eating coq au vin (anyway, there was none).

Nor had I the wit to appreciate the French Catholic culture around us: the glorious cathedral, the bishop's residence, the Convent of Jesus and Mary. (I admired the hospital's Grey Nuns, who plied me with ice cream after my tonsillectomy.) None of us Anglos seized the opportunity to broaden our horizons. None ever mastered French in school, awkwardly taught by teachers who had never uttered a word of it.

Here in Gravelbourg, it flowed effortlessly around us. Yet we, rather than learn from our bilingual neighbours, called them "peasoups" or "frogs." Sixty-odd years later, the language is fighting for survival, and this doughty island in its anglophone sea seems more important than ever.

In a nearby town, legend says, one man swears he will never set foot in Gravelbourg because of its francophones. When a French-only swimming pool was planned in town, outraged Anglos dubbed it the "Frog Pool." Other prairie people resent the French because they feel Quebec dips deeper into the federal trough than other provinces and that bilingualism was force-fed them by Big Government. Why not Ukrainian or German, nationalities that outnumber francophones by three or four to one in each prairie province?

"Many brave words have been spoken about the advantages of living in a country with two cultural traditions," Saskatchewan's then-premier, Allan Blakeney, told the Task Force on Canadian Unity in 1977. "That is a point of view which makes sense in Central Canada, but has much less meaning for Saskatchewan."

Nevertheless, the French belong. Their explorers and coureurs de bois were the first Europeans to open the Canadian West. Francophone pockets, ranging from St. Boniface, Manitoba, to St. Albert, Alberta, are dotted across the prairie. Gravelbourg is all of them in microcosm: their strengths, charms, struggles (including feuds within their own ranks).

The first settlers called the community La Vieille after the nearby Old Wives Creek. The waterway became Wood River and the town was renamed in honour of the Gravel family, Father Pierre Gravel in particular.

"There were five Gravel brothers," says Paul Boisvert, editor of the weekly *Tribune*, his droll eye seeming ever on the lookout for a joke. "Get a load of this: one was a priest, another a doctor, a lawyer, a pharmacist, and naturally the black sheep, who was a cowboy."

Over the years this clean green town with its sprinkling of planted trees has held its population at about 1,250. Retirees from the country replace young hopefuls headed for Alberta, but its institutions are dwindling. Paul Bonneau, local historian, and Louis Stringer, lawyer, count them off. The convent is now a bilingual elementary school. The local credit union folded into the Southwest Credit Union. The province closed Gravelbourg's judicial centre.

Cruellest blow of all, the Gravelbourg diocese of the Catholic Church was melded with the Regina diocese in 1998. Officially, the merger emanated from the Vatican, but feisty Paul Boisvert lays the blame closer to home: "It was integral to our culture, to our values, and it was the French in Regina who took it away."

At least Gravelbourg retrieved its French-language radio station (lost for a while to Radio-Canada). And the magnificent twin towers of Our Lady of the Assumption Cathedral still soar 175 feet at the top of Main Street, as they have for eighty-four years, a landmark unparalleled in southern Saskatchewan.

At 180 feet long by 85 feet wide, Our Lady could accommodate the town's entire population with pews to spare. With its stained-glass windows and interior murals by Monsignor Charles Maillard, a long-ago pastor who dedicated ten years of his life to the work, Our Lady is, as Pierre Trudeau once put it, "Le Bijou des Prairies." In classical fashion Maillard painted his child angels in the nude. A prudish public raised such an outcry that he had to dress them. He used local residents (clothed) as his adult models. Old-timers can still identify their kinfolk on the walls.

Along Main and its satellite streets, a few establishments bear French or hybrid names – Bouvier Seeds, Boquinerie Gravel Bookstore, Loisell's Confectionery, Le Petit Marché, Foyer d'Youville, Collège Mathieu – but more anglicized than I remember.

Jeanne Allard confirms that hunch. "When I was young most of the merchants spoke French. Now they could but don't." She was born into a family of ten in a nearby French-German community, spoke French at home and English in school. "I think we are losing our French."

"Some businesses will provide French if you want it," adds Boisvert, who grew up bilingual in nearby Willow Bunch (charmingly named Taille de Saule until the English got at it). "There's still a bit of a stigma. They'll be speaking French and the minute someone walks in, if they're not sure which language they speak, they switch to English. There's insecurity and the feeling that you must always speak to anglophones because you might lose a client."

Boisvert slips effortlessly between French and English worlds. He can become incensed with fellow francophones who, he says, are missing the boat.

"It's that stigma. We say, 'Give us our little cultural centre, we'll all hide in there and look out the window.' Well, it's not working, we're still getting assimilated at the rate of 75 per cent. And the language is going to be gone."

If so, it will not go down without a fight, and Henri and Maria Lepage will lead the charge. Henri is mayor. The forthright Maria, as co-founder and past president of Association des Femmes Canadiennes françaises, has routinely jetted from Gravelbourg to Ottawa, Singapore, and Luxembourg and worked with the nation's leading feminists. Maria is no country mouse.

"We want respect for our culture and our need for French education just as much as religious rights," she says. "It's a fundamental Canadian right, but a lot of people have trouble accepting that."

"We're often told, 'You can speak English, you shouldn't have to speak French,'" adds Henri, who taught physics, biology, and chemistry at Collège Mathieu before he retired. "But that is beside the point. I have been told when I am cheering for my college team in French that I should smarten up and speak English. I said, 'I'll speak French in my hometown and my home rink if I want to.'"

Gravelbourg was 98 per cent francophone until the late 1950s. Then schools began closing in rural communities, causing anglophone students to pour into town. The French constituency is now about 60 per cent.

"Ideally, with the school system we have here nobody should leave Gravelbourg without being perfectly bilingual," Maria says. "But that's not the choice all parents make."

The town is rich in options. Collège Mathieu, the only French-language residential school west of Ottawa, provides secondary education. So does Gravelbourg High School, with full instruction in English as well as a French-immersion program. The elementary school, with classes from kindergarten to grade seven, offers an English program with core French and French immersion with one hour of English per day. Finally there is École Beau Soleil, on the Collège Mathieu campus, with French-language classes from kindergarten to grade seven.

The school situation has, as Louis Stringer put it, "caused quite a ruckus in town." Claude Piché stood *not* on the francophone side, which irked some of his compatriots. He and partner Sam Hawkins operate the local funeral home. Sam is anglophone (his father was my rural-school classmate a lifetime ago). Claude, a francophone whose Québécois grandfather pioneered here in 1907, is of another era: warm, gregarious, the eleventh child in a big old-fashioned family, from a time when local French chose not to take umbrage at Anglo insensitivity.

"Some people will never give in, conflict all the time, it's too bad, eh?" Piché says. "It's nice to speak two or three languages, but to force people? That's not the way to handle it. But they decided they needed their own school. People got hot under the collar.

"I was the mayor at the time. I never sided with the French people and they got madder'n old hell at me. I told them, I says, 'Look we don't really need this building.'"

Neighbour turned against neighbour. Michel Vézina, a mild-mannered Québécois, came to Gravelbourg in 1986 to be director of an adult-education service connected with Collège Mathieu. He and wife Pauline helped set up Beau Soleil. "So we were on the bad side of the gang." But even amid the strife people were human. Vézina has a poignant memory. "During that time we had five children and the youngest one died. There was, like, a stop in the fight. Everybody for nearly a year helped us go through that. After that the fight went on."

All that aside, Boisvert says, "Everybody works together now." One reason is Gravelbourg's resolve to bring the world to its door. The locals decided to capitalize on the French ambience. Some anglophones shrank from that. Boisvert suggested a solution: that town council adopt the slogan "Come to Gravelbourg for a Taste of Europe."

Council knuckled its collective brow and rejected "Taste," for fear tourists would expect to find non-existent French cuisine. They settled on "A Touch of Europe," embracing the original French and Germans plus a sprinkling of latter-day nationalities.

"It allowed the people here to not think of Quebec," says Boisvert, with that amused Gallic roll of eye. "Suddenly it's not Bouchard and his separatist hordes. Suddenly we're Parisian and Eiffel Tower."

The concept caught on. Merchants spruced up their store-fronts. Main Street has a sidewalk café, paving bricks, and European-style lampposts. André Chevrier came back home from Vancouver and opened a different (for Gravelbourg) kind of store with a nifty bilingual name: Le Style/Styles. (Chevrier is a psychiatric nurse by trade, which perhaps fitted him for the town's split personality.) Le Style offers antiques, art prints, kitchenware, linens, bath products for spas, wrought-iron furniture, wicker, French soaps, and scents from France.

"It's a big success," reports Boisvert. "Finally we have people driving from the cities to shop in Gravelbourg. That has to be a first for rural communities."

Each summer Gravelbourg holds a Grand Prix (go-karts, not Formula One, but it sounds European). The annual Summer Solstice Festival brings out cowboy poets, literary readings, jazz, and old-time fiddling that will burn your hair off. On St. Jean Baptiste Day, revellers can feast on tourtières and sucre à la crème.

At the Maillard Cultural Centre, French culture is flourishing, largely due to Les Danseurs de la Rivière La Vieille, the first francophone dance group in Saskatchewan. The troupe of twenty adults and twenty children, in bright authentic folk costumes, has a repertoire of eighty dances. They perform locally, with bilingual narration, and at festivals around Saskatchewan.

"One of our mandates is to preserve the language as well as the culture," says administrator and artistic director Camille Bell.

"It helps kids, French or English, who want to improve their French. Dance has no language barrier."

Periodically, tourists from Quebec, en route to Vancouver, fly into Regina and are bused to Gravelbourg. A French-speaking guide leads them to the cathedral, maybe a grain elevator (Gravelbourg still has some), dinner at the cultural centre, a performance by Les Danseurs. "This is the only place receiving them in French," explains Vézina. "Most of them speak little or no English."

"It's almost like a family reunion," adds Solange Chevrier. "They are amazed at our French." So they should be; it is better than Quebec *joual*. "We still feel an attachment to Quebec. Most of our forefathers came from there. But I am not more attached to Quebec than to Canada. I am a Canadian of French descent."

And a Gravelbourger above all, she might add, for her town is increasingly pleasing. "I love to come back here," says young Joselle Stringer, who has lived in Regina, Saskatoon, and Paris. "I would like to stay here and start a little business. You can breathe and relax here. Everybody is so welcoming. I enjoyed the bigger cities, but there wasn't anything there I needed."

Michel Vézina's job takes him back to Montreal two or three times a year. "But – *phew!* – it's going too fast back there. Home is here."

And Gerald Legault sees no reason ever to leave. "My wife's buried here. I have a brother and sister here. My church is here. I have lots of friends. We'll switch to French to keep in practice . . ." He pauses, courteous to the core, and adds a gracious footnote: ". . . if there is no English [person] present, of course."

"Alone with God and Nature"

Margaret Boyd grew up near Kinistino, Saskatchewan, during the Depression. She had a fulfilling life as nurse, sciences instructor, director of nursing at a cancer institute, assistant executive

director in an Edmonton hospital, and finally ran her own con-
sultancy. "But I was robbed of retirement happiness due to the
early death of my spouse."

She moved back to Kinistino in 1994. Town and vicinity
number about four thousand. Hers is eloquent testimony to the
pleasures and imperfections of small town life.

"People on the street are friendly. Almost everyone knows
everyone else. The seniors generally speak, even if only a few
words: 'Nice day, eh?' 'Sure cold out!' 'That's a fierce wind!' At
the post office those who do not say hello are the young folk.

"Young people today are no different on the prairies. They
want for nothing; get their own vehicle at age sixteen, their Ski-
doos, CD players, boom boxes to irritate old ears! They cruise
around the town heaving empty beer bottles at signposts, so
broken bottles are a hazard on the street corners. There is no local
police service; by the time police get there, the teens are long
gone. Drugs, alcohol, and impudence are part of the school scene.

"Entertainment and fellowship here involve the seniors' Half
Century Club, a little café called The Place to Be, Jughead's
Drive-In, the Swen Café. Groups go for coffee three to four
times a day. What do they talk about? Weather, the old days,
curling, accidents. The men of Kinistino have gathered on
Coffee Row from time immemorial.

"Funerals are attended by almost everyone in the town and
surrounding area. Almost a social affair, with refreshments
served by the churches or other organizations. There are no
taxis, bus service, or trains in Kinistino. People in their nineties
continue to drive cars or trucks. This is dangerous, but other
drivers know their vehicles and steer clear of them.

"The land has been stripped of most of the bushes I
remember. There are no more fencelines ranged by miles of
chokecherries, saskatoon berries, raspberry bushes. There are

endless miles of fields, as far as the eye can see, with the odd old tree that has been saved, rock piles, the occasional old grey building falling into ruins. Because of the lack of bushes and trees in the countryside and herbicides and pesticides, the bird population has diminished. A few flocks pass through.

"In winter, snow whips across the barren landscape and across the highways, polishing the highway surfaces to black ice. Our winters are long, October to April. Most people have snow blowers. Teens are no longer interested in shovelling snow. A younger neighbour helps here when he can. Otherwise, I get into a Ski-doo suit, my kamik boots with extra socks, a pair of caribou mitts made in 1950, and a head cover, and out I go, using a shovel and small electric snow blower.

"You learn not to book dental or medical appointments in the whiter months if possible. You learn to get your snow tires on and the car winterized early, and you give thanks to the good Lord for safe trips and the strength to live alone in Saskatchewan.

"Spring comes, but not too long before summer. The sky is ever-changing, from cloudless and blue to cloud masses changing by the minute, a fascinating panorama. And of course sunrises and glorious sunsets; rainbows after a rain.

"What is nice here is you can get in the car and stop wherever you want, pick wildflowers, walk the dog, look for nice stones for the garden, and just be alone with God and nature whenever you feel like it. And if your car did break down, heaven forbid, you can be assured the first person coming along would stop and offer to help. This is Saskatchewan."

VIII

CITY LIGHTS

The western city has yet to take its place
of prominence in our mindscapes.

GEORGE MELNYK
The Urban Prairie, 1993

The City as Province

How about doing away with the prairie provinces and dividing them among the five largest cities? Prairie writer and editor George Melnyk floated that notion ten years ago: that Winnipeg, Regina, Saskatoon, Edmonton, and Calgary might be regarded as city-states in the ancient Greek tradition.

"An anti-urban bias runs through our heritage," he wrote in *The Urban Prairie*. "Westerners are an urban people like other Canadians. This fact must be recognized. At some point the city has to become a dominant power in both the cultural and political mythologies of the region."

He's right. Many of us idealize the rural prairie because our roots are there, but urban areas now account for 75 per cent of the provinces' population and the bulk of their economic product.

What if Alberta, Saskatchewan, and Manitoba ceased to exist? Melnyk speculated. "In their place would be a region divided into five city-states, having all the powers that the three provinces now have – five provincial capitals if you like. The rural inhabitants in each city-state would relate to the capital city and the smaller centres under its control, linking their economic future to that of the city-state. It makes more sense for a beet farmer in southern Alberta to have Calgary as his seat of government than Edmonton."

It wouldn't work, Melnyk concluded. Would Regina's territory extend to Saskatoon's boundary, leaving Saskatoon responsible for everything north? Would Winnipeg, already dominant in Manitoba, take over the province?

All the same, his idea casts a refreshing light on the West.

"The land cannot be the sole arbiter of our identity, nor the farmer our sole representative," Melnyk wrote. "We have been obsessed with the land and its meaning for more than a century. Perhaps it is time now to reflect on the cities."

Here, then, are snapshots of the Big Five and a few of their

people. Residents may say, "This isn't the city *I* know." Fair
enough. These are impressions only.

WINNIPEG

A Special Place to Live

As a youth James Carr played oboe with the Winnipeg Symphony.
He's been a columnist with the *Winnipeg Free Press*, board
member of the CBC, and deputy leader of the Manitoba Liberal
Party. At present he is CEO of the Business Council of Manitoba,
composed of fifty CEOs of Manitoba's leading companies.

With all of this at age fifty, personable and good-looking to
boot, Carr is, if not a Renaissance man, an attractive candidate
for premier or prime minister. But he'd be happy to go down in
history as a passionate Manitoban. Born in Winnipeg, he has
travelled the world, but "I've always come back here. Never
regretted it. I like just about everything that has made this an
exceptionally special place to live."

Carr cites a half-dozen reasons, but the most telling is
"advantages of scale." He rides a riverboat to work. The night
before we met, he'd taken the boat to the local ballpark. It took
him seventeen minutes to get back home, "and I didn't hear a
single horn being honked."

He warms to his theme. "If you like to be within fifty-five
minutes of lakefront property on the thirteenth-largest lake in
the world; if you want to be able to afford housing that leaves
you with enough money to travel to Mexico in the winter;
if you want to be able to buy season tickets to first-rate ballet,
theatre, music; if you want to be certain the water you're drinking
and the air you're breathing is relatively good; if you want to
have a public-school system where you have a high level of

confidence that your children will be graduating with enough knowledge that enables them to compete – then you stay here."

Seeing in Both Directions

"It's the greatest place in the world to live," agrees Winnipeg apostle George T. Richardson. For a century the Richardsons have wielded enormous influence in Winnipeg and beyond. They are its nearest thing to aristocracy, although the notion would appall them. They have shunned publicity. Their philanthropy is legendary but usually anonymous.

"We don't tell everyone what we are doing," the late Muriel Sprague Richardson told me nearly fifty years ago, "but we get things done." The dignified Mrs. Richardson was then a widow, mother of George T., and head of the family empire. My article for *Maclean's*, the first ever written about her, was extracted from her only after she had my journalistic ethics and ability investigated from stem to gudgeon.

The Richardsons do "get things done." They opened a Winnipeg office in the 1880s just before the CPR arrived, bought and sold grain, opened a prairie elevator chain. James A. Richardson, father of George T., moved the company to greater heights – airlines, brokerage, elevators, insurance, cattle, radio stations – before he died in 1939. His widow ran the firm successfully another twenty-seven years.

Today the family is still in grain and agribusiness – their Canbra Foods Limited in Lethbridge is one of Canada's largest oilseed crushing, processing, and packaging operations – as well as oil and gas, real estate, and high-tech. The *National Post* estimated the family's worth at $1.18 billion.

Why has Winnipeg held them for a century?

"We [Winnipeggers] have a different perspective," says George Richardson, seventy-eight, from his perch on the thirtieth floor of the Richardson Building at the corner of

Portage and Main, crossroads of the West. "People in Toronto or Montreal really can't see west of Winnipeg. People in Vancouver don't clearly see over the mountains because they're looking at the Pacific. We're in the absolute geographic centre of North America."

Manitoba prizes its location. The cover of the 2002 Winnipeg phone book depicted two buffalo beside a sign near the city that reads "Longitudinal Centre of Canada 96° 48' 35"," causing one buffalo to remark to the other, "Apparently Toronto *isn't* the centre of it all."

"The time difference is to our advantage," Richardson explains. "We're still going when Toronto offices close and when Vancouver is well into its day. We can see clearly both ways."

Occasionally one of the Richardsons' quiet philanthropies registers on the radar screen. As every child under eighty knows, there was once an orphan bear adopted by Winnipegger Lieutenant Harry Coleburn, on his way overseas in the First World War. Coleburn named the little bear Winnie (after Coleburn's hometown), and donated him to the London Zoo in England. There, A.A. Milne took his son, Christopher Robin, and Winnie-the-Pooh was born.

Winnipeg grew fond of its namesake. There's a statue of Pooh and Coleburn in Assiniboine Park. A group, Partners in the Park, is planning a six-million-dollar, fifteen-thousand-square-foot "Poohseum." Its prize acquisition is an original painting of Pooh by E.H. Shepard, who illustrated the Milne books.

For one terrifying moment it seemed that the Pooh painting might join Mickey Mouse and Goofy in Disneyland. The ubiquitous Disney company holds the rights to the Pooh name and likeness until 2026.

Luckily, Disney is bear-friendly. When the painting came up for sale Winnipeggers, led by George's son Hedley (currently president and CEO of the family firm), wanted it. Disney with its millions could have outbid them. "But they had been up here and were so impressed with the response that they agreed to back off," George Richardson says. "They just said, 'No, the painting should be in Winnipeg.' So when you get Disney working with you, well, it helps."

Winnipeg bought Pooh's picture for $285,000. Again, the Richardsons helped get a job done.

Laughing All the Way

When I lived in Winnipeg in the 1950s, it was — by today's frenzied standards — gentle and laid-back. The height of a good time was a house party where we drank too much rum and Coke or rye and ginger and smoked too many Player's. The most colourful neighbourhood was North Main Street, a mirror on Manitoba's ethnicity, where lunch counters echoed with the bickering of stubby men with warlike moustaches:

"Give me one of those."

"These?"

"No, no, no! *Them.*"

"The bagel? Why didn't you say?"

"You don't *sell* them maybe?

"Sure we sell, you tell us what you want already."

The mayor of the day was Steve Juba, the canny and streetwise son of a Ukrainian carpenter, who drove a lavender Cadillac and uttered such endearing malapropisms as, "No comment. I'm not gonna stick my neck out on a limb."

Vestiges of that old city still live in survivors like Mel Manichen. For fifty-five years he made a nice living as a Winnipeg sheet-metal dealer, but you suspect he would have liked to have been a stand-up comic. There's a permanent twinkle in his eye. He has hosted the occasional roast. Another time, another place, he could have been a Dean Martin, a Jackie Mason, a Henny Youngman even.

Humour is Mel's way of getting a point across. Through his one-liners – he's got a million of 'em – emerges a picture of the Winnipeg he has known and mostly loved. He talks of growing up Jewish and bullied, in the north end.

"That's where you develop a sense of humour," he says. "The north end was a very tough neighbourhood. If they weren't on relief they were bootleggers. You used humour to be accepted by the toughies. Where I lived, Euclid-Granville, you learned how to run at a very young age."

A one-liner is cocked and ready to fire. Mel eyes me hopefully to see if I know how to laugh. "When they had field days, Jews were very good runners. They started very early." You can hear the drum from the orchestra pit – *Kabum!* – punctuating the comedian's punchline.

There's reality in the joke. Manishen was part of a minority, and today he empathizes with Manitoba's growing aboriginal population. He thinks Canada has handled its native people worse than the United States treated its blacks. "We're really visitors to this country, so we should treat them with respect."

His parents came to Canada in 1905. Mel and five siblings grew up during the Depression. "You didn't have radios, you didn't have an awful lot of things. Saturday night's entertainment was to watch leeches swim around a bowl in the drugstore."

A pause for the laugh, then the kicker.

"We were so poor, my mother had to cut holes in my pants pockets so I'd have something to play with." *Kabum!*

The neighbourhood movie house showed two films, a cartoon and a serial on Saturday afternoon, all for five cents. But how were poor boys to find a nickel? Easy. They went down the street to the brothel and threw stones at the windows until the madam came out and gave them each a quarter to go away.

"Come on, Mel!"

"That's a true story!"

All the Manishen offspring did well. One brother became a French teacher; another owned a retail store in New Hampshire; one sister was a teacher; another a school librarian. Mel's first job was with the Hudson's Bay Company. Then he was a wireless air gunner in the RCAF. Afterwards he joined his father's Empire Sheet Metal Manufacturing company. When his father retired, Mel and a partner bought it out. Life was good. "Somebody would say, 'Mel how's this recession affecting you?' I'd say, 'I didn't know we had one.'"

His own sons turned out admirably. One has a master's in music and writes a music column for the *Free Press*. Another is a doctor. A third is a criminal lawyer.

"A lot of people say, why live in Winnipeg? I say, it's simple, those with brains moved to Toronto so it's an easy place to make a living." No, that's a joke. He's proud of Winnipeg's famous sons. "We kept the best brains here. Izzy Asper: Manitoba can be proud of what he's done, he is a class act. Winnipeg was good enough for him and good enough for George Richardson, it's good enough for me."

He ticks off Winnipeg's charms. He can get to the office in eight minutes. He has friends dating back sixty years. The pace is sane. "I'm seventy-seven, I couldn't last to seventy-seven if I lived in Toronto. You have a quality of life here. You can belong to a golf club for twenty-five hundred dollars, and get to the course in eighteen minutes." Time for a joke. "Golf is an excuse to go for a walk."

Winnipeggers in their once-famous geographical isolation – before jet travel and the Internet melted distance – invented their own fun.

"In my younger days, we had a very active social life. We'd play bridge on Friday night, go to the movies on Saturday, have people over for dinner during the week. We had so much socializing then, to get me out of the house now it's a big chore. I burnt myself out."

He is a voracious reader of non-fiction. "I'm a book-oholic. I have an insatiable curiosity. I feel sorry for young people today who don't have that [reading habit]." Pause. "Knowlton Nash once said television is chewing gum for the eyes."

When Mel and I met in the summer of 2002, Israel Asper was in bad odour with many journalists for his centralized editorial control of thirteen daily newspapers in his CanWest Global Communications empire, and for firing one of his publishers. Manishen remained loyal. Asper – who rose from modest beginnings in Minnedosa, Manitoba, to (according to the *National Post* in 2001) a fortune of $1.25 billion – is famed locally for his charitable donations, but Manishen wasn't awed by the dollars.

"I'm attracted to people that are passionate about what they do and are good people. You could be very wealthy and very smart, but if you're not a good person, keep away. Izzy Asper is the kind of guy if you drop him a note, you get an answer. He likes people. When Izzy grew up in Minnedosa, it was so small, when they had a parade there was nobody left to watch it." *Kabum!* "I'm not kidding you!"

We'd been lunching at Rae and Jerry's, another remnant of the comfortable old Winnipeg, where corned-beef aficionados have dined for a half-century. Now it's time to go. Mel's lean, friendly face telegraphs one parting joke.

"Somebody once told me, 'You spend most of your time selling Mel Manishen.' I said, 'Yes but it's a good product, isn't it?'"

That's the truth, no kidding.

SASKATOON

In August 2002 a pollster sampled four hundred people in each of Regina and Saskatoon: How did they feel about their respective cities? It was Regina's worst nightmare come true. Growth prospects? Good! exulted 80 per cent of Saskatonians; not so good, said half of Reginans. Beautiful city? Ninety-seven per cent of Saskatoon respondents said yes, compared to only three-quarters of Reginans.

Good place to raise a family? Ninety-six per cent of Saskatonians gave their ringing endorsement, compared to 56 per cent of Reginans. Only half of Reginans felt safe in their city, compared to 80 per cent in Saskatoon.

Almost a Camelot

Yet part of Saskatoon's west end is the aboriginal ghetto, what the *Globe and Mail* in 2000 called "the Indian quarter . . . a Canadian Harlem . . . a square mile of reckless inebriation. . . ." Here, among small, pitiful houses, among pimps and hookers and nightly brawls, social agencies struggle to break a vicious cycle of welfare, poverty, drunkenness, and drugs, where natives cry racism and cops are bitter and frustrated because aboriginals, who make up only 3 per cent of the population, account for 15 per cent of those in jail.

On the other side of town, a different society. The Delta Bessborough Hotel, like a feudal castle, dominates the bank of the South Saskatchewan River as it has for seventy-five years. Across the river – where summer theatre-goers can see Shakespeare on the Saskatchewan – fine homes overlook shady avenues. The university campus, with its handsome greystone buildings and strong component of agricultural education and research, is an amalgam of learning and picture-postcard elegance. A kind of prairie Camelot for those whom fate has dealt a better hand.

Scenically, Saskatoon has it all, says local artist Darlene Hay. "There is prairie to the south, forest to the north, and the South Saskatchewan with a beautiful deep valley running through it. It is well treed, truly an urban forest, and a major flyway for migrating birds, 340 species."

The river creeps into every conversation. Tall, balding Robert Brack is not given to flights of fancy, but the South Saskatchewan stirs him: "It has added so much to the beauty of this city." He and his wife, Joyce, now in their early seventies, have spent most of their years here, not always easy ones. Joyce has had multiple sclerosis since 1957.

When it struck she was twenty-eight, teaching grade one, and had a year-old baby. She spent a thousand days in her sickbed, at times too paralyzed to lift a finger, swallow, or even shed a tear. For fifteen years she wore leg braces. During remissions she doggedly kept on with her life, because, as she says, the alternative was to exist in a wheelchair or flat on her back.

Bob and Joyce's seven brothers and sisters surrounded her in turns and helped her through the worst times. The Bracks raised two healthy sons. Joyce carries on today without medication (fearing side effects at her age).

"I feel good most of the time, with extra rest. I've learned how to ration my energy." She uses a wheelchair if she needs it and does daily exercises to increase her strength and mobility.

The Bracks could have been forgiven for giving up on Saskatoon. It seemed to be jinxed. At the time, its rate of MS cases was more than double that of other Canadian cities. But moving wouldn't have changed her disease, and the city's comfortable size (about two hundred thousand), its university (where Bob spent his career as professor in the extension department), and its showpiece river helped sustain them. Saskatoon has enhanced its riverbanks with the Meewasin Valley Trail, sixty kilometres of paths, parks, and six bridges (with talk of building two more).

"On any given day you'll find people out there doing their daily exercise," Bob says. "At Diefenbaker Park near the Exhibition Grounds, you can drive right to the edge of the valley and look across. In fall the colours of the trees on the riverbank range from the reds of the saskatoon to the bright yellow of the birch. In the summer the pelicans stay close to the weir near the CP railway bridge and you can watch them catching fish."

It's a tonic for the spirit.

Serenity Amid Chaos

Wayne Shaw rises up from a wild confusion of books stacked floor to ceiling on shelves, spilling out of boxes, teetering on piles on the floor. One small book-filled room leads on to another, leading back to who knows where.

Trim and grey-haired in his early sixties, slightly resembling the actor Steve Martin, the proprietor of Saskatoon's the Book Hunter is something of a thespian himself. Shaw talks non-stop, at gale force, in capital letters. He springs upright, gesticulating, in what he calls "my excitable pissed-off way." He rises to furious heights of indignation, but his voice modulates in mid-tirade to answer the phone with a dulcet "Hello, the Book Hunter." He is by no means the typical Saskatonian, but is proof that Westerners are anything but dull.

Paradoxically, Shaw prizes Saskatoon for its serenity. He has lived in Regina and Winnipeg, and has often visited Calgary and Edmonton, but "I have never found any part of those cities where I could feel as close to rural or small-town life as here. I recently bought a house three blocks from my store, and it feels like small-town Saskatchewan when I walk to work."

His roots are a farm near Davidson, Saskatchewan. He took his grade twelve at Notre Dame Wilcox under the iconoclastic Father Athol Murray. Père Murray had a rare talent for dialogue; some of it rubbed off on Shaw. Wayne attended University of Saskatchewan, played football for the Saskatoon Hilltops when they won the Canadian Junior Championship in 1959, joined the Saskatchewan Roughriders – the team that belongs to the province – and played linebacker for twelve years.

On this fine summer morning a friend from football days drops by. Ted Urness, towering and amiable, played centre for the Riders for ten years and made the CFL Hall of Fame. He plucks a copy of the *Western Producer* from Shaw's desk.

"LOOK AT HIM!" Shaw shouts. "He's a MILLIONAIRE, but he comes in here to read my newspaper instead of buying his own!" Ted smiles benignly, keeps reading. Over the next hour Ted (who's heard it all before) and I are treated to snippets of the world according to Wayne (proving that not all of the West's angry old men are in Alberta):

"Politicians and bureaucrats don't read, don't think. If they do they get fired because they cause trouble."

"I CAN'T STAND THOSE ARROGANT ONTARIO PEOPLE! Ontario and Quebec think they're the centre of the world, think they know more than everybody out west."

"Our Ottawa government is a sick, sad bunch of people. The federal government doesn't give a fuck about doing business with small businessmen in Western Canada. THEY DON'T GIVE A SWEET FUCK!"

"I'm addicted to open-line programs. I phone 'em all the time" (They must love him.)

For a while Shaw ran service stations, then a car-rental business. He's content now among his books. His core clientele is from the nearby university. He deals mostly in used copies, claims he has no idea how many are in inventory, yet when customers call he briskly turns to the computer, right on top of their requests.

"I have loved every day in the book business and have never been bored," he declares. "More people read in Saskatoon than in any city in North America. Another reason I like it here."

"So maybe you're finally settling down?" I ask before leaving the maelstrom of the Book Hunter for the calm of high noon in Saskatoon.

"Only way I'd move east is if some real gorgeous old woman said 'I have a bookstore in Ontario, come and run it,'" Shaw cries. "I LOVE WOMEN!"

REGINA

Learning to Love It

Regina has seen its share of tribulations in its hundred years. It shucked off the original Pile O' Bones name for the more elegant appellation (honouring Queen Victoria). Having no river, it transformed its bare plain with 315,000 planted trees and the artificial Lake Wascana. It survived a devastating tornado in 1912 and a riot of unemployed workers in 1935. It became a laboratory for social change under Tommy Douglas and the CCF.

And then – wouldn't you know it – that poll of Reginans and Saskatonians in 2002 found that the folks in Saskatoon cherished their city much more on almost every count.

"We should be boasting of the great things about our city," a chagrined Mayor Pat Fiacco told the press. "About the quality of life, that we're one of the least-expensive places to live in the country, that we have one of the highest [per capita median] incomes in Western Canada. There's so many great things about raising a family, all of those things."

The city set out on a course of self-adoration. Fiacco launched an "I Love Regina" campaign. The mayor – who "sees selling Saskatchewan as a marketing challenge not unlike selling Coke," claimed the Moose Jaw *Times Herald* – even stormed the 2002 Calgary Stampede in an "I Love Regina"

T-shirt, hoping to lure back some of the estimated hundred thousand Saskatchewanites who – ah, the shame of it – left to live in Cowtown.

At least two Reginans of my acquaintance – both Eastern expatriates – didn't need T-shirts or civic exhortations. They were already converts. Fate plunked them down on opposite sides of the same Regina street, women of the same age, same occupation, same convivial outlook. Maggie Siggins and Gail Bowen didn't plan it that way; serendipity was at work.

Bowen, of enormous cheer and energy, is an English teacher, Sunday-school teacher, mother and grandmother, and acclaimed writer of mysteries (her Joanne Kilbourn character has appeared in eight novels and six films). Siggins has written eight non-fiction books, including Governor General's Award winner *Revenge of the Land*. Two have been turned into films.

Both came from Ontario, and romance held them in Regina. Toronto-born Bowen met her future husband at the University of Waterloo, where both were doing graduate work. She followed him to Regina thirty-five years ago.

"I am so ashamed," she confesses, "I didn't know the order of the prairie provinces when I moved out here."

Siggins, when I met her thirty-three years ago, was a tough investigative reporter (*Toronto Telegram*) beneath her blonde good looks and disarming smile. I couldn't imagine her in Saskatchewan. Nor could she. In 1983 she took a one-year appointment at the University of Regina journalism school. She married professor Gerry Sperling, who was prepared to relinquish his tenured job to move back east.

Then Regina worked its magic.

"I like the place," she says. "I'm not sure why. It's not a pretty city. There's a beautiful park, but downtown is the absolute pits. No, it's the lovely ease of living here."

"Nice pace of life," agrees Bowen. "I walk to work, winter and summer." (Listening to them together is like watching Wimbledon: they swoop in and out of the joint conversation, *serve, volley, thwack, thwack.*) "You can do what you want to do. People don't give a rat's ass if I write a book or not. Nobody sits on the edge of their chair to see if I succeed or fail. So you're relaxed and can take some chances."

Maggie's serve.

"When you come out of northern Saskatchewan – we have a cottage there – and suddenly hit the prairie, I always have this incredible lifting of spirit."

"Me too," Gail says.

"My mother moved out here towards the end of her life," Maggie says. "She came from Toronto; she was a real downtowner."

"Maggie brought every person in her family here."

"Two things bothered my mother: she was afraid to get too close to the edge of the sidewalk, because if she did, every car would stop! Absolutely true."

The courtesy of Regina drivers – unlike Toronto, where pedestrians are considered bothersome blips in motorists' gunsights – is truly awesome. (Similarly, in Brandon I saw a man cycling slowly down a main street with a dog on a leash. A car behind waited courteously until the pair rounded a corner. In Toronto the savage SUVs would have blasted them into oblivion.)

"The other thing was the bus system," Maggie says. "Mother thought it was insane: on several occasions when it was cold, the driver dropped her at her door!"

Gail's serve.

"We're very political," she says. "You don't feel that social problems can't be solved. Increasingly, it's not connected with party, it is just activism."

Siggins: "Liberals don't do well here, because there isn't much room for namby-pamby nothing."

New game: time for Regina to get its lumps.

"There's a kind of lack of sophistication here that drives me crazy," Maggie says.

"Saskatoon is a little more sophisticated," Gail agrees.

"People are Pollyannaish. There is a lack of questioning. The Regina *Leader-Post* is the worst newspaper of all time. When I was doing investigative stuff on the Thatcher case, documents were stacked high in the courthouse and nobody had looked at them." (Siggins wrote *A Canadian Tragedy*, on the Colin Thatcher murder case.)

"Everybody knew about the scandals in the Devine government," Gail chimes in. "Regina is a political town, a company town. But nobody talked about it. It was shocking."

"I'd phone up for an interview, the man says he would be glad to see me," Maggie continues. "Then I show up and they'd absolutely refuse to say anything."

"Because it'd be rude to turn you down," Gail explains. "I've been a teacher for twenty-seven years, and my students are the nicest and least questioning of any I've known."

"The other thing about Saskatchewan," Maggie says, "there's a sense of inferiority here."

"I resent that attitude down east: that we're here because we've missed the boat," Gail says. "Of course, it isn't true."

"My mother, at a party out here before she moved, said, 'But of course all of you would move to Toronto if you could.'" Maggie smiles and winces at the memory. "But when she moved here she was never happier."

Game, set, match.

Music, Verse, and Hard Work

Police chief Cal Johnston acknowledges the local tendency to self-deprecation, but looks beyond it. "There still remains here in Regina a very strong and alive sense of community, and a deep appreciation of the diversity of community. Also the work ethic. People work hard. They're not afraid to work hard, they don't apologize for working hard, they don't expect that they will do anything other than work hard. A few people can get a lot of things done. And if they pull together they will do so in a very strong way."

Maybe the "I Love Regina" campaign will puff out their chests.

A city's culture is a window into its soul. Regina has had a symphony orchestra since 1908. "The music program here is just incredible," says University of Regina professor John Conway. "They have more kids in the National Youth Orchestra than any other city in Canada. The devotion of resources to children, to their education, to their cultural endowment, is just amazing for a province of this size."

In the 1960s an avant-garde group of painters, the Regina Five – Ken Lochhead, Art McKay, Ron Bloore, Ted Godwin, and Doug Morton – received international acclaim for their works and drew attention to prairie art.

"Art in Saskatchewan has changed a lot in ten to twelve years," says Mary Weimer, in her mid-twenties, director of the Assiniboia Gallery. "We've moved to acrylics and oils. People are going more colourful and bold. Subjects are representative but very impressionistic."

What about that old calendar classic, the grain elevator?

"Elevators are coming back," Weimer says, "because more people look back to the days when they were still around. In the summer we get lots of former prairie people and more Easterners. They want the quintessential town with elevators. There'll always be a place for prairie landscapes."

Vesta Pickel was two months from her ninetieth birthday when we met, and an active member of the Saskatchewan Poetry Society for sixty-seven of those years. A lady in every sense of the word, Ms. Pickel wore a pink flowered frock, pink flowered light summer jacket and white button earrings and small white necklace for our interview. She poured mid-morning tea, and served shortbread and jam tarts, assuring me they were not too sweet.

She worked forty-eight years as a secretary for one company, but poetry poured from her pen in every free moment. In 1993 she published a collection, *Under the Prairie Sky* (see epigraph, Chapter II). In 1999 she was an honoured guest at the opening of the provincial legislature, where excerpts of two poems were read as part of the Speech from the Throne.

As a child she lived in many prairie towns, where her father was a school principal. She liked their friendliness, a quality that drew her to Regina. "I used to go downtown every day on the bus and meet friends in Eaton's for coffee or tea. I got to know a lot of people even though I didn't know their names."

Regina is still welcoming, and has another gift to set a poet dreaming.

"The space," Ms. Pickel says. "The distance. Go up to the McCallum-Hill Centre, top floor. The whole wall is glass. You can see forever."

A Mini-Calgary Without Lineups

"I was born and raised in the teeming slums of east Regina," says the *Leader-Post*'s Will Chabun, knowing it'll get a laugh. "My Ukrainian grandparents were those men and women in sheepskin coats that Clifford Sifton wanted."

Somewhat to his surprise, he has been with the newspaper a quarter-century. He studied journalism in Ottawa. A scholarship took him to Syracuse University in New York for a master's in journalism and business, although "it's the most useless goddam degree ever created, because trying to administer journalists is like herding cats."

He had taken a semi-paid leave of absence from the *Leader*, so felt obligated to return. "I got married, my wife was working here; my parents, her parents were here. Next thing I know I've got two small children, a minivan, a house in the suburbs, and twenty years have passed."

Chabun senses that Regina's glory days were during the tenure of Premier Tommy Douglas. The Saskatchewan Arts Board, created under Douglas, became a model for the Canada Council. Douglas famously brought in medicare.

"That sense of innovation seems to have disappeared," says Chabun, although he was too young to have experienced it. "There was a charged sense of energy. Good-intentioned people, idealists, often highly educated, poured into Saskatchewan in the latter forties and early fifties. Regina, only sixty thousand or so people, had all these intellectuals coming to town. It must have been a very exciting place."

Then, he says, it wound down to a form of day-to-day survival. "Instead of being something wild and eccentric and distinctive, we've become much more ordinary, much less distinctive. There are times when Regina is just a mini version of Calgary, without the lineups."

Still, it's home. "If I move I don't think I would leave the prairies. At the risk of sounding corny, it's nice to be in touch with your roots. Some people see monotony here. To me it seems very lively and evocative."

EDMONTON

"I can't believe this place," an actor from Montreal recently told a friend. "Edmonton is the best-kept secret in the country.

We love everything about it, the culture, the quality of life."

Conversely, a visiting British journalist, snotty as only Fleet Street types can be, dubbed the place "Deadmonton." Fact is, Edmonton doesn't want to be a tawdry Las Vegas, a troubled New York, or – especially – a twitchy Calgary. The decades-old Calgary-Edmonton rivalry endures.

"Calgary is more hyper than Edmonton," says economist Mark Anielski. "I sense that we are more in touch with what makes life worthwhile, less frenetic than Calgary."

"Edmonton is an understated place," agrees local banker Earl Andrusiak. "People here are not showy with material trappings, and they're much more community-minded." The sixty employees in his office contributed more than thirty thousand dollars from their own pockets for a recent United Way campaign. Calgary, he says, doesn't raise half that much in dollars per capita.

"The number-one thing here is the sense of community," playwright Conni Massing confirms. "The Fringe Festival is run with about thirteen hundred volunteers. Lots of people take their holidays so they can work at the Fringe."

The Fringe is the largest of its kind in North America. Edmonton also has more than seventy art galleries, a nineteen-hundred-seat concert hall, and a multi-million-dollar pipe organ, newest and grandest in Canada. Its restaurants vie with anything in the East (how about the Hardware Grill, where the menu offers "Soya Lacquered Duck Breast, an Interesting Potato Waffle, Grilled Endive, Butternut-Pear Hash, Pine Nuts, Molasses-Whiskey Glaze"?).

Once, long ago, I scribbled in my Great Canadian Novel notebook, "All the men in Edmonton look like Nikita Khrushchev [leader of the Soviet Union in the 1960s]." It was, of course, a wild exaggeration, a fanciful view of certain stocky citizens with fur hats hugging their Slavic features. I carried the analogy further: on savage winter days, with pillars of steam and smoke spiralling high in the frigid sky, Edmonton reminded me of Siberian cityscapes in old copies of *Life* magazine. But that was fifty years ago.

The city is admittedly more blue-collar than Calgary. The latter has oil-company headquarters; Edmonton has drilling contractors, pipeliners, construction companies. "Calgary does the designing and finding money," says Andrusiak. "The people who make it happen come from here."

"It's gritty," sums up author and former Edmontonian Katherine Govier. "People don't have airs."

Especially not in the Mall.

Mall Heaven

An Albertan holidaying in Florida once mentioned her province by name to some of the sun-fried locals. Puzzled stares.

She tried again: "Edmonton?"

Their faces cleared. "The Mall!" they cried.

Americans worship malls and all that is huge. The West Edmonton Mall fuses their heart's desires in one gargantuan sprawl of 5.3 million square feet. The *Guinness Book of Records* calls it the world's biggest mall, with all the wonders and horrors that entails.

It is open every day of the year. You could live here for months – an unnerving thought – sampling every kind of junk food known to child or obese adult in more than one hundred eateries, and sleeping in one of the outlandish theme rooms in the Fantasyland Hotel. How about bedding down on a dogsled in an igloo? In a bunk on a pretend train? Aboard a pretend catamaran under sail, or in an actual half-ton truck? Tourists' favourites, say Fantasyland custodians, are the Polynesian (catamaran) and Roman (round king-size bed, marble fittings, and nude marble maiden overlooking the Jacuzzi).

It is teen heaven. "I know of people who sold their house

because their teenaged children had too easy access to the Mall," says Edmontonian Cora Taylor.

You can shop your brains out in more than eight hundred stores; attend two movie houses, play blackjack or the slots, lose yourself in the bedlam of a fun fair with twenty-five rides. (For three terrifying minutes I *was* lost there until an exit sign beckoned, a straw for a drowning man.) You can watch the dolphins (Howard and Mavis by name, when I was there) perform for fish snacks. They seemed to be having more fun than the people, but some Edmontonians have waged a Free the Edmonton Mall Dolphins campaign, so what do I know?

You can ice-skate, glide underwater in a mini-submarine, swim in a man-made lake under glass, or laze on a pseudo-beach where the temperature is held forever at thirty Celsius. There is a Rock 'n' Ride Dance Party every month, surely an exquisite form of hell. Visitors with faint hearts or fallen arches can rent electric carts to traverse this indoor acreage, unencumbered by kiddies or pets (there is children's and doggy daycare).

About twenty million people visit the place in a year, pouring $1.2 billion into this already wealthy province. Edmontonians have mixed feelings. "We don't go there unless we have to, which often is to take out-of-town friends," says one. "We're not exactly proud of it."

The Mall, incidentally, was the brainchild of the entrepreneurial Ghermezian family, who also had a hand in building a monster mall in Bloomington, Minnesota. That one, at last count, covers only 4.2 million square feet with a piffling 520 retail stores. If size really matters, ours is bigger than theirs.

Unsinkable Ted

Edmonton's Ted Byfield – writer, editor, entrepreneur, gadfly, the provocative voice and sometime conscience of Western

Canada – has been called many things, but no one has ever called him lazy. If Edmonton is gritty, Byfield fits right in.

The seventy-five-year-old Byfield writes a weekly column for the Calgary and Edmonton *Sun* newspapers and until recently monthly essays for his own *Citizens Centre Report*, a national newsmagazine. Each piece of writing is a model of wit, clarity, and incendiary opinion. In 1998, the best of his essays were marketed in hardcover as *The Book of Ted: Epistles from an Unrepentant Redneck*, selling more than five thousand copies.

Between times, to fill those idle hours, Byfield – tall, greying, raspy voice, mischievous eyes – delivers speeches and publishes books. Western United Communications (Ted Byfield, chairman) sold twenty-four thousand copies of an Alberta atlas and is completing an acclaimed twelve-volume journalistic history, *Alberta in the Twentieth Century*. Byfield conceived the series, edited several volumes, and wrote many chapters. The first volume sold forty-seven thousand copies, a best-seller many times over. In total the series has sold a hundred thousand copies – marketed primarily through the magazine. Currently Byfield and a fleet of writers are deep into a fifteen-volume history of Christianity.

Since his working regimen requires the constitution of an ox, one would assume that Byfield keeps fit. One would be right, more or less: he runs a bit, and most weeks takes a seventeen-mile walk through Edmonton's river valleys. Five hours later he ends up at his favourite tavern, the Beverly Crest Hotel, where he celebrates with a few light beers, shots of rye whisky, and spirited conversation with whoever happens by. His wife of fifty-four years, Virginia "Ginger" Byfield, also a journalist, drives him home.

The story of his magazine read like *The Perils of Pauline*, but the unsinkable Byfield always soldiered on. Friend Ralph Hedlin credits it to his "spirit of sheer cussedness." Once, during a postal strike, Ted and his merry band set up their own delivery service in defiance of Canada Post and devised a stamp which – if hugely enlarged – showed a clenched fist displaying the one-finger salute. More than once, Ted and family and friends pulled the magazine from the brink of financial oblivion. One of his angels was brother John, a California physician.

"You want to buy a magazine?" Ted asked in one of his hours of need.

"How much?" said brother John.

"About $100,000 to $250,000, American."

"Why not?" said brother John, a true Byfield. He put up $125,000, Canadian, and Ted retained a controlling interest. That is what brothers are for.

The thirty-year-old magazine, once the centrepiece of Byfield's journalistic stable, had 40,000 subscribers, and a readership of about 320,000 in the Western provinces and beyond. *Report* was not to everyone's taste. To many in the East, it was a dirty word.

On the one hand, it had some of the brightest writing and most incisive reporting in the land. (The nineteen-person editorial staff was a bit of a family compact. Son Link was publisher; son Mike was editor; wife Virginia, daughter-in-law Joanne, and grandson Eli were reporter-contributors; daughter Philippa Dean had worked on staff. During the magazine's formative years, Ted's father, Vince, a veteran Eastern newspaperman, came out to help.) Their take on national politics and local issues was refreshing and sometimes unmatched. Byfield had enormous sport with Canada's sacred cows. He said of the CBC, "the people's network became more arrogantly independent of the people than any private corporation could ever become." He called the *Globe and Mail* a "cornucopia of asininity." Last autumn he suggested in print that Jean Chrétien was suffering a mental breakdown.

On the other hand *Report* was unabashedly right-wing – Ted was a moving spirit behind the creation of the Reform Party, although his magazine never hesitated to give Reform or its offspring, the Canadian Alliance, an editorial tongue-lashing – mixed with a back-to-the-Bible brand of Christianity. Byfield believes in God and a life hereafter and is one of the few persons I know who is not self-conscious about saying grace before a restaurant meal. In the mid-1990s Ted and Virginia, former Anglicans, joined St. Herman's Orthodox Church. At the time he described it as "seemingly more Catholic than the Catholics and more evangelical than the evangelicals." Parishioners greet one another with "Glory be to Jesus Christ."

Report stood four-square against abortion (an abortion doctor's premises might be called an "abortuary") and was militantly homophobic (homosexuals have been labelled "sodomists"). It looked askance at environmentalism or animal rights when either seemed to impinge upon ranching, farming, or Alberta industries. It called aboriginals "Indians" rather than the politically correct "First Nations people." One of its columnists devoted a whole page to the evils of masturbation – "Most of us still think it's distasteful and shameful" – although she did not claim that it would make you go blind.

The Byfields' view of today's society might be summarized in this passage from a publisher's letter by son Link: "Most people in my grandfather's day would have considered the morally bizarre world we now inhabit to be impossible . . . homosexuality protected and advocated, human reproduction deplored, animals given rights denied to humans, religion despised, selfishness codified and even deified. . . ."

Kenneth Whyte, former editor of the *National Post*, once worked for Byfield, as have many other top Canadian journalists. "I can't begin to explain, let alone justify, Byfield's excesses, tantrums, tyrannies," he once wrote in *Saturday Night* magazine. "I just know he's very complicated, and that you have to look at him whole: good Ted as well as bad Ted."

Did *Report* reflect Albertans' thinking?

"In some ways, yes, but not in all ways," says Calgary political-science professor Tom Flanagan. In its advocacy of smaller government, lower taxes, and direct democracy, its suspicion of control by Ottawa and hostility to special privileges for Quebec, the magazine was, he thinks, in tune with most Albertans.

"Its positions on several other issues you couldn't take as typical of Albertans in general. In polling on issues like abortion or gay rights, opinions of Albertans, on average, are not that much different from opinions anywhere else. I think a lot of readers of *Report* just accepted some of those positions as part of the package. They regarded Ted as having earned the right to have his own views."

"I don't agree with Ted's anti-gay and anti-abortion stance – but so what?" adds influential Albertan Jim Gray, a force in the energy business. "Out here we honour people for their honesty, integrity, and energy. We don't have to agree with every element of their opinion."

Byfield's views on too much central government, on the dangers of an electoral system that forever weighs against the regions, and "his strong voice for the energy, spirit, and vision of Westerners does epitomize the West, particularly the prairies," Gray says. "I'd argue that it is the tolerance for a spectrum of opinions that describes the West. People out here, Ted Byfield–type people, are not mushy middle ground. They take strong positions that stimulate debate and discussion, and we honour them for it."

Byfield was born in Toronto (nobody is perfect) and his first reporting job was on the now-defunct *Ottawa Journal*. He and new bride Virginia moved through newspaper jobs in Timmins and Sudbury, started a weekly newspaper and "went awfully broke." Ted found his way to the *Winnipeg Free Press*, where his energy and ingenuity made him a star. In one memorable stunt, he climbed into a ventilation duct above a men's washroom, crawled to an air vent next to a meeting room, and reported a secret debate on a city scandal.

In 1957, distressed by permissiveness and the lack of direction in society, he and a friend founded Saint John's, an Edmonton area boys' school run by a partnership of teachers who worked for a dollar a day plus basic expenses. They stressed scholastics, chores, rigorous sports, and strong Christian content. From this sprang *Saint John's Edmonton Report* which begat *Alberta Report* which begat *Western Report* which in 1999 begat *Report*, a national edition.

Ted became something of a Western legend. The Western Magazine Awards recognized this, honouring him with a Lifetime Achievement Award marking fifty years in journalism. The National Citizens' Coalition named him recipient of the Colin M. Brown Freedom Medal.

On a September night in 2002, 150 friends of the Byfields and their magazine met in Edmonton for a $150-a-plate fundraiser and silent auction. Pauline was in Peril once more: she was tied to the tracks and the express train was coming; the evil landlord was about to evict her; the lascivious squire was having his way with her pearly white body. In short: *Report* was strapped for dollars yet again.

Ted Byfield, with his customary wry humour and elo-quence, explained why: in twenty-nine years, his magazine had stuck to its original principles, but society had changed. National advertisers had fallen away as *Report*'s stances annoyed and angered certain groups. Then Link Byfield explained their plan: turn the magazine into a non-profit organization, renew its mission, stay alive. (It would be operated by the Citizens Centre for Freedom and Democracy.)

It was a good try. In June 2003, Link announced that *Report* would close (barring another Byfield miracle). But that September night all the people who believed in what Ted does, who especially believed that Ottawa should keep its grubby paws off Alberta, and who admired this gritty guy who stuck to his principles and could grin even on the verge of financial disaster, all those people rose and gave him a standing ovation.

CALGARY

A City of Immigrants

"In 1947 or '48 there were maybe ninety thousand people in Calgary," Jim Gray is saying. "Now there's more than nine hundred thousand. So we're a city of immigrants. We're all new out here. The West is built on risk and is built around great distances and around very strong traditional values. We have different outlooks. In Calgary there is no establishment. Who's the establishment in Calgary?"

People like you, Mr. Gray – veteran of the energy business, holder of multiple directorships, very big man around town?

But Gray, perhaps anticipating that, adds, "There's not an *ingrained* establishment that goes back generations and generations. I just love it here. I've had so many experiences of being able to *do* something here, whether it's successfully raising a family or building a company. It's a great size of community, big enough yet small enough. Big enough to be an international player, yet a relatively small community. I see that situation deteriorating a little bit because we're growing way too fast but still . . ."

We are dining in the Owl's Nest restaurant in the Westin Hotel. Two waiters arrive with the entrees in tureens, remove the lids in one sweeping coordinated motion like a U.S. Marines drill team, and cry in unison "Voila!" Definitely not the raw-boned Calgary I knew in the early 1950s, when it was prudent to dine at home.

"Calgary is becoming a very international city," Gray says. "The airport here is the third-busiest in Canada. An all-time-record number of countries came to the World Petroleum Conference in 2000, partly because it's Calgary. We had a thousand volunteers. We had vice-presidents dressed up in cowboy outfits taking tickets at the door. And in typical Calgary fashion, we ended up with a five-million-dollar surplus, so we're starting a big scholarship program."

Cowtown is really Oiltown. Energy's contribution to Alberta's gross domestic product is markedly less proportionally than, say, fifteen years ago, but is still the biggest factor in the province's and Calgary's prosperity. Yet there is more.

Almost Like Toronto?

"Images of the West tend to be very stereotypical," says Dr. Roger Gibbins, president and CEO of the Canada West Foundation. "Calgary has an image of being a white-bread kind of city and there's a lot of negative commentary on the lack of diversity. In fact, as a cultural environment Calgary is more diverse than Ottawa or Montreal."

Calgary has opera, ballet, symphony, galleries. Traffic is relatively sane, property taxes are low, there is no sales tax, and homeowners get subsidies for natural-gas home heating. Still – perhaps because it *is* Calgary, forever doomed to its stereotype – some visitors cannot be pleased. William Thorsell, once editor of the *Edmonton Journal*, then of the *Globe and Mail*, now president and CEO of the Royal Ontario Museum, found Calgary lacking in "urbanity."

"Downtown Calgary is characterized by a seamless conformity of buildings and spaces," he wrote in a 2002 *Globe* column.

"The featureless structures and 'Plus 15' pedestrian bridges that link them create a unified organism – an undifferentiated singularity that wipes away the distinctions that make for anything memorable in a city. There is nothing but the whole to grasp in downtown Calgary – a kind of fascist unity (like downtown Edmonton) that repels lovers of cities, and leaves the rest of the population blithely indifferent."

Having laid waste to both cities, he praised with faint damns: "The absence of urbanity in places such as Calgary is a big part of what makes them such good places to live for so many."

Calgary and Toronto are in some ways alike (a comparison both would find appalling). Both teem with glass and steel towers, luxury cars, lumbering SUVs and poseurs pacing the sidewalks with cellphones clamped to their ears. Each city has a tall pointy thing: Toronto's CN Tower is higher, but the Calgary Tower has the finer view (overlooking the Rockies).

There the likeness ends. Toronto traffic rages deep into a weekday evening. In Calgary the downtown road warriors have mostly vanished by seven, early to bed, the better to rise healthy, wealthy, and ready to get wealthier.

"I'm the patron for a number of dinners," says Jim Gray. "If a business dinner is over at nine-thirty p.m. you're 50 per cent of the way to success. Doesn't matter what the dinner's about or what the food is like. If you can get people out by nine-thirty, they're forever grateful."

Most Calgary businessmen are in the office by eight, partly because that's when eastern stock markets, two hours ahead, open for trading.

"Partly it's the oil business: there's a tradition that at eight in the morning everybody phones in from the rigs," adds Gray, of the early-rising habit. "And partly it's our agricultural roots."

Yahoo!

Those roots – "Yahoo" to you, stranger – are mainly ranching. Calgary clings to its Cowtown legend. It presses white cowboy hats on astonished visitors such as Luciano Pavarotti. A sign on the wall in Buzzards restaurant advises: COWBOY PARKING ONLY. VIO-LATORS WILL BE CASTRATED. An establishment called Cowboys has line dancing and serving girls with cowboy hats and cowboy belts. Other cities have freeways, Calgary has trails: Macleod, Deerfoot, Bow Valley, Sarcee, Glenmore, Crowchild, Blackfoot. *If yer drivin' into Cowtown, Pilgrim, yuh better know yer trails.*

The ultimate expression of pseudo-cowpoke mentality is the ten-day Calgary Exhibition and Stampede in July, attended by 1.2 million people. Riley & McCormick, outfitters of western clothing and accessories since 1901, does a land-office business in cowboy boots and hats.

"Just a chance for the locals to get falling-down drunk," a non-believer told me sourly of the festivities, but added hastily, "Don't quote me!" He feared, perhaps, that a white-hatted rider on a black horse would rope, throw, and tie him and snip off his testicles for a prairie-oysters brunch on Eighth Avenue.

For all of its estimated $136 million economic benefit to the city, and its avowed purpose of preserving and enhancing Alberta's agricultural and historical legacy, the Stampede is a cosmetic implant. Indeed, says Roger Gibbins, there's talk of doing away with the Stampede: "The fear is that it reinforces redneck perceptions of the region."

Maybe so, but it won't go away in his lifetime or mine.

IX

FOOD FOR BODY AND SOUL

The everyday experience of a person's life,
that's what cowboy poetry is all about.

DALE "DOC" HAYES, PH.D.
Brandon University professor and cowboy poet

Pass the Teriyaki Jerky

In certain Toronto sidewalk cafés, where trendy black-clad persons huddle at curbside to inhale coffee and noxious fumes, a psalm of jubilation soars above the rumble of SUVs: "How fortunate are we to be here at the Centre of the Universe, sipping lattes in traffic instead of eating hot beef-and-gravy sandwiches in some flyspecked Western shanty!"

Well, that is *so* fifties. Shanties? There are prairie homes so elegant, so spacious, so impeccably furnished that Lord Black of Crossharbour would happily rent them as summer cottages. Flyspecks? The fly problem is abating, thanks to fleets of diligent Eastern summer students equipped with swatters and Canada Council grants.

As for sandwiches, certainly you will find, in less upscale rural joints, the toasted western (scrambled eggs, minced ham, pepper, and onion) between the kind of white bread that, untoasted, will bounce back to your hand if dropped. But the hot beef sandwich bathed in glutinous gravy is as rare in the West as a Liberal cabinet minister.

Face it, Rest of Canada, this is no longer total heartburn country (except when diners get their bill, which can rival anything in Montreal). Every conceivable ethnic food may be had, from Middle Eastern and Cajun to Thai and Vietnamese. But reaching culinary nirvana has been a tortuous path paved with cholesterol and acid indigestion.

In the beginning, prairie residents ate buffalo, prairie chicken, bannock, beaver, and pemmican (meat mixed with fat). Sometimes they chewed rosehips, not for their vitamin C – which nobody knew about – but because the guys liked to spit the pits. It was a male statement, a tradition that endures with sunflower seeds, an important Manitoba crop. For prairie loogans in turned-back baseball caps, the appeal is less in seed-eating than in husk-spitting, a form of basic training for professional sports.

Early explorers ate anything as long as it was meat. In crises they resorted to strips of dried jerky, as tasteless as their boots but nevertheless meat. Pioneer settlers ate whatever ran by. Ukrainian Maria Adamowska, who arrived in the West in 1899 when she was nine, was herding a cow near Yorkton when she came upon an aboriginal family roasting an animal. They offered her a piece.

"How I enjoyed that meat – as though it were some rare delicacy!" Adamowska wrote later. "I discovered afterwards that it was gopher."

Fair enough. Gopher was meat. A history of Sundre, Alberta, tells of an early resident who had two prairie chickens and too many dinner guests. He shot six gophers, skinned the legs and tossed them in the stew. His guests loved it, never pausing to wonder how two prairie chickens could have twenty-eight legs.

In the desperate 1930s, circumstances forced us to eat more sensibly. We children were dispatched to the ditches to pull pigweed (also known as lamb's quarters), which tasted like spinach when cooked. The homely cabbage grew when other plants withered, and, says Calgary home economist Beulah "Bunny" Barss, saved lives. "Sauerkraut in winter helped prevent scurvy. Cabbage rolls, coleslaw, sauerkraut . . . what a food! Cabbage should get a Governor General's Award for the good it has done."

Ingenious prairie women made nutritious sandwiches of radish and vegetable marrow layered in hearty homemade bread. My mother concocted a refreshing summer drink from vinegar, water, and sugar. Jaded Torontonians would pay fifteen dollars a glass for that drink today and christen it Sweet and Sour Summer Cooler. We called it Vinegar.

And now? Prairie people still eat meat, berries, and jerky, but it's called gracious living. Barbecue is no longer the only option. Valbella Meats in Canmore sells air-dried buffalo prosciutto, smoked pepper duck, venison paté, and Moroccan lamb sausage. (You need not be dressed in black to order it.) Jerky is twenty-first-century chic, available at corner stores in flavours from cracked pepper to barbecue to teriyaki.

The berries of choice are saskatoons, like blueberries only better. Sometimes it is left to a newcomer like Bep Hamer to take a saskatoon berry and run with it. Bep, a chubby, cheery soul in her sixties, emigrated from Holland in 1952 with her parents and four siblings. Her father lost the job awaiting him at an Alberta poultry farm because their ship was late. After seven days in Winnipeg's immigration hall, a "very courageous man," Jack Hamer, rescued and employed them. He trucked them over a snowploughed trail to his farm at Central Butte, Saskatchewan.

"It was colder than a witch's kiss and we had never seen so much snow in our entire lives," Bep remembers. "We didn't speak any English. When we met Jack's mother and brother, they said 'Hello' and we all politely said 'Goodbye'!"

Bep eventually went into business with Hamer and married him. They created a mini-empire in Swift Current: two flower shops, a bakery, a bridal boutique, a food-processing operation, and a restaurant. They specialize in saskatoons, once abundant in the wild, now grown commercially.

She claims her saskatoon pie is the best in the West (hundreds of prairie cooks with flushed faces and hot ovens might challenge her on that). She and Jack also market prairie specialty baskets under the Gramma Bep brand name (she is a bona fide grandmother): chokecherry syrup and jelly and saskatoon-berry pancake syrup, dessert sauce, jam, and vinegar. The saskatoon-berry vinegar is for fries, salads, sauces, and dressings. There is wild-cranberry salad dressing called Cranberry Zinger, a saskatoon chutney, a rhubarb chutney, and pickled garlic.

For a touch of Old World gentility, pause for afternoon tea at From the Prairie, a Brooks, Alberta, teahouse; or That's Crafty, near Rosebud, specializing in tea and local crafts; or Pinky's, near Grande Prairie, where you can order scones and clotted cream in an old house painted vibrant pink. (As a fringe benefit, you won't find any loogans or rednecks eating scones in a pink house.)

For other gastronomical exotica, take knife and fork to Gimli, the Icelandic community on Lake Winnipeg, for vinarterta, a seven-layer cake, each layer separated by a sweetened prune filling. Sumptuous enough, surely? No. People of comfortable girth insist it should be eaten with butter icing.

Vinarterta is but the tip of the Icelandic-berg. My Gimli agent, Helen Kristjanson, speaks highly of pönnukökur, a whole wheat crêpe. "Mix the batter, make sure it's thin, pour it in a pan, and don't answer the phone," she advises (the crêpe could burn while someone is selling you aluminum siding). "Add brown sugar and roll."

There's skyr, a kind of yogurt made when buttermilk at room temperature is left to drip through a cheesecloth filter. The whey oozes out, leaving skyr, a low-fat replacement for sour cream. "Great with strawberries," says Linda Goodman, editor of *Gimli Today.*

Kleinur are inside-out doughnuts, cut and twisted to take on a diamond shape. "*Not* low-fat," Ms. Goodman warns. Neither is rúlapylsa, a luncheon meat made from mutton, sprinkled with saltpetre, and flattened into an oval log. "After it cures, it's ready to eat, if you don't mind a lot of visible fat with your mutton," Goodman says. "Not my personal favourite, but extremely popular around here."

Gimli gourmets who own hammers are also fond of hard fish – pickerel fillets hung in the sun until well dried. Then, says Helen Kristjanson, break off the pieces with the hammer, dip in butter, and enjoy.

Man cannot live by rúlapylsa alone. Take it from Ed McNally, the man who built a better beer. From his southern Alberta home, with sweeping views of the outdoors he loves,

McNally – a big, greying man with an unwavering dark gaze – tells how it happened.

He grew up in Lethbridge, studied law, got acquainted with barley growers during a court case, and discovered that Alberta raises some of the best malting barley in the world. He began growing it. Ed liked beer but found the local products bland and overly carbonated. Alberta had great barley and excellent hard water; why was his barley being sold for cattle feed?

Through a sometimes harrowing and occasionally hilarious process McNally studied the market, found backers, located a brewer in Zurich, built a brewery, and named it Big Rock, after a locally famous eighteen-thousand-ton glacial erratic of that name sitting in a farmer's field west of Okotoks.

He now has a line of flavourful unpasteurized beers with such showstopping names as Grasshöpper, Warthog, and Big Rock Springbok. Other breweries rise and fall, but Big Rock rolls on. If you order Grasshöpper in a Calgary restaurant they may serve it with a slice of lime. Local galoots recoil in horror – how unmanly can you get? – but lime goes good with Grasshöpper.

The ginger beef at the Peking House in northwest Calgary sneaks up on you like a gentle lover. Next thing you know, the flavour blossoms into a slow burn at the bottom of your throat – delicious, with three sips of water for a chaser. Better yet, it was invented in Calgary, says my companion, the gracious and animated Dr. Josephine Smart, University of Calgary anthropologist.

Smart, née Yau, came here from Hong Kong in 1974, married a fellow student, and is completing a three-year research project into Chinese immigrant cuisine and identity politics. The idea came when she discovered that Chinese restaurants abroad all have local variations on Chinese food: "Local colours, as I call it."

Pork is a staple of Chinese food in China and North America, but some countries eschew it for religious reasons. Others replace traditional ingredients with whatever is at hand. Once, in Spain, Smart asked for chow mein and was served spaghetti. Where were the thin yellow egg noodles she expected? Not available, the proprietor said. Yet all such local variations are called Chinese food.

"What could this tell me about the integration of Chinese in local societies?" Smart wondered. "About local consumer demands, about differences around the world, articulated through the Chinese restaurant as a physical place where all these stories could be told?" It took a long time to propose the project because it sounded like too much fun. "Every time I mentioned it, my colleagues laughed, 'You just want someone to give you money to eat your way around the world.'"

Chinese food as we know it is westernized because its cooks have "a pervasive notion that non-Chinese customers like food in a certain way." And that, Smart says, is how ginger beef emerged in Calgary. "Canada was dominated for a long time by southern [Chinese] cuisine because the immigrants who came here were primarily from southern China. When the first northern Chinese restaurant was started in Calgary in the early eighties, one of the dishes offered was beef cut into very thin strips. It was lightly coated and deep fried until crunchy. Almost like beef jerky. Over the years cooks began modifying it to appeal to the mass market."

Calgary's ginger beef was possibly one chef's way of counteracting Alberta's winter climate, says Dr. Smart. And what does she eat? Many Chinese dishes, especially won ton noodles. "I tend to avoid thickly battered and deep-fried food, except fish and chips. I *do* love fish and chips."

The Prairie as Palette

Artist Darlene Hay, tall, fair-haired, and sunny of disposition, was born in Gravelbourg, Saskatchewan, on one of those rare, blessed January days when a balmy chinook wind creeps in from Alberta and kisses the snowdrifts. It was a fitting entry into the world of one who grew passionate about every detail of her environment.

She has a mission: to show in her art the diversity in Saskatchewan's landscape and to fill a universal need. "I think there is an urge in everyone to renew their spirit and bring peace into their lives by feeling close to nature, whether through being out in nature or seeing it in a painting."

From her Saskatoon home, she specializes in Saskatchewan landscapes: rich vivid oils on subjects ranging from marshes, fields, and cliffs, to sand dunes, sloughs, and river rapids, all dispelling the cliché concept of prairie.

"They help me feel closer to the farming community and closer to my dad. One of the happiest times in my growing-up years was living on a farm for a year and a half. My dad took pride in his good crops and the land he owned."

Much has been said of the prairie's clear light. Hay sees *many* shades of light that would escape a less discerning eye. "Prairie light makes the images have strong, clear, sharp colours because of the low humidity and absence of industrial pollutants in the air," she explains. "There seems to be a yellowish golden glow with deep greens and rusty reds.

"It takes a long time for the sun to set in the summer, which makes the warm colours in late afternoon last for a good while. The long shadows contrast with the brightly lit areas, which causes a luminous glow. The colours change dramatically across the sky from the west to east and are different each day. The light in winter is still warm, affecting the colours of the snow over the different landscapes."

Her work, which one curator says "combines elements of both abstraction and realism," has been shown throughout the West and in Ottawa and Montreal. But Hay is happy to stay in Saskatoon, free from the pressures of the art world's main centres.

How can she find inspiration in Saskatchewan's reputed monochrome? That's a myth, she says. "We have vast fields of rusty-red ripe wheat, intense yellow canola, blue flax fields that look like large lakes, rich-coloured hayfields, ditches, and sloughs with multicoloured wildflowers." Her prairie is a kaleidoscope.

CHARLIE LOVED KRISTÍN

Every Icelandic delicacy can be found at Gimli's Wevel Café, plus smoked goldeye, pickled herring, and the touching story of Cartoon Charlie. Originally, the Wevel Café was in Winnipeg, and in the 1930s a favourite haunt of Charlie Thorson. Charlie, cartoonist for Icelandic publications, fell in love with Kristín Sölvadóttir, beautiful dark-haired waitress at the Wevel.

In 1935 Thorson went to Hollywood, worked briefly for Walt Disney, and contributed to the creation of Snow White, basing his drawings on his Kristín. (Although the finished Snow White resembled Kristín, the character was the product of many other designs.)

Thorson had a falling-out with Disney, moved to Warner Brothers, and was invited to design a rabbit for a new cartoon. Thorson's rabbit was deemed too cute but the name he gave it stuck: Bugs Bunny. (Bugs Bunny did not work at the Wevel Café.)

There was no Disney-style romantic ending for Charlie Thorson. After he left Winnipeg he never saw Kristín again.

All the West's a Stage

Mothers, don't let your daughters grow up to be actors, if they can't dodge an insult or a flying object. The worst moments in acting, says Winnipeg performer Sarah Constible, twenty-seven, are "when the audience turns on you. It happened when I did a children's theatre tour. At a couple of schools, especially in the richer areas, the kids were demons. They would throw pointed objects at you. It was an interactive show where you had to ask what should we do in such-and-such a situation. They would answer 'commit suicide.'"

Apart from guided missiles, life is fulfilling for a prairie actor who is willing to hustle. Constible is busy with local stage plays, films, improv, and the occasional made-for-TV movie.

Constible and her partner, Rob McLaughlin, thirty-eight, have both worked Fringe Festivals. Rob – well, let's come clean, he is another of my shirt-tail cousins – is tall, with a deadpan gaze that hides a thousand characters. That, and impeccable timing, make him a natural for improvisation. One of his finest hours was when he and his mother, Pat, went to claim a mint-condition 1942 Oldsmobile that had belonged to his grandfather. Rob got behind the wheel, turned, said, "Where to, Miss Daisy?"

He has done improv since high school, has played the lead in a detective movie and, to help pay the rent, has a regular gig as one of several voices of Monty, meeter and greeter at a Winnipeg casino. (Monty, an animated dummy, looks and sounds so real that some patrons pour their inmost secrets into his plastic ear.)

"The cost of living is still low enough here that artists can work at their profession and somehow patch together a living and do things other people do, like buy houses and have children," says Conni Massing, forty-three, an Edmonton playwright with a long list of credits. "It's difficult to make a living just from theatre, but actors supplement their theatre wages through TV and film work. You can be happy here."

So, all over the prairie, theatre thrives in communities large and small. Edmonton's Fringe Festival (recently with more than 140 theatre companies from around the world in more than eight hundred performances over ten days) is second-biggest in the world, after Edinburgh. It is perhaps a measure of prairie theatre's vitality that neither Massing, Constible, nor McLaughlin pine for

Toronto, New York, or even Hollywood. If a slick-talking producer in funereal black, wearing two-day stubble and opaque
shades, sidled up to them in a bar and murmured, "We're
shooting in Tuscany next week, I got a part for you, babe," they
would thank him and catch a cab home.

"If Winnipeggers stay here and make their own projects,
they don't have to move to Toronto," Sarah Constible concludes.
"We don't have to export our culture."

Egypt in Edgerton

Is it the solitude? The space? The long, boring winters? Why
have the prairies produced such a disproportionate volume of
fine writing? Their outpouring reaches back through Ralph
Connor, F.P. Grove, Sinclair Ross, W.O. Mitchell, and Margaret
Laurence, and latterly includes Guy Vanderhaeghe, Carol
Shields, and Sandra Birdsell. Two thousand other writers or
wannabes belong to the three prairie writers' guilds.

"I think it has something to do with what they write about,"
says Regina's Ken Mitchell, English professor, veteran author
and playwright. "Prairie writing tends to deal with more universal and enduring themes, in particular the relationship with
the land and the landscape – the essence of Canadian literature.
The ideas and the works are often more simple and directly
expressed [than those of the Eastern CanLit establishment],
without literary 'refinement.' In other words, they are closer to
the people and the land."

There is another, rare specimen of the genus *literati*: the
near-reclusive writer who steadily produces best-sellers, gets
respectable-or-better reviews, shuns groups where writers read
aloud to other writers, does not idealize the prairie, has never
been lionized by CanLit – and makes pots of money. English-
born Pauline Gedge of Edgerton, Alberta, population about
three hundred, is queen of the category.

Gedge, fifty-eight, fair-haired, soft-spoken but tough-minded, has eleven published novels, eight of them in her favourite historical period, ancient Egypt. They've sold more than seven million copies and have been translated into seventeen languages. Her trilogy *Lords of the Two Lands* earned her more than a million dollars in royalty advances from Canada, the United States, France, Germany, and Spain.

Gedge's own story is the stuff of fiction. In the early 1970s she was a single welfare mother trying to raise two sons by teaching piano and voice. Alberta launched a search-for-new-novelists competition. Gedge, who'd written nothing but unpublished poems, came fourth on her first try. The third time around she won first prize and a fifteen-thousand-dollar advance from Macmillan for her first published book, *Child of the Morning*. Her second novel, *The Eagle and the Raven*, won France's Société des Gens des Lettres award.

Edgerton people never regarded her as a freak (her father was the local minister when she moved there). She writes from September to June, five days a week, three or four pages a day, not waiting for the muse to inspire her, but always wearing makeup and several pieces of jewellery. "They bolster my self-confidence. If I feel that I look bad, then my work is going to be shoddy." She is, in fact, rather glamorous; one interviewer deemed her "voluptuous."

Her second husband, Bernard Ramanauskas, who "loves ferreting out minutiae," compiles her voluminous research from their home library and other archives. "He gives me the blueprint and I build the house."

She has "never lost the sheer wonder of being a writer," but loathes book tours. "They leave me literally shaking. . . . I resent being forced to expose myself. . . . To make matters worse it was considered very bad manners in my family to 'blow one's own trumpet.'"

A magazine article called her "Alberta's millionaire author." "Ah, money!" Gedge says. "It buys me freedom. That's what I love about it. I am comfortable but not rich." She hates to shop – she doesn't buy art, antiques, or excessive clothes – but indulges heavily in books.

Does she mind not being embraced by CanLit? "Perhaps I can diplomatically answer this way," Gedge says. "If I go into a bookstore and find that my novels have been put in the Canadiana section, I ask that they be moved."

Strings and Keys in Sundre

Alberta-born Jamie and Laurie Syer travelled, worked, and studied afar, then returned to their beloved big skies. For a while they lived in Calgary, but wanted to be "where we felt we were making a difference." As classical pianist and violinist respectively, they could have chosen almost any place in the West (where every major city has a symphony orchestra plus smaller musical ensembles). "But," says Jamie, "we were ready for another adventure."

They settled on an eighty-acre farm six miles from Sundre, population twenty-two hundred, near a crossroads called Bergen (a sign at the outskirts says "Beautiful Downtown Bergen," meaning gas station and general store). The land had been in Laurie's family for generations. They started a community-shared agriculture project that provided organic vegetables for twenty-five Calgary families every week, but expected to earn most of their living in cities. Laurie was already playing full-time with the Calgary Philharmonic.

"But we found a community much more artistically active than we expected," Jamie says. Sundre has a strong amateur theatre group and an arts centre built mainly with volunteer labour. Families were hungry for their services: Laurie has thirty violin students; Jamie's piano classes grew so large he stopped taking students in Calgary. Nine years ago they launched Strings and Keys, a summer music program for children from ages ten to fifteen. Now, with the help of a dozen additional teachers, they instruct about seventy students a year.

The Syers, in their late forties, have performed in major cities at home and abroad (every year they go to Europe) but are devoted to their receptive and open-minded home-town audiences.

"This community has helped us to develop in ways we couldn't have imagined before we arrived," Jamie concludes, "and taken us in directions quite different than if we'd stayed in the city. It's hard to imagine being anywhere else."

Laurie adds a cherished memory. For a while she raised sheep, and used to get up in the middle of the night to check the lambs.

"The stars would be brilliant, it would be biting cold, the snow crunched under my feet," she muses. "It was just magical. It was like the world is out there and nobody's seeing it."

Before we parted, they agreed to play for me. And for a while the house was alive with piano and violin in Aaron Copland's "Ukulele Serenade." Would that every interview had such a glorious finale.

Poems for the Lariati

Down by the river underneath the old railroad bridge
The Cross Bar M had disposed of an unwanted fridge
And left it there to gradually rust away.
Until one time it became part of a little boy's play. . . .

A hush hung over the Elks Hall in Maple Creek as Dale "Doc" Hayes recited his poem. It was uncommon fare for a gathering of cowboy poets, a poem about a refrigerator cast off in a river and the little boy who hid in it – and died. Then a burst of sustained applause as Hayes, a straight-backed man in black hat, shirt, and jeans, finished his poignant verse.

Most other poems that day at the Maple Creek Cowboy Poetry Gathering were about cows, bulls, bucking horses, roundups, the joys and trials of a cowhand's life. The audiences warmly received them all. Cowboy poetry is a hot ticket in the rural West. The literati spurn it because it's usually simple, usually rhymes, and habitually drops its *g*'s (*sittin'*, *ropin'*, *ridin'*). The lariati, as some jokers christen the cowboy-poet fraternity, respond, "People *pay* to hear our poetry."

At its best – Doc Hayes is a headliner because he reads well, and writes of thoughtful themes – it appeals to people who remember, or yearn for, a dwindling way of life, a simpler time when grass was taller and cities were smaller, when it was horse and rider against the elements, when a handshake was a promise.

"The everyday experience of a person's life, that's what cowboy poetry is all about," says Hayes, who grazes cattle near Nesbitt, Manitoba, and teaches language arts at Brandon University. "It's a document of an occupation," adds Glen McKenzie of Medicine Hat. McKenzie, in his early seventies, ranched thirteen thousand acres for thirty-seven years, still rides his horse, began rhyming fifteen years ago, and has self-published two books of poetry. "I've lived most of the poems I've written."

There are more than two hundred annual cowboy poetry gatherings in North America (most of them in the United States, where it has become showbiz). Gatherings like the 2002 show at Maple Creek, in southwestern Saskatchewan ranch country, are as pure as they come. Its half-dozen venues (Elks Hall, Armoury, Curling Rink, and more) drew forty prairie poets, as many more musicians, several dozen purveyors of saddles, western art, clothing, whips, and spurs, and several hundred enthusiastic spectators who paid five dollars each for the three-day event.

The crowds, in a sea of cowboy hats worn indoors and out, were mostly middle-aged or older, ambling about with coffees, soaking up nostalgia and laughs. McKenzie brought down the house with a tale of a man who shot a moose, crawled into its carcass to take shelter from a storm, woke to find he was frozen in, began reflecting on his past, remembered he had once voted Social Credit, and "felt so small I crawled right out that moose's ass."

Self-deprecating humour is a sure hit. Take Lee Bellows of Moose Jaw, livestock inspector for the provincial department of agriculture, poet, and rodeo clown. His whimsical "Masculinity" begins:

> I've thought about it a long, long time
> And y'know it's just not fair
> There's no one that is more maligned
> Than a fellow what's got no hair
> No, I'm serious. I'm tired of this abuse.
> All my friends got hair that's turnin' grey
> Mine, she's turnin' loose . . .

Bellows began rhyming to keep himself awake on long, boring highway drives, and because "most people are three or four generations removed from the farm, and I wanted to share my pride in my lifestyle." When he retires from government, and from being battered on the rodeo circuit, he'll take up poetry full-time.

Canadian star Bryn Thiessen, a Sundre, Alberta, rancher, has produced CDs, videos, a book of poems. Thiessen cuts a fine figure on stage with his flowing black moustache, high-laced boots, and black hat (the round overturned-kettle style, a standard in the Old West). He, too, is a comic but also a practising

Christian. On the last day of the Maple Creek gathering he led a church service in the skating rink.

Doc Hayes (he has a Ph.D. and an M.A. but says, "As an Alpha male, wouldn't you rather be known as "Doc" than "Ma"?) grew up in Arizona and moved to Canada in 1968. At Brandon University he taught teachers how to use poetry, storytelling, speaking, listening, thinking, writing, and reading, and taught graduate courses on diagnostic reading, and on aspects of language-learning problems.

"Poetry permeates my day, often my night," Hayes says, who took it up seriously seven years ago, "and is my third love after God and wife and family." Now sixty-six, he plans to rhyme his way around North America. "Fair money and a lot of fun."

Fair money indeed. The top American performers attend 75 to 150 gatherings annually for fees of three to five thousand dollars (U.S.) per two-day event, plus expenses and the right to sell their books, tapes, and videos on-site. One poet claims he earns more than President George W. Bush. So much for the lariati versus the literati.

X

FAITH

The Holy Spirit has bypassed us.

REVEREND DWIGHT RUTHERFORD
Foxwarren, Manitoba

How Big Is the Bible Belt?

So what about it? Are the three provinces a nest of ranting, raving, foaming-at-the-mouth preachers? Elmer Gantrys in bib overalls? Shrivelled zealots standing silently on street corners with blazing eyes, mouths set in unforgiving lines, and placards proclaiming THE END IS NEAR?

Sorry, but the prairies are *not* a hotbed of religion, fanatical or otherwise. A 2003 StatsCan survey found that adult church-going in Canada has dropped to 32 per cent. Prince Edward Islanders are the most devout (53 per cent attend church at least once a month). The prairies hover near the bottom of the scale: Manitoba's attendance has fallen to 36 per cent, Saskatchewan's to 39 per cent, Alberta's to 31 per cent. Many prairie people – from 15 per cent in Saskatchewan to 23 per cent in Alberta – have no religious affiliation.

Such figures may even be inflated. An American source claims that half of respondents habitually lie to pollsters about church attendance. Not very Christian of them, but they apparently hate to admit they don't attend. But the empty pews in mainstream churches in small communities show they are hard hit. In part it is a backlash against modernization. By accepting gays or jazzing up hymns and worship, churches alienate conservative members who cling to old beliefs and traditions.

"In the country many of our congregations are aging," adds Reverend Dwight Rutherford, a United Church cleric in the Foxwarren area. Fewer young families attend. "There is much fear, especially among clergy, about the future of the church. As one colleague says, 'I think the Holy Spirit has bypassed us.'"

He thinks small rural churches may have to partner, adding a third church to a two-point charge. "This is not always easy," says Rutherford, who already serves two charges. "Distances will increase, and many clergy, me included, do not want to do three services on a Sunday." There's also a trend towards two denominations – United Church and Anglican or Lutheran, say – sharing a ministry with turnabout Sunday services.

What of the so-called prairie Bible belt? The label had its beginnings in pioneer Alberta, when many immigrants were Americans with evangelical leanings, explains David Marshall, professor of religion at the University of Calgary. They couldn't relate to mainstream churches so congregated on their own. Being poor, they attended rural Bible colleges rather than universities.

Bible colleges and radio evangelism flourished in Alberta, in part due to its preaching premiers, William "Bible Bill" Aberhart and Ernest Manning, whose popular evangelistic radio show, *Back to the Bible Hour*, was heard across North America. "Bible belters" became a catchphrase to describe right-wing fundamentalists and for Albertans in particular.

Today, writes Calgarian Graham Chandler, in a thoroughly researched 2001 article for *Alberta Views* magazine, "There's no record of Albertans being any more evangelical than anywhere else in the country."

Those who claim Christian Orthodox or other Christian (including Apostolic, Born-Again Christian, and Evangelical) as their faith account for a mere 4.3 per cent of the population in Saskatchewan, 5.4 per cent in Manitoba, and 5.7 per cent in Alberta. Professed Roman Catholics and Protestants (including United Church, Baptist, and Lutheran) outnumber them by far in all three provinces.

There are indeed prairie churches where the minister exhorts his flock to speak in tongues, where the congregation whoops and weeps with outstretched arms, where backsliders face warnings of eternal hellfire. Although they are a minority, they delight the media and perpetuate the myth. A national television show about Alberta in 2002 singled out that kind of church – and that alone.

Some evangelical groups, like their mainstream brethren, are feeling a modest pinch. The Evangelical Missionary Church in the West increased attendance from 6,579 to 11,147 between 1993 and 2001 (that included B.C. with no prairie breakdown). The Evangelical Lutheran Church in Canada, strongest in Alberta, but with sizable numbers in Saskatchewan and Manitoba, is hurting in small communities, says spokesman Reverend Kenn Ward. Baptized membership (approximately 100,000 overall) has decreased by about 8,000 in ten years. The Lutheran Church of Canada, separate from the Evangelical, has 37,000 members in the three provinces; membership has slipped slightly. The Christian and Missionary Alliance in Canada had about 16,000 prairie members in 2001, stable over ten years.

So, the Bible belt, while still firmly in place, looms larger in the minds of Easterners than in reality.

Pilgrim

Would today's world have a place for as pious a soul as Margarita "Gretta" Graffin? In the late 1950s this Manitoban made a solitary pilgrimage to Roman Catholic shrines in Italy, France, Spain, Portugal, Britain, and the Republic of Ireland.

She trudged three thousand miles through rain, heat, and snow, begging clothes, shelter, and meals of bread and water. She roamed penniless, ill-clothed, and sometimes barefoot. Yet when I wrote about her for *Maclean's*, she was back teaching grades seven and eight at Holy Cross School in St. Vital, regarding her exercise in asceticism as no big deal.

Gretta was a tiny forty-three-year-old brunette with dark eyes and full lips, slightly resembling Judy Garland. She would have hated the comparison. She was intensely devout, a million Hail Marys away from Hollywood glitz and fakery. Yet she was also down-to-earth and self-deprecating, with a beguiling sense of humour.

"There was nothing heroic about it," she told me of her journey. "Oh, it was uncomfortable at times. Some people say the more uncomfortable you are, the more holy you become. If so, there were days I became holy by leaps and bounds!"

Such as the day when her shoes literally fell apart or when dinner one night was a single bread roll washed down with water from a pump, or when a speeding car in Italy knocked her down (she got up with a nosebleed and refused a lift). Or when a French housewife turned her out into the rain, saying, "Pay up or get out." That night Gretta slept on a pile of damp sacks on a garage floor.

For her the true accomplishments were her visit to the Chapel of the Holy Shroud in Turin, an audience with the Pope, a visit to Lourdes, and hours of prayer at countless other shrines and cathedrals along the way.

Graffin started with some assets. She had always lived simply, so poverty as penance was not far from her normal daily life. She was born in Belfast and began her education in a convent, hence her humour and religious grounding.

Her father, a railway section hand, brought his family to Manitoba. In school she thrived on work, and her nimble mind was too quick for her teachers. She told one of them, "We're just wasting time in class" and was temporarily expelled. At fourteen she decided on a whim to live like a Hindu and to her parents' consternation spent six months not eating meat and sitting cross-legged on the floor. She hiked and worked around Canada during the Depression, received a B.A. in languages from the Université de Montréal and spoke fluent French and passable Spanish.

Her pilgrimage started in Rome. She gave away her spare clothing and her $2.98 cardboard suitcase and donated her last twenty dollars to an emaciated Gypsy woman carrying a baby. She averaged twenty-five miles a day with her long swinging stride. She wore a blouse, a dirndl skirt, and low-heeled shoes, carried a sweater for chilly nights, a rosary and her passport pinned to a picture of *Madonna della Strada* (Our Lady of Travel). Her documents in French and Italian from her parish priests back home stated that "Miss Margarita Graffin, schoolmistress, of this parish, enjoys a good reputation. We know of no occasion on which she was the cause of a scandal or any other difficulty." With this, nuns and priests gave her food and shelter without question. She insisted that she be fed only bread and water.

Once she fended off a gang of youths, who left her alone when they realized she was penniless. Another time, when hitching a ride on a motorcycle, the driver refused to let her off. She jumped, split her forehead, and had to have it stitched.

At the tomb of St. Francis of Assisi, she prayed, saw a tattered robe that was said to be the saint's, looked at her own rumpled self, and thought, "How delighted he'd have been with me!" But later, walking through rainstorms and recalling St. Francis, who regarded a walk in the rain as "perfect joy," she muttered, "I've got news for you. This *isn't* perfect joy!"

After six months of steady plodding she entered Spain in January. She was freezing in her thin skirt, two sweaters, kerchief, umbrella, and a piece of plastic with a hole for her head that sufficed as raincoat. She had fleas. "I hope I don't meet anyone from Winnipeg," she thought.

She could barely walk. The sisters at a Spanish convent put her to bed. The local priest refused to hear her confession unless she broke her fast. She gave up her bread-only diet, after six months, and "really fell off the wagon." In the end her parents sent money for her passage home.

She had achieved her goals but shrugged off praise. "Thousands of Catholics go to shrines and thousands more face just as many difficulties as I did, of a different kind."

Recently I tried to find Gretta again, or at least some word of her later life or death. No luck. Nuns in Manitoba remember that she resumed teaching for a while, then dropped out of sight.

Presumably her God knows. Which is all Gretta Graffin would want.

"And They Need No Candle . . ."

Emil Strand was showing off for me, just a little. He jogged from his farmhouse across a hundred yards of prairie that led to his barn, crawled through a barbed-wire fence, slipped a bridle on his mare, Polly, and took off at a gallop down a hilly dirt road.

Nothing unusual about that – except that Emil Strand was blind. He had retinitis pigmentosa, a hereditary disease that atrophies the retina. His vision, weak since birth, failed completely at age twenty-eight. Yet here he was at fifty-three acting like a sighted man.

Emil had no education. As a child of Norwegian parents, he spoke no English until he was six. That, coupled with his failing eyesight, made school a nightmare and he dropped out after a few weeks. He grew up knowing nothing but farming. It's an occupation that cripples many a sighted person, and is perilous for a blind man. Barbed-wire fences, power machinery, skittish livestock – any or all could kill or maim him.

Around his hometown of Readlyn, Saskatchewan, everyone assumed he would go into an institution. Emil feared that more than barbed wire or fractious bulls. He stayed on to prove a blind man could run a farm.

His only helpers, when I met him in the mid-fifties, were his older sister, Lena, small, stooped, and also blind, and his friend and hired man, Alex Strubech, a gentle slow-spoken man with an honest, homely face. Lena cooked on a coal-burning stove, tended the house, and never left the farm. Strubech, then seventy-six and diabetic, operated machinery with whirling belts or gears. Emil did almost everything else.

He was of medium height, with a strong, weather-beaten profile, shaggy, unkempt grey hair, and a quick grin that revealed a broad gap in his upper teeth. He walked briskly in a slight crouch, bristling with energy. After an hour or two of inactivity, he paced restlessly around his house, flexing his powerful hands or snapping his jackknife open and shut.

When his vision failed entirely, aggravated by influenza, Emil had to learn how to farm all over again. He gashed his hands on fences, ran into barn doors, often fell. Once he tumbled from a bale of hay but merely sprained an ankle. A wagon wheel rolled over his foot, but no bones were broken. An angry bull knocked him down, but his dog held it off until Emil could get away.

He memorized every contour of his barnyard. The wind became his compass. Partly from memory, partly from riding over it, he acquired a phenomenal knowledge of the surrounding land. Once, a truck driver asked directions to a farm four miles away. Emil gave them in detail and added, "Watch that last quarter-mile, there's a bad bump." There was, too.

He chopped wood, patched fences, pitched hay, stooked grain, drove fence posts with a heavy maul. He rounded up his cattle on horseback, guided by a tinkling bell on the lead cow. Sometimes he plodded the fields on foot, and claimed he was lost only once, when the wind suddenly changed direction.

Possibly his hardest task – "harder than pitching sheaves," he told me – was learning Braille. But he mastered it, with the help of a CNIB home teacher: he eagerly worked his way through books and magazines, and became a more stimulating conversationalist than many farmers with sight and schooling.

Not long after I met them, the faithful Alex Strubech died. Emil carried on. Then Lena lost her hearing and went into a nursing home in 1972 (she died ten years later, aged ninety-three). Emil sold his remaining land but lived ten more years in the house with his dog. During blizzards, he strung a line from the outdoor well to his house so he wouldn't get lost fetching water.

His greatest fear was that he, too, would have to go into a home. But in 1981 he took his first plane ride, to Chilliwack, B.C., where a niece welcomed him into her home to spend his last days. He hated to leave the farm, but, he said, it was "God's will."

Emil leaned on his God, and on his Braille Bible. One of his proudest moments was reading from his Bible by invitation in an Assiniboia church. Before I left him that time in the 1950s, he asked, hopefully, "Maybe you'd like me to read for you?"

He scrubbed his hands meticulously, pulled out a thick green-bound volume, and turned to Revelation 22. Afterward, I wondered if he deliberately chose that passage as a going-away gift for the journalist, a ready-made ending for the story.

It was evening, the drab little farmhouse was dim with shadows, but Emil read aloud softly, his fingers flickering over the pages, a half-smile on his face: ". . . and they need no candle, neither light of the sun; for the Lord God giveth them light."

Away from the World Out There

The private world of the Swift Current Hutterite colony – an island of humility, faith, and hard work amidst a seething secular sea – begins at a farm gate a dozen miles northwest of the city. Past a regiment of mammoth tractors standing at attention along the drive. Past workshop, chicken barns, milking parlour, feed mill, fertilizer silos, a gaggle of geese, some pheasants, and a wandering peacock.

The core of the community is a cluster of trim one-storey stucco buildings – dining hall, church house, school, and row-housing family apartments. It is seven in the evening; the day's work and meals are over. The people watch me with interest from their front steps: men in dark trousers, black hats, sober blue shirts; women in long dark dresses and dark babushkas. A stranger from "out there," as some Hutterites refer to the outer world, is an object of mild curiosity.

A young man, his beard signifying he is married, meets me. I ask for Curley, the secretary, or Jake, the boss. "Curley's away," the young man says cautiously. No mention of Jake, implying that passersby can't just roll in off the road and expect to see whomever they want.

"He's expected," a woman calls out, referring to me. My cousin Bonnie Currie in Swift Current has phoned ahead. Her parents, the late Ruby and Arnold Zabel, were loved and respected schoolteachers in a neighbouring Hutterite colony. Their names open doors and kindle smiles.

The young man guides me to Jake – Jacob Hofer, president and minister, senior among the eighty-one men, women, and children on this colony. He is tall, bespectacled, bearded, solemn of visage in the mandatory black hat, dark trousers slung with dark suspenders, pale-blue shirt with a thin dark-blue stripe. Hutterites shun bright clothing and jewellery; theirs are humble colours. Jake shakes hands, wary and a trifle stern. Writers have not always done right by his people.

Have I read up on Hutterites? Jake demands. Not much, I confess (I'd been saving history reading for a rainy day back home).

"You should have done, there's lots of books," he scolds.

I pull out the tape recorder. "Okay if I use this?"

"Don't you take shorthand?"

Then, having established that I am probably harmless if not very swift, Jake settles back and in a sonorous voice answers every question freely, with surprising flashes of dry humour – surprising because Jacob Hofer takes his responsibilities seriously. For the rest of this day he is a generous host and tireless tour guide, proud of his colony and warming to my genuine interest

The prairie at its most idyllic, in 1927:
perfect stooks of grain and the
landmark grain elevators (now sadly
vanishing everywhere) in Alberta's
Fort Saskatchewan district.
(Glenbow Archives ND-3-3755)

The soul of every small town used
to be the general store (like this Little
Bow Trading Company in High
River, Alberta) – wooden counter,
shelves heaped with all that settlers
could desire, and hangers-on with hats
worn from dawn to dusk, and possibly
in bed. (Glenbow Archives NA-370-26)

Technology-wise Warren Jolly of Mossbank,
Saskatchewan, uses two computers, fax, scanner, and
Global Positioning System to help farm eight thousand
acres. Record keeping is vital. Warren's wife, Paula, says,
"He spends more time in the office than he does on the
land." (Robert Collins)

Patti Scott
looks like a fashion
model, but she's a
fourth-generation
rancher, running
150 cattle in the
Alberta foothills
with the help of
daughters Birch
and Cassie and
a very loving
Montana.
(Robert Collins)

This glorious horse chestnut had stood in downtown Edmonton for nearly eighty years when it was threatened by a parking lot. Earl Andrusiak, vice-president of the next-door HSBC Bank, led a campaign to save it. Now, every spring its blossoms still burst out "like an explosion of white fireworks." (Robert Collins)

Saskatoon's iconoclastic book-seller Wayne Shaw is audible proof that Westerners aren't dull: "I can't stand those arrogant Ontario people!"; "Politicians and bureaucrats don't read, don't think!"; "Our Ottawa government is a sick, sad bunch of people!" And more. (Robert Collins)

The plains are alive with the sound of music. Violinist and pianist Laurie and Jamie Syer moved to a rural property near Sundre, Alberta, and discovered a local appetite for classical music. Their "Strings and Keys" teaching program draws about seventy youthful students each year. (Robert Collins)

Betty-Marie Hofer and sons Aaron and Christopher of the Swift Current Hutterite colony live modestly and happily with seventy-eight others on an island of faith, humility, and hard work amidst the secular sea of the world "out there." (Robert Collins)

The petroleum that made Alberta rich still lurks beneath
its fields. Here, the roughnecks of exploratory Rig
616TE pull up drilling pipe west of Claresholme in
search of natural gas. (Robert Collins)

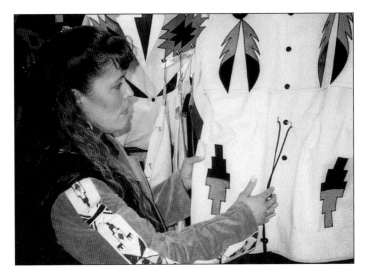

When Patricia Piché was small, her Cree mother and
grandmother taught her to sew. Now, with her own
fashion design company, Piché, of Bon Accord, Alberta,
makes spectacular coats, vests, and jackets with aboriginal motifs, selling for $250 and up. (Robert Collins)

As far back as 1912, the East was shafting the West. This *Regina Leader* cartoon from that year suggests collusions between railways and eastern manufacturers, forcing the prairies to payer higher freight rates to move goods east, while Ontario and Quebec enjoyed special rates to ship finished products back west. (Glenbow Archives NA-3055-20)

Throughout his tenure, Pierre Elliot
Trudeau was the eastern lightning
rod for prairie wrath. As *Calgary
Herald* cartoonist Tom Innes saw it,
the Western premiers stuck it to the
prime minister at a joint meeting in
1976. (Glenbow Archives M-8787-313)

in these admirable, hard-working people who have stood by their beliefs throughout centuries of persecution.

Hutterites are a prairie phenomenon. About 27,900 of them, almost the entire Canadian population, live in the three provinces, with 140 colonies in Alberta, 55 in Saskatchewan, and 96 in Manitoba. In one significant respect they are like most other immigrants: they came here to be free.

Their history began in 1528 when a small group of Anabaptists (meaning "to rebaptize") under the leadership of Jakob Hutter fled religious persecution in the Tyrol to set up a communal society in Moravia, now a region of the Czech Republic.

Their religion was based on strict separation of church and state, and on New Testament teachings, with particular attention to Acts 2:44-45 ("And all that believed were together and had all things common, and sold their possessions and goods and parted them to all men, as every man had need"). In 1536 Hutter was burned at the stake for refusing to renounce his beliefs.

Over the centuries his people moved from country to country, migrating to North Dakota in the 1870s, then to Western Canada during the First World War. Here they live much as their forefathers did almost five centuries ago: praising Jesus, eschewing war, holding to their community, and trying to avoid the lures and pitfalls of the outer world.

"Coffee?" Jake asks solicitously. "Would you care for cream? A dab of milk?" and "Here's some cookies that they baked at the beginning of the week sometime." Around his kitchen table with his wife, Rachel, the story of the Swift Current colony unfolds. There are eighteen families in residence on this day, from couples to groups of four or five. Each has its own apartment of about fifteen hundred square feet with private entrance in one of the long four-unit buildings. They branched off here in 1976 from another colony that had outgrown its space.

"They built all these buildings without any architect schooling," Jake says proudly. "We make all our own furniture – rockers, tables, beds, couches, cabinets, we made them all. And we do all our sewing except our underclothes. We have patterns, we buy the raw material."

They also bake their own bread, buns, and pastry, make cottage cheese, crank out noodles, preserve pickles by the hundreds of jars, and concoct their own wine from strawberries, rhubarb, sometimes rye. "We don't need much outside help except for doctors and dentist," Jake sums up. They raise most of their vegetables but buy most of their fruit by the truckload from afar.

"We take enough to can for the winter and the spring. How many two-quart sealers would we have, Mom, a couple thousand?"

"Oh yes," Rachel says, as though preserving two thousand sealers of fruit wouldn't raise sweat on her brow. Rachel is mother of their seven children. Although writings on Hutterites say women have "an official subordinate status," she seems an equal partner here.

"It works out pretty nice. You can pick it a little riper this way and your fruit is more tasteful," Jake is saying. "Bring a few cherries, Mom. They are just in." Sure enough, they are better than anything in the supermarkets.

"We used to grow tomatoes, but we never had any luck with them," Rachel says ruefully. "If we got a cold rain it would take forever for them to recover. By the time it's supposed to be a tomato it's not very much of a tomato. So it's cheaper for us to buy by the case. We can about sixty cases. But we grow our own potatoes and everything else."

Jake's grandchildren – Jennifer, Aaron, and Christopher – have squirmed into the kitchen, wriggling with curiosity. All are blond with shining pink-scrubbed faces, the boys with neat haircuts (not the designer hairdos of city kids) and dark trousers hoisted up with white suspenders. Children have a little latitude in colour: Aaron's blue shirt has vertical strips in geometric design; Jennifer's dress is a jaunty floral with matching headgear, a kind of cloche.

Hutterite children get a lot of parental attention. They are the future of the colony, but it's not easy to hold them from the material delights beckoning "out there."

"We'd like them to stay in the colony, but not all do, not any more," Jake says with a tinge of regret. "We have no control over them, everybody is here of his own free will. If he goes away he can come back again if he has no debts out there – the colony can't pay their debts – and is not in trouble with the law. A lot of them come back. When they do find work out there, it's hard work." That's because Hutterite children don't go on to higher education.

"It's not all roses and sunshine," Rachel says. "The ones that don't come back, they can come visit." Then she reveals gently, matter-of-factly, what must be a sorrow for them both. "We have a son out there. He comes back once a year. He works for the oil patch. We exchange birthday cards. We can talk on the telephone between six at night and six in the morning. He has children, nine and seven."

"The big secret," Jake forges on, "we are born here and brought up here. You get a good start, you don't worry what's happening out there. Because we can see a lot of things happening out there that even the people out there wish they could get away from."

Now, an awkward moment. Hutterites do not like having their photos taken. Still, nothing ventured . . .

"No, we don't," Jake says firmly to my question. I produce a photocopy from a book, of two winsome Hutterite kids. Would Jake permit one like this of his grandchildren?

He studies it. He says something to Rachel. He thinks the picture was taken in another colony in Alberta or Saskatchewan. Well, if the other colony permitted it . . . Courteously, they assent. Daughter-in-law Betty Marie corrals Christopher – who at first wails like a banshee – and Aaron and Jennifer. They pose charmingly.

Afterward Jake explains, "The reason we don't want photos taken, it goes against the Ten Commandments, and we try to live up to the Commandments." A photograph seems to defy "Thou shalt have no graven image before me."

We begin a tour of the colony: schoolrooms, kitchens, and dining rooms, church, a glimpse of the apartments – everything bright and immaculate. Seven-year-old Jennifer tags along, chattering in a mixture of German and English, singing, capering, watching me intently, full of questions.

"Jennifer, you be good!" and "Oh, be quiet, now, Jennifer," Jake admonishes repeatedly, almost absently. ("When you have children," he told me earlier, "they entertain you. But you got to keep them in line.") His granddaughter carries on, not unruly, just lively, knowing that grandfather, stern preacher and head of the colony though he is, dotes on her.

From ages three to six the children attend their own kinder-garten, supervised by older women of the colony. They recite their German verses and prayers, have lunch and a nap.

"They bring their own little blanket and pillow and every week take it home to have it washed. At three-thirty they go home to their families . . . Okay, you be good, Jennifer . . ."

At age six the children start grade school. They start the day by helping their mothers with light housework, then an hour of

German studies conducted by a member of the colony. "It's mostly Bible study, they learn where Jesus was born and things like that," Jake says, "and songs our forefathers have left behind." Then English schooling taught by a teacher from outside.

The small voice beside me: "What's your name?"

I tell her.

"What's that?"

"A tape recorder."

"Jennifer, you be good!"

Even playtime is serious. "We'll allow swings, tennis balls for children, but we don't want to be carried away; the older folks join in it, you know."

At age fifteen the young people leave grade school and begin learning the work of the colony. Jobs are assigned, and changed every fourth year. There are cattle, hogs, chickens, geese, and ducks to tend. The boys do field work under supervision, from picking rocks to helping harvest. The girls at seventeen take turns cooking in the huge communal kitchen and eventually join the older women, divided into work parties, in the vast canning operation of pickles and fruit. Soon all are proficient in many aspects of running the colony.

"This is what I call education for our work," Jake says. "A lot of people go to university to learn that. We have a university right here."

Jennifer: "Why you take my picture?"

"'Cause you look pretty."

"Okay, Jennifer, you run along now . . ."

Hutterites have not always been warmly received by their neighbours, partly because of their exclusivity, partly because of the scale of their operations (although large-scale prairie farming is now the norm). At least one community tried to ban a new colony on the premise that the Hutterites bought all their supplies in bulk from big cities or out-of-province. In the ensuing court case, the Hutterite boss produced receipts for their machinery and building supplies. Most of it was purchased in the area. Case dismissed; colony built.

"On the whole, I think people regard them as good neighbours," a Swift Current friend told me. "For some farmers who want to sell out, the choice is either to Hutterites or to a very big farmer, and at least the Hutterites support a lot of people on their land."

The Swift Current colony owns about eleven thousand acres, only 148 acres per colony member, not much by today's standards. They grow wheat, oats, barley, canola, and a few chickpeas ("anything there's a market for, because we use very little of what we grow"). They have a hundred head of cattle plus hundreds of geese, duck, turkeys, and pigs.

Everyone works and everyone shares in the colony's affairs – up to a point. A board of trustees buys or sells off land. Colony members can speak up if they're not satisfied. The secretary takes in all money earned and pays all expenses. Any surplus goes into savings until needed. The people get a little spending money every month, for personal toiletries or a soft drink in town. If the young men get into the beer parlour, Jake doesn't want to hear about it.

He leads me enthusiastically through kitchen, dining hall, milk parlour. The kitchen has a deep fryer, a chiller for canned vegetables, cooler for slaughtered poultry, sausage mixer, dough mixer that handles fifty pounds of flour, and an oven big enough for a hundred loaves. Many appliances are of shining stainless steel. Everything is scrubbed, even the walls.

Jennifer is with us all the way. "Do you have a friend?"

"Well, yes, I have friends."

"What's her name?" Then I get it: she means girlfriend.

"Not *that* kind of friend. But I have two daughters."

"Jennifer! You know too much English already!"

The colony has four or five vehicles, including multi-person vans for group travel. Their two-way radio system has a range of thirty miles, to track down members on the farthest reaches of their land or in Swift Current.

"But you have no television or radio?" I ask, back in the kitchen.

"Not *supposed* to," Rachel says with the slightest twinkle of eye, which seems to confirm rumours that perhaps a few illicit radios are sneaked in.

"We don't allow them," Jake says emphatically. "The folks have always been against the radio, even years ago, when there wasn't that much bad stuff on radio. People would sit and listen to a ball game or a boxing match instead of being at work. In the colony we have to work pretty steadily to make a living, we can't be at every hockey game or watch TV."

They do read newspapers and Jake concedes that some members probably read magazines. "We like them to be clean magazines if they do read 'em. Pocketbooks, we like them to be clean, not too much murder or things like those.... Jennifer, you be good, now! Okay, you run along, now.... It's not that they are gonna go through life without experiencing it, but it's better if the young folks don't read about it or hear about it."

But every child and adult sings, lustily, in church or at weddings – rousing old German hymns written by their people centuries ago, sometimes with guitar and mouth organ. In the church house, the minister leads, singing a line, the congregation repeating it after him. The men sit on one side, the women on the other, oldest at the back, children up front.

"I was raised and born in Alberta, but Saskatchewan has been home for forty years," Jake says as I leave. "I'm glad when

I get home from Alberta. They seem to be in the fast track out there. We couldn't survive on the spending they do out there. It seems like everyone likes to live like the Joneses down the road."

We shake hands. I have grown fond of this honest man who is striving to maintain his cherished way of life against the current of society. We take a long look at the big darkening sky.

"I *love* it out here," he says fervently.

"Yes, when I come home from town I am *so* glad," Rachel agrees. "I get tired of the noise."

But what of the young ones? Will Jennifer marry a Hutterite from another colony, move there, carry on the tradition? Will peace, faith, and simplicity be enough? Or will she, with her bright inquiring mind, be lured by the world "out there"?

XI

TALES OF THE OIL PATCH

*Swaggering, superconfident Marlborough Men with
Oklahoma or Texas accents who winked at the girls,
drove big cars and came from a different world.*

JOHN BARR
on the post-Leduc invasion of American oilmen in Alberta

The Legend of Dry-Hole Hunter

In 1947 we went drilling at Leduc,
Upon a rural property of stubble, straw, and stook.
We really drilled for water, but by some outrageous fluke,
The oil just poured and poured.

Glory, glory hallelujah,
Glory, glory hallelujah,
A little dab of oil would do yuh,
But ours just pours and pours.

"Alberta Anthem" – lyrics, Robert Collins; tune, "The Battle Hymn of the Republic"

So firmly entrenched is the late Vernon Hunter in prairie oil mythology that someday someone will surely put his feat to song for guitar, harmonica, and nasal voice. They might call it "The Legend of Dry-Hole Hunter," although legend it was not. Hunter was the real-life toolpusher (rig boss) who on February 13, 1947, brought in Leduc #1, the well that lifted Alberta into unprecedented riches.

Both he and his employer, Imperial Oil, came to Leduc with calamitous records. In the previous thirty-five years Imperial had drilled 133 dry holes, and Vern Hunter, a lean, fair-haired man with a wide smile and unquenchable sense of humour, had dug his share of them. (Stories vary on whether he arrived at Leduc with his "Dry-Hole" nickname or whether he invented it post-Leduc for a little colour. Regardless, he bore it amiably for the rest of his life.)

By then the prospects for new oil in Alberta were grim. There had been no significant discoveries since Turner Valley in the 1930s. By 1946 Turner's production had dropped to about

17,000 barrels a day. The whole of Canada that year produced 21,000 barrels of oil per day – and consumed 200,000. The rest was imported, mostly from the United States. Post-war Canada was hungry for new energy, but more than half of it still came from coal.

Imperial Oil had spent twenty-three million dollars since 1912 on Western exploration. It had done half of all the industry's geological work in the prairie provinces and a quarter of the drilling. For all of this it had only a share of the declining Turner Valley field and a field in Norman Wells, Northwest Territories, far from southern Canadian markets.

Before 1947, much of the province's oil – including Turner Valley's discovery well – had been found in the Cretaceous level, laid down between 146 and 165 million years ago. There'd been one strike at the deeper Devonian level, formed between 410 and 360 million years ago, but no one paid it particular heed.

In the spring of 1946, in an aura of gloom, a skeptical Imperial Oil committee in Toronto recommended one more deep-drilling effort, in an area of central Alberta reaching from northwest of Edmonton and south beyond Leduc. If that failed, the company would have to build a plant to make synthetic gasoline, using natural gas as the main ingredient, instead of crude oil in the long-established refining method. Leduc #1 – initially known as Wildcat #134 ("wildcat" means a well in untried territory) – would be the last-chance well.

Imperial acquired rights to almost two hundred thousand acres over twenty-four townships around Edmonton. Seismographic crews, studying the underground formations, came up with two possibilities: one near Leduc in the Cretaceous zone, and a better-looking prospect near Pigeon Lake about thirty miles southwest of there.

Leduc was near a highway and closer to Edmonton's services and to the Saskatchewan River. If the wildcat well turned up only natural gas, steam essential to the process of making synthetic gasoline would be provided by river water. So, through expert hunch and sheer good luck, the company chose Leduc.

Time to call in the drillers.

Vernon Hunter was born in Nanton, Alberta, son of a Baptist minister. His father demanded strict Sunday observance: no swimming, fishing, or anything else that qualified as fun. Reverend Hunter was more often paid in farm produce than in cash. His son, who came through childhood with his humour intact, later claimed that he grew up thinking the only vegetables on earth were potatoes and turnips.

He finished grade twelve at sixteen, worked as a clerk and truck driver in Turner Valley, and got his first roughneck job (oil-well labourer) with Royalite, an Imperial subsidiary, in 1927. He and his wife began married life in a tarpaper-lined shack in Poverty Flats on the outskirts of Turner. Laid off by the Depression, Hunter scraped together a living digging ditches, chopping wood, and selling eggs from his three hundred hens.

Royalite rehired him in 1935. In the early forties he caught the eye of Walker Taylor, at the time Royalite's western manager. Out hunting pheasants at four in the morning, Taylor dropped in on a Royalite rig. He found toolpush Hunter working with his roughnecks over a broken diesel engine.

"Why are you out here in the night doing this?" Taylor said. "Let the crew do it."

"It's pretty hard to sleep when you've got an engine broken down," Hunter said. Taylor never forgot it. He chose the dedicated toolpush to be his drilling superintendent at Imperial's Norman Wells site. Now, never mind all those dry holes, the forty-one-year-old Hunter was picked to drill Leduc #1.

Hunter went ahead to check the site – fourteen miles north-west of the town of Leduc and sixteen miles south of Edmonton

– and meet the landowner, Ukrainian-born Mike Turta. Mike's little farm was typical of the time: horse-drawn implements, kerosene lamps, and battery-operated radio. He didn't own mineral rights, so he wasn't going to become oil-rich. But Mike and his family seemed delighted to greet the oilmen. It was a fillip of excitement in their work-filled lives.

Hunter offered to build a road to the well site around the homestead, but Turta refused to give up that scrap of crop land. "Come through my yard," he said.

Hunter didn't like that. The constant truck traffic would surely annoy the family, endanger Mike's children, maybe flatten some of his chickens and geese. But Turta stood firm, so Imperial paid him $250 a year ($50 an acre for five acres) for surface rights. (Two years later the company sweetened the deal: $3,000 for extra acreage plus $500 a year for surface rights.)

Now came Hunter's rig and crew of four drillers and twenty-eight roughnecks from Provost, Alberta, where as usual they'd been disappointed: two wells drilled, one with a modest show of gas, the other with a trace of oil that turned to water. They didn't expect to find oil at Leduc.

"Too close to Edmonton," Hunter said. It was the oilman's version of Murphy's Law: you never found oil near a big city with movies, comfortable hotels, good restaurants, lots of single women. You found it in some desolate gopher-pocked prairie backwater with no beer parlour and no restaurants (or at best a Chinese café serving burnt fried eggs).

Leduc #1's derrick rose section by section, towering over the flat land like a huge windmill without the vanes. The well was spudded in (started) on November 20. Day after day it ran, around the clock, engines rumbling, pipe clashing. The hospitable Turtas often invited the crewmen in for cups of tea or a snack. The oilmen in turn bought their cream, eggs, and chickens on the farm. There was only one hazard, according to the droll toolpush.

"Walking through Mike's yard was dangerous," Hunter liked to say, "with his ganders snapping at your heels like the hound dogs after Little Eva." (He meant Eliza, the embattled heroine of Harriet Beecher Stowe's *Uncle Tom's Cabin*, who escaped the savage bloodhounds of a wicked slave-owner by skipping across ice floes.)

For a while nothing happened. Then, the core tests (cylindrical sections of perforated rock pulled up from the oil-bearing zone) at about 2,000 feet began to show heartening signs. At 5,029 feet, in the little-known Devonian level, they ran a test that brought oil to the surface. Afterwards, geologist Steve Cosburn stopped by the Hunters' trailer in Leduc. Hunter's wife, Dean, and a friend were having coffee. The other woman, a Turner Valley veteran, sniffed the tarry stuff on Cosburn's overalls and instantly knew: "You've found oil!"

By the end of January, Hunter "knew we had a damn good well. The whole thing was *alive!*" On February 3, a geyser shot forth, drenching a roughneck in mud and light crude. Hunter's bosses urged him to name the day he'd bring it in (let the oil flow), before an invited crowd. It would be a nice piece of public relations for Imperial after all those rotten years. The toolpush hated the idea. He knew from bitter experience that oilwells, like children, rarely come in when called.

"The crew and I were experts at abandoning wells," he said later, "but we didn't know much about completing them. I named February 13 and started praying."

True to form, Hunter spent part of the previous night at the well site, helping his crew coddle their unborn baby. About eight in the morning of February 13 he went home. He was nicely into breakfast when the bad news came: breakdown. They'd been swabbing the well, cleaning out the worst of the accumulated mud before going on-stream.

"The rig was fairly new, but there was one old part that we never used because we never had to bring in wells before,"

Hunter recounted later. "That bloody piece of machinery must have been twenty-three years old, and the shaft broke."

The crew worked feverishly all morning to clear the obstruction as onlookers gathered. It was windy and minus-ten Fahrenheit (-23.3 °C). By noon the snowy side road to Mike Turta's farm was clogged with half-ton trucks, venerable Chevs, and dilapidated Fords. Their occupants, a shivering crowd of five hundred, huddled outside Turta's barnyard. Imperial had invited the *crème de la crème* of press and Alberta dignitaries. Hundreds of ordinary folk also got wind of the event and crashed the party.

Tall, solemn Nathan Tanner, provincial minister of lands and mines, was there, a fashion plate in dressy overcoat, pearl-grey hat, and high-zip boots. So was Edmonton mayor Harry Ainlay and assorted Imperial bigwigs. "Dry-Hole" Hunter and his hard-hat overalled crew wore the harried looks of men wrestling a den of grizzly bears.

Although Imperial had prudently said only that it "hoped" to bring in the new well at one o'clock on this day, that in itself was giving Vern Hunter heartburn. Nothing happened at one. Imperial treated the restless chattering throng to coffee, sandwiches, pickles, cake, and doughnuts catered by Edmonton's Cottage Tea Room.

Two o'clock came and went. No oil. Nothing at three nor three-thirty. Some of the frostbitten crowd called it quits. Mayor Ainlay headed back to a meeting in Edmonton, thereby missing his date with history. But when the four o'clock crew came on shift, the road to the well site was still so cluttered they had to park their trucks a mile away and walk in.

Then it happened. Just before four the wellhead cleared. There was a rumble, the likes of which few of the bystanders had ever heard.

"Here she comes!" a voice shrilled. "She's coming in! It's OIL!"

The roughnecks on the derrick floor spun valves at the wellhead, turning the flow into the sump pit, clearing more of the drilling mud (a special concoction that lubricates and cools the drilling bit). Another spin of valves, and the stream – from 5,066 feet down and four hundred million years back in history – snaked through a three-inch flow line into a vertical elbow of steel pipe.

The oil and gas were still contaminated with mud, water, and drilling chemicals that had to be burned off. The honour of flaring went to roughneck Johnny Funk, at twenty-two the youngest man on the crew. He'd practised the day before. He twirled a burning, oil-soaked sack around his head like a lasso and let it fly at the spewing mixture. With a mighty WHOOSH it erupted in smoke and flames. Then a perfect smoke ring rose, widening and floating high in the crisp air. Old hands said it was a good omen.

Nathan Tanner, Walker Taylor, and Vern Hunter posed stiffly in a row for a photographer, all staring fixedly into the camera. The air reeked of crude. Then the crowd surged in with bottles and jars to scoop up a souvenir of the miraculous stuff that would revolutionize Alberta.

Vern Hunter moved from Leduc #1 to be toolpush on #3, his last job in the field. Walker Taylor then named him first district supervisor of the Leduc field. (Later Imperial drilled at Pigeon Lake, which had been a strong contender for that last-chance well. It was a dry hole.)

Hunter would ultimately move into bigger managerial jobs and live until 1985, but Leduc #1 and the "Dry-Hole" label would be forever associated with him. A modest man, happiest when yarning with old cronies, he would nevertheless become a regular on the rubber-chicken speech circuit, would be a guest on CBC's *Front Page Challenge*; would discover that some people believed he personally drilled the famous well single-handed.

But all that was later. The night after Leduc #1 came in, Imperial threw a full-blast party in Edmonton's Macdonald Hotel. Vern Hunter, man of the hour, was "too damn tired to go." He hadn't slept much the night before. He went home to his bed, swearing he would never again be coerced into producing an oilwell on demand.

> *There's oil upon our highways and there's oil upon our grass,*
> *The oil lies underneath us in one great enormous mass.*
> *The oil extends from Dawson Creek right up our Crowsnest Pass,*
> *The oil just pours and pours.*

> *Glory, glory hallelujah,*
> *Glory, glory hallelujah,*
> *A little dab of oil would do yuh,*
> *But ours just pours and pours.*

SAFETY FIRST

In the wilder, woollier days of petroleum exploration, the arrival of oilmen was, to peace-loving town folk, as welcome as a social call from Attila the Hun.

Seismic and drilling crews, particularly the single men, were notorious for drinking, fighting, and womanizing. The good burghers of Leduc had their fears confirmed one Sunday morning in the winter of 1946-47. Churchgoers passing the local hotel saw a geologist's car parked at the curb with a used condom frozen to its window.

A while after Leduc #1 spudded in, Imperial threw a banquet for its crew, honouring its shining safety record (a year without a lost-time accident). By the end of the safety banquet, one crewman had a broken arm from either falling over a chair or being heaved out a door (stories varied). Others were badly bruised.

Magic Suitcase

For seven years in the late fifties and early sixties I laboured in the vineyards of Big Oil as editor of *Imperial Oil Review*. It was a good job. We had a generous mandate, hired some of the country's finest writers, photographers, and artists, and, apart from the obligatory "oily" article, could have passed for a first-class consumer magazine.

Around us in the public-relations department, less fortunate souls toiled in less subtle fashion to put a happy face on Big Oil. For some, the task was to carry the Magic Suitcase to schools or service clubs. It was an actual suitcase, with samples of the myriad products that came from petrochemicals such as nylon, Dacron, Teflon, detergents, latex paint, and synthetic rubber. Imperial's emissaries displayed these wonders to the multitudes with silver-tongued narrative, much as sorcerers performed their legerdemain for dazzled crowds in ancient marketplaces.

Fulsome though it sounds, "magic" was not a bad description for what oil had wrought and the effect it has had on the prairie provinces since 1947.

Within weeks of the Leduc strike, Alberta was bristling with oil derricks. Suddenly Imperial could do no wrong. New wells came in rapid succession, one winner after another. Even before Leduc #1's great day, the company spudded in #2, a mile and a half to the southwest. It found nothing at #1's so-called D-2 level, so the crew kept drilling to 5,370 feet. At dawn on May 7, oil began flowing from a completely new and fruitful Devonian zone, to be known as D-3.

In essence, the company had found a multi-level oil field. It had tapped into a second "reef" – literally a coral reef from Alberta's prehistoric tropical times. Oilmen knew of reefs but never dreamed they would be found here. It took Imperial's technical people several months to accept the fact. Then it would lead to one dazzling discovery after another.

There was little caution in the oil patch, just a headlong rush to get in on the action. By late March 1947, ten independent companies, some formed specifically because of Leduc, had acquired land. The first independent to strike was Globe Leduc West #2 in August. By December a record-breaking 195 barrels an hour was pouring from Globe Leduc West #3.

All the majors were on the scene: Shell, British American, McColl-Frontenac, Anglo Canadian, California Standard, Gulf. Landowners around Leduc were already counting their cash from land leases alone. Widow Kate Manchak leased acreage for a reported $41,000 and went vacationing on the west coast. Pete Harysh got $130,000 from Leduc Consolidated. William Sycz leased to Home Oil for $58,400. The Rebus family hit the jackpot in September with $200,000 from Atlantic Oils Limited for a quarter section of land. They also held mineral rights and at year's end were awaiting more riches. By the end of 1947 the Leduc field had thirty-one producing wells, twenty-four of them drilled by or for Imperial, and had produced a total of 372,427 barrels.

Edmontonian John Barr, in later years public-affairs director for Syncrude Canada (the tar-sands enterprise), wrote in "The Impact of Oil on Alberta" about the dramatic changes after Leduc. "Prior to this time, Edmonton was a backwater. If you wanted to see a really big city, you drove all the way to the 'big apple' – Spokane. If you wanted to go out to dinner you either went to the MacDonald Hotel or the local Chinese café.... If you wanted to amount to virtually anything in virtually any field, whether business, academia or government, you had to move to Toronto, or Vancouver if you could not quite make it in Toronto."

After Leduc, Barr wrote, the province was awash in "swaggering, superconfident Marlborough Men with Oklahoma or Texas accents who winked at the girls, drove big cars and came from a different world. The Edmonton Eskimos hired a coach who later returned to the United States and came to symbolize big-time college football. His name was Darrel Royal, and he lived down the street from me. He was handsome, he had a beautiful blonde wife who used to be a cheerleader and he called his little girl Sugar. He symbolized the beginning of a different kind of Alberta."

> *Well, that was fifty years ago, the oil is flowing yet.*
> *We've paid off all of Premier William Aberhart's bad debt.*
> *Just keep the royalties coming, we'll take all that we can get,*
> *While the oil just pours and pours.*

> *Glory, glory hallelujah.*
> *Glory, glory hallelujah,*
> *A little dab of oil would do yuh,*
> *But ours just pours and pours.*

Statistics can be mind-numbing, but they best explain what energy means to Alberta, and to the rest of Canada. The province accounts for nearly 70 per cent of all the energy produced in this country, including more than half of our conventional oil and 80 per cent of our natural gas. Energy provides about 21 per cent of Alberta's total GDP, and 70 per cent of its exports ($24 billion in a recent year). The provincial government owns 80 per cent of Alberta's mineral rights; those rights paid $10 billion in the fiscal year 2000–2001.

The tar sands in northern Alberta are the world's largest; approximately three hundred billion barrels of oil may ultimately be recovered from them. It's estimated that by 2005, Alberta's sands will account for 50 per cent of all Canadian crude-oil production. Alberta's petrochemical industry produces $8 billion worth of products annually.

Oil came with less flamboyance to Saskatchewan and Manitoba, but it made its mark. In 1999 Manitoba collected approximately $3.7 million in Crown oil royalties and taxes on oil production. In Saskatchewan, revenues from crude-oil royalties and taxes and sales of petroleum leases was an estimated $795 million for the 2000-2001 fiscal year. That was about 10 per cent of government revenues.

Swimming Across Canada: One Kind of Oilman

"I was at the YMCA by five-thirty this morning, same as usual," Jim Gray is saying. "I'm swimming across Canada."

And Gray smiles his amiable smile. What's a guy of his stature doing at the Y instead of some exclusive gym, and what's with the swim across Canada? Gray was co-founder and is former chairman of Canadian Hunter Exploration, a major oil-and-gas player that in the summer of 2001 posted a 184 per cent increase in second-quarter net income. Subsequently, the international giant Burlington Resources bought Hunter for $2.1 billion.

Today, Jim Gray is Mr. Everything in Calgary. In 2002 the province named him to the Order of Excellence, its highest honour. He is a director of eight major corporations, including CNR, Nova Scotia Power, and the Hudson's Bay Company. He chaired the sixteenth World Petroleum Congress, which drew four thousand delegates to Calgary in 2000. He is chairman of the Canada West Foundation, a Calgary think-tank. The list goes on.

And the swim? It's his incentive to keep fit.

"I started in 1993. I swim about a mile, slow. I'm not a good swimmer, but I swim and I keep track on a map in my office. I'm in Ontario now. It's gonna take me five years to get through Ontario, I think" (moving east).

He'll make it. Gray finishes what he starts.

He was born in the mining town of Kirkland Lake, Ontario, which may have whetted his interest in the depths of the earth. He studied geology at UBC, worked at it for sixteen years, and in 1973 hooked up with partner John Masters. The latter, Gray says, was "an exploration genius" who could sniff out oil and gas where others failed. Gray, said Masters, was a "whirlwind whose greatest talent is in getting things done." Together they found major natural-gas fields and turned Canadian Hunter into a powerhouse, especially in finding huge, previously undetected deposits of gas.

Twenty-five years ago Masters told me, "Jim and I already have far more money than we will ever be able to use." Yet Gray has never been the stereotypically flashy oilman. Some oil-rich entrepreneurs in the half-century after Leduc amused themselves with the trappings of wealth. Many owned Lear jets; one had a Boeing 727; another had a three-million-dollar Grumman Gulfstream II with gold-plated faucets in the washroom. Mercedeses and Cadillacs were as common among oil tycoons as power mowers among lesser folk. One oilman had a six-car garage with its own automated car wash. Another had a thirty-one-room ranch-style house with nine bedrooms and a TV in the ceiling of the master bedroom. Another gave his grandchild a helicopter for Christmas.

Gray (and Masters, who has since moved to the United States) were not of that ilk. They shunned fancy cars and mahogany office walls, strolled the corridors in shirt sleeves, and insisted their employees call them Jim and John.

Gray is still refreshingly down-to-earth: a stocky man of seventy, happily married with three grown children, white hair cropped short. He drives a medium-size four-by-four. He gets his kicks from community work. He's been a director of the YMCA for more than twenty years and conceived the idea and led the drive for funds to set up a children's wilderness camp in the foothills. He raised the corporate funds for the Indian Friendship Centre in downtown Calgary for local and visiting natives. He was a founding director of the Calgary Academy, a private school for children with learning disabilities. In 1987 he co-chaired the local fund drive for Rick Hansen's "Man in Motion" world tour and helped raise $2,675,000.

Gray played a major part in establishing the Canadian Centre, a residential and treatment facility for drug-addicted youth. He and wife, Josie, have been instrumental in alerting the local business community to domestic violence and helping its victims. Gray is also on the board of governors of the Duke of Edinburgh's Award Charter for Business, devoted to "at-risk" youth.

His prominence in Calgary is evident one night when we leave a local restaurant together. There's a lineup at the entrance for seating, ranging from college students to greying business-men. Gray can hardly get out the door for the greetings and handshakes: it seems all remember a contact with him, a helping hand he gave them.

Gray tries to breakfast at least once a month with someone under thirty. "Just anybody. It can help you be young yourself. You hear about their frustration, their challenges, which are not all that different than your own when you were that age. They make you think. It energizes me. They're not in ruts."

Neither is he. About now he's swimming somewhere in northern Ontario. One of these years he will, figuratively, dip his toe in the Atlantic.

Where It All Begins

Off to the west, the slim tracery of the derrick soars 127 feet against the drab brown backdrop of Alberta's Porcupine Hills. Jim Gray's four-wheel drive follows a muddy trail up into the foothills, west of Claresholm, where exploratory well Precision Rig 616TE is searching for natural gas.

"This is where it all begins," Gray says. There's a tinge of excitement in his voice. After forty-six years in the energy business, the gamble of the search still turns him on.

Everything in the business, he means, starts out with these wildcat wells, probing in untried ground for the oil or gas that could be a big field and make big money. Or fail.

Near the rig, the trail is freshly carved from the surrounding ranchland, topsoil and subsoil peeled back and piled separately alongside. When the drillers move on, the soil will be restored and seeded with native grass. Oil drillers are more environmentally conscious than ever before, although still not enough to please some.

One of a small cluster of trailers is rig manager Chris Coffey's office and home away from home: small bedroom, fridge, stove, TV, exercise bike, fax, phone, printer, and the office nerve centre, a sophisticated computer system that shows precisely what's happening on the rig at every moment.

Coffey, forty-three, dark hair and moustache with a clean-cut profile that TV producers would kill for, has been working the oil patch for twenty-four years. Back home near Dauphin, Manitoba, he has a wife, nine children, and a farm. He makes the eleven-hour drive back as often as he can. Coffey likes his job and his company, Precision Drilling, but looks forward some day to farming full-time.

"It's not for everybody," he says of wildcat drilling. "The travel, the being away, can be stressful. We see a lot of marriages fail."

Coffey and Gray begin talking in oilmen's code. For me they might as well be speaking Urdu, so I watch the rig outside. Up on the drill floor a five-man crew (from Alberta, B.C., Ontario, and Newfoundland) is working its twelve-hour shift. Another five will take over later. A third crew is on its week off.

A powerful electric motor is twirling a rotary table on the floor. A square chunk of metal called, inexplicably, the kelly is embedded in the centre of the table, spinning the drill stem. The stem consists of thirty-foot lengths, or joints, of pipe, screwed together and attached at the bottom to a thick-walled pipe called the collar. It supplies weight, and the rotary drill, worth about fifteen thousand dollars, screws into it. Its teeth on three rollers are studded with tungsten carbide to bite through underground rock, but they regularly wear out. There goes another fifteen thousand.

The crew spudded in five days before our visit, and already are down to 4,593 feet. At about 9,800 feet – according to the geological and geophysical data that brought them here – they should strike natural gas. Or not. No time-wasting here: operating this rig and paying its crew costs about thirty to forty thousand dollars a day. It doesn't take long to spend a million.

If Precision 616TE turns out to be a dud, they'll abandon the hole, dismantle the rig in two sections, patch up the damage to the soil, and move on.

"An exploration geologist has to be almost pathologically optimistic," Gray had said earlier (he was one himself). "Approximately 85 per cent of wildcats don't turn out. People *want* you to be right, because the product is so valuable. But it's very difficult, intellectually, to handle so much repetitive failure."

Coffey looks at his computer screen. "They're tripping," he says. "Would you like to watch?" A "trip" means the crew is pulling up the entire drill string to change the bit. We put on safety helmets, safety glasses, and earplugs to deaden the high-pitched whine of motor and drill works, and climb metal stairs to the doghouse, a small office beside the rig floor.

The five men on the floor are, you might say, a synchronized drill team. The driller operates the motor that lifts joints of pipe, *tons* of pipe, with draw works and cable. As each joint emerges, three roughnecks wrestle mammoth tongs to grasp the stem. With a whine of motor the driller unscrews one length. High overhead, at the top of the rig, the derrick man guides it to a vertical stack at one side of the derrick. *Clang, whirr, crash; clang, whirr* . . . It's as smooth, as intricate, as ballet, although the three roughnecks would hang me from the highest derrick for such a fanciful analogy. Real men don't perform a *pas de trois*.

Tripping is dangerous for the careless or unwary. *All* drilling, with its heavy high-speed equipment, is dangerous. Safety is a top priority, but men still get bruises or strains, on rare occasions lose a finger. Industry-wide, there are still a few fatalities.

For this the roughnecks get twenty dollars an hour and up, plus a ninety-five-dollar tax-free daily living allowance (unlike some rigs, this one doesn't have live-in trailers, so the men lodge at nearby Claresholm). A driller earns thirty-one dollars an hour. A toolpush gets a salary of $92,090 to $98,660 a year.

Two weeks after our visit, rig 616TE was dismantled and moved to Claresholm to await a new assignment. As an exploration well, its results would remain confidential for one year. By autumn 2003 the outer world would know if Chris Coffey and the boys had lucked in or not.

XII

THE THIRD SOLITUDE

Will it always be us and them?
Maybe only when they are totally celebrated
as them, *can there be an* us.

SISTER LESLEY SACOUMAN
Rossbrook House, Winnipeg

Street Waif

Words from a Regina police interview with a sixteen-year-old native girl in custody. Her father lived on a reserve. Her mother was dead. Her four sisters and three brothers were scattered among various relatives.

She had lived with an aunt and uncle on the reserve, moved to her grandmother's in the city "because the reserve was boring," left "because I didn't like the way she kept me in the house all the time," and went to another aunt's down the block.

"What happened at Auntie's?"

"Ummm, I drank while I was staying there."

"Did that go over well with her?"

"Just as long as I didn't break something."

Still drinking heavily, she moved in with a sister, smashed a car into a fence, and was charged with impaired driving.

"You talked about other girls, what they do on the street. Do you mean prostitutes?"

"Yeah."

"Do you work the streets at all, or have you?"

"No."

"Hey?"

"Uhhh, well I have, but it just kinda grosses me out."

"When was it?"

"When I stayed at my auntie's."

"How long did you work the streets?"

"I don't know, like, a month."

"A month?"

"A month or two."

"Were you working for anybody?"

"No, just working to get beer money."

"Was it every night, or . . . ?"

"No."

"How often, would you say?"

"I think every weekend."

Chasm

For generations the gulf between French and English has been known as Canada's two solitudes. On the prairies, there is a third solitude. Despite earnest efforts on both sides, and billions of dollars spent, the chasm between aboriginal and non-aboriginal people remains.

To some natives, whites are racist and insensitive. To some whites, aboriginals are chronic drunks, layabouts, and recipients of endless government largesse that has done little to improve their lot. To others they are the pitiful casualties of ancient treaties, reserve ghettos, and the residential schools.

Bridging the gulf is essential, and frustrating. Of Canada's nearly 1.3 million aboriginals, 38 per cent live in the three prairie provinces. In Saskatchewan and Manitoba, about 14 per cent of the people are natives. Those under age fifteen make up 38 to 42 per cent of the native population, which represents a growth rate almost double that of non-aboriginals. Given an aging non-native population and a high native birth rate, the relative size of the groups will change dramatically. By 2045, some projections say, aboriginals will form one-third of Saskatchewan's population. Presently, Winnipeg has more natives than any other community in Canada, around 63,000, or 9.5 per cent of the population.

The problem is, almost one in four members of Western Canada's aboriginal labour force is unemployed. In all three provinces, aboriginal personal income is approximately ten thousand dollars below the provincial average. A large proportion of their income (about twice as much as in the general population) is welfare or otherwise government-derived.

Looking ahead, Tom Flanagan, University of Calgary professor of political science, says, "If a third of your people are not working and on welfare and not paying taxes, what are you going to do?"

Flanagan is either devil or realist, depending on which side of the chasm you stand. His *First Nations, Second Thoughts* won the 2001 Donner Prize for best book on Canadian public policy. (The fifty-three-year-old Donner Canada Foundation supports projects that emphasize self-reliance, individual initiative, and independence.) Donner jury chairman Grant Reuber called the book "well-written, fully documented and effectively guarded." Phil Fontaine, grand chief of the Assembly of First Nations, called it "nothing more than racism."

Like it or not, Flanagan's book highlighted some crucial elements of the aboriginal situation:

1. "Unless there is serious public debate . . . Canada will be redefined as a multinational state embracing an archipelago of aboriginal nations that own a third of Canada's land mass, are immune from federal and provincial taxation, are supported by transfer payments from citizens who do pay taxes, are able to opt out of federal and provincial legislation, and engage in 'nation to nation' diplomacy with whatever is left of Canada."

2. The federal government pays $6.3 billion annually for the care and upkeep of status Indians. This includes medical treatment – drugs, eyeglasses, prostheses, ambulances – beyond what medicare provides for everyone else. Among its ill effects, Flanagan contends, are that people tend to not economize on things that come to them without cost, and it creates a sense of entitlement among those "inside the magic circle" while fostering resentment among those who are not.

There is not enough space here to address the huge, intricate problem of aboriginal land claims or self-government. This is simply a glimpse of prairie native people, their strengths, and their challenges.

The Aboriginal Industry

Each year a multitude of organizations across Canada spends untold billions – federal, provincial, and municipal dollars as well as contributions from such agencies as the United Way – in faithful efforts to improve the well-being of aboriginal people: providing education opportunities, finding jobs, reducing crime and addictions, and, under the embrace of "cultural healing," helping restore their sense of self-worth. These efforts, in addition to the actual benefits and services dispensed to native people, employ scores of natives and non-natives in the aboriginal industry.

Is it paying off? If you measure success by white standards – good job, decent house, nice car – there are plenty of examples of achievement: native M.D.s, Ph.D.s, teachers, lawyers, police officers, judges, hotel owners. The Federation of Saskatchewan Indians is developing a program to sell bison meat in Europe. There are aboriginal recording studios in Saskatchewan and Alberta, a financial consulting firm in Winnipeg, and an aboriginal oil company in Edmonton.

"Twenty five years ago, everything about being Indian was bad," says Regina novelist Gail Bowen, who teaches at the local Indian Federated College.

"Now," adds her friend Maggie Siggins, "these real tough, smart aboriginal businessmen – this is what is going to save this province. And they have access to government funds."

So they do. But sometimes, happily, accomplishment has less to do with the aboriginal industry or government dollars than with the individual's own sheer determination.

After Barbie

When Patricia Piché was little, her Cree mother and grandmother, experts in needle- and beadwork, taught her to sew. Like many small girls, she made outfits for her Barbie dolls. Unlike most, she parlayed them into a career.

Today, as proprietor of Patricia Piché Contemporary Fashion Designs, she makes spectacular outerwear – coats, vests, jackets of varying lengths – from denim, leather, canvas, and synthetics, adorned with silkscreened or appliquéd aboriginal designs. They sell for $250 and up throughout Western Canada.

Piché is soft-spoken but resolute, a poster girl for those old-fashioned virtues, talent and hard work. She graduated with honours from the tailoring program at Northern Alberta Institute of Technology, worked for other designers, then branched out on her own. She's completing a course in business management from an Edmonton community college. When she's not visiting fashion shows around the West she's home at Bon Accord ("If you blink your eyes, you'll miss it"), twenty miles north of Edmonton.

While her partner, Scott, attends to marketing, she labours in her basement workshop from eight in the morning to eight at night, sewing eight hundred to a thousand outfits per year. Her motifs are stylized bear paws, eagle feathers, buffalo, eagle heads, and more from aboriginal culture, in bright reds, rich browns, turquoise, black on white, whatever springs from her fertile imagination.

Being slim and comely with dark eyes and long black hair, she sometimes models her own fashions. And because mother and grandmother (still around, and very proud of their protégé) taught her traditional dances, she sometimes performs at native powwows, in costumes of her own design.

Patricia once lived in the city but found it too distracting. "It took too much of my concentration. This job needs 100 per cent of my brain, or I make mistakes." So far, the girl who played with dolls is right on target.

Hobbema to Hollywood

For Jonas Applegarth, thirty-two years old at the time, it was luck, coupled with his own willingness to take a chance, that plucked him from a Cree reserve at Hobbema, Alberta, where he was a farmer, to that most bizarre outpost of the world of fantasy: Hollywood.

Warner Brothers, preparing to shoot a horse opera called *Saskatchewan* near Banff, sent an advance man around the province to find Indian extras (the appellation "First Nations" was decades away). The recruits would have to ride horseback, shoot Mounties, be shot themselves (taking dramatic falls from the saddle), and mutter in crowd scenes.

To Jonas – a six-footer with a strong, white smile, sharp, bronzed features, and a 210-pound tapering build – it seemed like an okay way to pass the summer. The job paid $9.80 a day, not bad in the mid-1950s. He'd spent a decade on the Alberta rodeo circuit, handling mean broncos and learning to fall without breaking his neck. When it turned out that Hollywood would pay ten dollars extra per fall, Jonas bit the dust with enthusiasm. The director, Raoul Walsh, liked his style.

When it was over, Jonas went home to his wife, Helen, his daughters, Rachel and Bernice, and his oats and barley. The next winter Raoul Walsh began casting for *Battle Cry*, a Second World War movie that would star Van Heflin, James Whitmore, and Aldo Ray. The script had a bit part for "a full-blooded young Indian, tall and husky." Hollywood crooked its fickle finger at Jonas.

He took a horse-drawn sleigh to Hobbema and a bus to Calgary, where he was turned away from two hotels because he was native. At the airport, *Calgary Herald* reporter Myron Laka asked, "You pretty excited about going to Hollywood and acting with all the stars?"

"Don't think I'll like it," Jonas said.

Things took a better turn in Los Angeles. A company limo whisked him to a decent hotel. The next day the studio fitted him into a U.S. Marines uniform, gave him a crewcut, and introduced him to his role: Shining Lighttower, native recruit.

Only Hollywood could have concocted such a name, but Jonas didn't mind.

He felt bashful, he admitted later, but for the first time in his life whites were treating him as an equal. He learned his few lines and delivered them competently. After hours he hung out with the cast. ("That Van Heflin, he treated me like his brother.") He now had a stunt man (Applegarth the actor was no longer expendable, as Applegarth the extra had been) and an agent who took 10 per cent. Fans asked for his autograph.

When the movie was finished Jonas happily went home. He had a cheque for fifteen hundred dollars in his pocket for back pay. The reserve held a dance in his honour and Jonas made a speech, saying he would do his best to give Hobbema a good name. He bought new furniture and clothes for his family, and a half-ton truck for himself.

Two weeks later he flew back to Hollywood for a part in *Drumbeat*. For five weeks he earned $350 a week for riding horse-back, shooting cavalrymen, and behaving like a Hollywood Indian. His daughter Judy in Hobbema (Jonas and Helen had more children) reports that he made a fourth movie. Who knows what he might have accomplished? But Jonas died in a train accident in 1965, only thirty-eight years old.

The last night I saw him, Jonas asked, "Could you buy me a case of beer?" I did, keeping one eye cocked for the Mounties: in the 1950s Jonas Applegarth – minor movie star, earning a better-than-decent wage – was in Canada just another Cree. As such, he couldn't legally buy alcohol.

"Everything Happens for a Reason"

She could pass for a model: tall, poised, long black hair, great smile. No hint that Diane Redsky was once a foster child who repeatedly ran away, whose aboriginal parents died of alcoholism, who used drugs and booze, slept wherever she could find a bed, and by nineteen was a single mother.

Now, at thirty-three, she is programs director for Ma Mawi Wi Chi Itata Centre (commonly called Ma Mawi, meaning, in Ojibwa, "We all work together to help one another"). With an annual budget of about five million dollars, Ma Mawi offers family support, family-violence prevention, foster care, home-maker services, and youth support services. It is directed by neighbourhood councils; community residents have a stake in their own betterment.

Redsky is suited to the job. She laughs often, talks fast, and is ever in motion.

"I've seen lots in my life and really feel like I have a duty to do something about it," she says. "We're not given these experiences just to keep them to ourselves."

On any given day some five thousand Manitoba children (the majority aboriginal) are in care: about two-thirds of them are in foster homes.

"Some of that is warranted and some of it is not," Redsky says. "We think it more appropriate that kids be with aboriginal families and neighbourhoods. The kids can keep the same school, same friends."

(To this implied criticism of the Winnipeg Child and Family Service, a white foster parent replies, asking anonymity, "We all struggle to provide the urban aboriginal population with appropriate supports, but this is a diverse group of folks who don't necessarily have a lot in common except daily survival." Legislation was afoot in 2002 to turn over the task to two aboriginal authorities. "Every individual community has its own identity and culture; how these will all be taken into account when the authorities take over the city, I have no idea.")

Most of Ma Mawi's clients are aboriginal single mothers. It has a residential learning centre for teenage parents, where mothers can acquire basic parenting skills, and absentee fathers – if they can be found – can get to know the babies they sired and, maybe, help the mother. Ma Mawi holds retreats for couples to redefine their relationship and has an Honourable Men's Society to help men accept their responsibility to family and community.

As a child, Diane spent much time at her family reserve at Shoal Lake. "I could go into anybody's house if I was hungry or scared or whatever. I had a whole community. There was a strong sense of connection." That sense of community clings in the urban setting. "We laugh about it. We say, 'Yeah, we travel in packs.' One car and everybody will just get in and we go off."

As a teen, Redsky fled every foster home because it *wasn't* home. Even so, she went to school each day and graduated from grade twelve. "It's not because I loved education," she says with cheerful candour. "It was where my friends brought me food and where I got my drugs. Then I'd figure out where I was gonna sleep that night."

She went into adult education, became a community worker, and "being an aboriginal woman, a single mom, and a bigmouth, got involved in some causes." Ma Mawi offered her a job.

"Actually I lied to get the job," she says merrily. "I did!" She told them she understood budgets, knew all about child development, and could write the proposals so dear to bureaucracy. "I knew nothing. I just knew that I cared. And that I loved kids. So I got the job and I stayed up many nights, all night, just reading things, figuring it out, asking for help."

Redsky is convinced that everything happens for a reason. When Ma Mawi asked her to develop the residential learning centre for teenage mothers, she dipped into her past. "I knew exactly what not to do. We're not locking nobody nowhere." In one foster home she was kept locked in her room. "And I understand being scared and not really knowing where you fit."

Now she knows where she fits.

"I'm at that point where I can appreciate everything that has happened. I wouldn't be able to do this stuff, wouldn't have the heart and the commitment to do it, if I didn't believe it."

A Place to Be Safe

"We recognize that sometimes kids cannot be at home," Diane Redsky says. "It's not safe for them at home."

Other establishments are likewise offering a safe haven for natives, adult or child: the Main Street Project, Rossbrook House, and the Boys and Girls Clubs of Winnipeg.

Winnipeg's six Boys and Girls Clubs deal with six- to eighteen-year-olds who are deemed at risk. They offer alternatives to street life, with after-school and evening programs including leadership groups, recreation, cultural pursuits, anti-racism sessions, sports, and counselling on substance abuse. Roughly 70 per cent of its nearly four thousand membership is aboriginal, many with major culture trauma.

"There's probably more culture shock for aboriginal kids than for kids coming to Canada from countries far away," says executive director Michael Owen. "If you're coming from a community where there's 97 per cent unemployment and move into a city, where culture is defined by employment, you're lost."

The clubs recently analyzed their results: 62 of 112 gang members who were club attendees were no longer in gangs; 18 of 36 actual or potential arsonists have kicked the fire-setting habit; 7 of 31 suicidal children are no longer considered at risk; and of 117 kids considered "socially withdrawn," 50 have come out of their shells.

Sister Lesley Sacouman, fifty-five, co-founder and executive director of Winnipeg's Rossbrook House, is slim in a plain dark-blue dress. Her hair, lightly sprinkled with grey, hangs becomingly just above her shoulders. Compassion and humour play over her face.

A member of the Sisters of the Holy Names of Jesus and Mary, she has lived and worked in the inner city since 1971. Rossbrook House is where children can be safe from the strains of dysfunctional homes or the perils of the street. They play games, sing, study in Rossbrook's schools, or just hang out. In a typical year, five thousand different children pass through its doors, nearly half of them aboriginal.

They've been coming here for twenty-seven years. Before that they were filing into Sister Lesley's home down the street. Then her friend and associate, the late Sister Geraldine McNamara (a saintly soul who died of cancer in her forties), quit her job as lawyer and teacher and rented Rossbrook, a vacant United Church building, for a dollar a year.

Rossbrook is open around the clock on weekends and whenever school's out. For many native children it is a second home. Some live on the streets for a while, then bounce from house to house, then go back home, but Rossbrook is always their fallback. And they are always included in the decision making.

"Because they've had to grow up so fast in some ways, they're used to making decisions," Sister Lesley says. "Their survival skills would run circles around yours and mine any day. We feel we must never weaken those skills."

"Will it always be us and them?" I ask.

"Maybe only when they are totally celebrated as *them* can there be an *us*. One day, maybe."

Seeing aboriginal people as she does – up close, daily, and with a trust not accorded the rest of us – she has unbounded admiration for them.

"They've given me a lot of life. They carry a tremendous burden but have gifts that could redeem us as a society if we could see them. Their honesty. Their family involvement. Their value on time, which breeds a different kind of efficiency than what the white world projects, allows people to live healthy and reflective lives. They are affectionate people. They're inclusive. They'll allow anyone into their circle.

"They face problems straight on. That's how they survive, being honest and open and not hiding things. And I believe that that's a very healthy way of living."

To the inevitable question – does Rossbrook House succeed? – there is an inevitable response: How do you measure success?

"Everybody's life here is better, because kids here experience respect and love," she says. "In terms of success in the world's eyes, whether kids have gone on to complete university, yes, there are a handful. Others have jobs at banks or recreational centres or in their own community.

"But I couldn't live my life on those. My success story, what gives me energy, is seeing a child come here who looks down in the dumps and seeing them playing pool or badminton and smiling. Then I know that they can cope with the things that I can't help them cope with."

She walks me to the stairs.

"Where did you park?"

"On the street."

"Well," says Sister Lesley, with a mischievous smile, "I hope your car is still there."

And with her spirit and sense of humour intact, she goes back to keeping her children safe from those mean streets.

The Main Street Project started in 1972 with a walking street patrol: two dedicated souls prowling the neighbourhood for those needing shelter or medical help. Today it provides a refuge for people every day, twenty-four hours a day, and offers them a chance to change. Two-thirds of its clientele is native.

Executive director Joan Dawkins is a former lawyer who opted to leave the corporate towers for the grittiest basement level of Winnipeg's streets. "I was never very happy practising law," she says. "It took me twenty years to figure it out."

She has flecked grey hair crisply cut, a firm handshake, an unwavering gaze, and is as clear-eyed and pragmatic as anyone I met on the problems of those who "cascade down through the cracks in the social-service chain."

With a staff of fifty-five, the Main Street Project still runs a modified patrol, as well as a homeless shelter and a drunk tank for the Winnipeg police. "Other services say, 'If you're drunk, don't come here.' Main Street Project says, 'You can come here even if you're drunk as long as you're not hitting us.'"

Some clients have held jobs but no longer can. Others have never worked steadily. They are eighteen and older; a growing number are seniors. For Main Street that means over fifty-five; by then, if you've lived a street life, your body is old.

"Our clients experience a lot of violence and they perpetrate a fair amount of it," Dawkins says. "They come looking for a place to be safe."

Here they find it: a hot meal, a kind word, a TV to watch, a place to shower or wash clothes, a quiet night's sleep, a respite from the hard world outside.

"We see past the dirt and past the violence and see the humour and the spirit that still exists in there," Dawkins concludes. "They're just folks like you and me. Their experience of life is different, but these guys have a wonderful sense of humour. They're amazingly loyal and supportive to each other. Even though they may be fighting one day, the next day they may be sharing what little they have. They're probably the most resilient human beings I have ever met."

Drugs, Drink, and Crime

For all the effort, hope, and good intentions, the aboriginal story remains very dark in places. Life on the reserves is not idyllic. Sometimes those in authority siphon off money, leaving the rest of the people in poverty. Sometimes young women are impregnated by their fathers or grandfathers.

Around parks and bus stations in most major prairie cities, natives hunch in the familiar despondent slouch of the down-and-outer. David Martin, adviser to the Peguis Reserve, drives me around one of Winnipeg's seedier sections north of the CPR tracks. Street signs read, "No Turns 6 p.m.–6 am," an effort to discourage the johns who cruise for teenage prostitutes, David says. If the signs keeps them from circling until they find a girl, maybe they'll give up and go home.

In Regina, far from comfortable suburbia, there's a stretch of shabby houses marked by graffiti, broken stairs, torn screen doors, plastic sheets on broken windows, abandoned couches, discarded tires. Sometimes, clusters of laughing children. Sometimes, older kids with wary eyes and street-tough grins flashing finger signs that identify their gangs. Most of the residents are native, renting these pitiful places from absentee landlords. They are breeding places for hopelessness and crime.

Aboriginal crime in Saskatchewan is high throughout the province but twice as bad on the reserves. For violent offences the rates (in a 2000 study) were almost five times higher. Fifty-two per cent of accused persons in Regina and Saskatoon were aboriginals, who represented only 9 per cent of the population.

Relationships between police and natives are often strained. Police grow weary and cynical of the inordinate number of natives they take into custody. Natives say the police are racist. In 2001, two Saskatoon police officers were convicted of the unlawful confinement of an aboriginal man. They left him in a field south of the city on a frigid January night. (He made his way to a nearby power station and survived.) Both officers were sentenced to eight months in jail and discharged from the force; they finished their sentences in a halfway house.

Regina police chief Cal Johnston acknowledges that 74 per cent of people imprisoned in Saskatchewan are aboriginal. "What's going on? Are we picking on them? Not necessarily. From a police point of view, we start with a crime and follow it through to the offender on the other end."

He cites poverty, school dropouts, single-parent families, addictions, the high growth rate of the aboriginal youth population, and "the dysfunction that has been going on for generations." The Regina Police Service, Johnston says, is learning about traditional native practices and values. A previous police chief bought a teepee and asked local First Nations elders how to paint it to capture the proper symbolism and meaning. Now, each spring, the cops raise the teepee in an inner-city neighbourhood and invite people to a pipe ceremony followed by a traditional feast.

Substance abuse, crime, and poverty go hand in hand among urban aboriginals.

"Poverty breeds that need to find release when you can't go on a holiday, or you can't go to a movie and then to dinner," says Winnipeg's Sister Lesley Sacouman. "Crack and cocaine imprison people far more tightly than alcohol. It is so immediately physically addictive and so expensive, you have to become involved in a life of crime to afford it. And it's promoted by gangs." The gangs recruit girls as young as eight for prostitution.

Alcohol remains a familiar, almost routine addiction for those who can't afford drugs. "Almost every aboriginal child that I know grows up in an alcoholic environment," says Sister Lesley. "Nobody has just a glass of wine with supper. The pattern they grow up in is, 'Oh, you've got some money, we can celebrate.

Let's have fun. Buy a ton of it. Drink it.' So there's always drunkenness. I don't know if I've ever been in an aboriginal home where it's just one drink. I've been in aboriginal homes where there's no drinking. It's all or nothing. If you grow up in that environment, you have a propensity towards it."

The New Buffalo

"A reserve is a nice place if you don't need a job," Wayne Helgason is saying. He is big, bluff, self-confident, hair down to his collar, his robust features reflecting more of his Icelandic father than his Saulteaux mother. "A lot of seniors move back to the reserve. It's a country setting. You're given a house by the band. Nobody on a reserve owns their house, because it's federal land."

Helgason is president of the Aboriginal Council of Winnipeg and played a major part in the acquisition of the old CPR station in the heart of downtown, which would become the Aboriginal Centre. But today he wants to talk about young people who leave the reserve to seek higher education. A chief of the Federation of Saskatchewan Indian Nations once said that education is the "new buffalo," replacing for natives the real buffalo wiped out a century ago.

Nearly everyone applauds education for native youths. In "Looking West 2003," 51 per cent of Western respondents cited lack of education and training as the root of native unemployment. (Another 30 per cent think it is because natives are unwilling to work.)

In some cases, native bands help supply living costs for city education. "Unfortunately," says Helgason, "they may have a grade ten or twelve on the reserve, but when they're tested here for academic proficiency often they test at a grade-seven or -eight level." It's one of many harsh realities of the switch to urban life.

Helgason grew up with a foot in both worlds. His mother attended residential school, returned to the Sandy Bay reserve, and subsequently married a handsome Icelandic lad. Residential school left her ashamed of her background; the Icelanders were proud of their roots. "So I always had two cultures at play. On the reserve, I'd see violence and chaos. The Icelandic side was no better economically, but most of their kids went on to careers."

Wayne obtained a degree in psychology at Carleton University in Ottawa, returned to Manitoba, worked in group homes and treatment facilities and became a social worker in the inner city with the Children's Aid Society, then executive director of the Ma Mawi Centre for five years.

A community campus in the Aboriginal Centre offers a university-entrance upgrade. Helgason is something of a role model to the students. "I meet with them the last Friday morning of every month. It's called Coffee With Wayne. It's a chance for me to tell them how important what they're doing is, and that their struggle can be just as hard, being back to school, as it is to win a prime minister's election."

Thirteen years ago the Peguis Band Educational Authority hired David Martin to help mentor young people going into Winnipeg to study. Its students were dropping out of university at two or three times the normal rate. Martin, now forty-three, with a B.A. in economics and political science, had worked in university-student counselling. Now he is the Peguis students' link between reserve and city.

Although Martin is white, the young people, who may be shy or suspicious, trust him. He is hefty, gregarious, most comfortable in jeans and workboots, and drives a big red truck. He coaches them on studying and writing tests, and helps them learn city skills: how to navigate public transit; what neighbourhoods are safe to live in; how to find a family doctor; how to write a resumé and hunt for jobs.

"When you come into a city, everything costs money," Martin says. "You can't seem to cross the street without having to pay for something." Most kids from the reserves don't know how to budget. He teaches them.

"You can't steal somebody else's life," he sums up. "Their skin and features never change, so they can't expect to become a carbon copy of white people. You simply have to point them in directions that seem right for them."

On those terms the program succeeds. The number of Peguis graduates is increasing. At year's end aboriginal kids have a separate convocation, a powwow. Parents who'd be reluctant to attend a convocation attended mostly by whites usually go to the powwow.

"They say that, in time, 15 to 25 per cent of the potential workforce in Manitoba will be First Nations," Martin says. "If they aren't equipped for jobs, that means a potential 15 to 25 per cent unemployment rate."

Putting native kids through university is costly, Martin admits. With tuition, books, and allowances, he reckons it averages about fifteen thousand dollars per student per year. Yet it is an investment in everyone's future.

Miracle at Peerless Lake

Sometimes, getting an education is as simple, and as difficult, as finding a brilliant educator.

In 1998, when the division superintendent invited David Newman to be principal of the all-native school at Peerless Lake, it was known as the worst school in Alberta. Its scores on provincial examinations were abysmal: every grade-three student had failed language arts and math; every grade-six and grade-nine student had failed them too, as well as science and social studies.

Newman was something of a wunderkind. He had grown up on the Stoney Reserve at Morley, Alberta, where his father was principal, then education and economic coordinator; his mother was a nurse before becoming an elementary-school teacher. Throughout his career he had taught in native schools by choice, turning down a job offer in Calgary. ("I like a challenge. It seems to me that a monkey can administer a thriving school.")

He had just finished fifteen years at Calling Lake, where he had briefly tried out some innovative theories. Peerless Lake, a community of 450 roughly midway between Peace River and Fort McMurray, was not a dream posting. The superintendent offered some bait. "You can hire a completely new staff," he said. And Peerless Lake would become a three-year pilot project, meaning Newman could experiment.

The lean and congenial forty-three-year-old – born in New Guinea, with several years in Australia and a year in Denmark before Canada – seized on it. He hired nine teachers, leaning heavily on maturity in life experience, not necessarily teaching experience. If they had no preconceived ideas about education, so much the better. He also flouted conventional wisdom by hiring an equal number of local teaching assistants. That first autumn he briefly waited, watching the performance of his 130 Cree students.

"Then two or three teachers came to me and said, 'Omigod, Dave, what can we do?' They were primed for change."

And change they got. Over the months that followed, Newman and staff:

- Put the seniors on a noon-to-six school day. "They were out on the street until three in the morning and got here dragging their tails, no good to us at all, for the first couple of periods." It worked; they came alive in the afternoon.
- Began serving breakfast at school. "They were coming in hungry. You could hear their tummies grumbling before

lunch." The school fed them a varying menu of cereal, muffin or pastry, and yogurt or fruit. (Eleven other schools in the division now also serve breakfast.)

- Hired a physical-education specialist (something of a luxury in budget-strapped schools, but Newman felt it was essential: "When we look good and feel good, we do good") to teach forty minutes of phys. ed. to every student, every day. The kids try everything from volleyball and cross-country skiing to wrestling and, of all things, archery, rugby, and cricket.
- Delivered report cards to the parents' homes. "It's a marvellous thing," Newman enthuses. "Every school should do it, especially native schools where you don't necessarily get parents coming to parent-teacher night. We reach 93 per cent of them in their own homes. And I have yet to have an irate parent come in to my office!"
- Grouped students in creative ways. During a day a student may be in three or four groups, exposing him or her to the teacher with the most expertise in a given subject. Newman also separates boys and girls in nearly all junior-high classes. It cuts down on flirting, teasing, swearing, and obscene gestures. "Teachers love it," Newman adds. "The students' behaviour, progress, and achievement have improved markedly."
- Found an oil-and-gas company in the area willing to train senior-high-school kids. "They pretty much walk right into a job, if they graduate."

The results are spectacular. Peerless Lake is now ranked in the top 30 per cent of Alberta schools. Seniors need to gain 100 credits over their high-school experience. In Newman's first year, the eight or nine seniors managed only 15 credits, total. Last year they amassed 325. Their teams often bring home medals from tournaments. One student won a gold medal in wrestling; another represented the school division at the world track-and-field championships in Edmonton.

What next for David Newman? Could he be a professional troubleshooter, going from problem school to problem school, a kind of pedagogical Lone Ranger?

"That has certainly been mentioned," Newman admits. "There are a couple of things I would like to finish off here. But I would like to spin the gospel, go in a school and say, try this and this and this, come back later and see how it worked."

Taking Charge

There's a feeling among some in the aboriginal industry that no amount of federal money or white liberal guilt will alleviate the native "problem" until natives themselves clean up their act, specifically, the mess on some reserves. Which brings us to Rita Galloway and her doughty compatriots in the First Nations Accountability Coalition. Galloway, a Cree in her mid-forties, is an achiever, and she's helping tackle some of the thorny problems head-on.

She was born and raised on northern Saskatchewan's Pelican Lake reserve. Her parents separated when she was young. Her father was illiterate. She had no role models "except my grandmother who, though not educated, was very loving." Regardless, Rita got through school on the reserve, looked around at the aura of hopelessness and despair, and knew she wanted something better.

"Sometimes I almost wished I'd attended a residential school," she reflects. "I know abuse went on at some of them. But I know some people who went to those schools who have turned out very well. Some of the things we went through on reserves were horrendous. The notion of the loving, supportive aboriginal family has been romanticized."

She put herself through university, doing odd jobs to help pay her way, and became a teacher. (Three of her sisters are also teachers, a fourth is a therapist.) Today she lives at Holbein,

Saskatchewan, where she and her husband raise cattle and run a fishing-and-hunting lodge. Her son is an accountant. Rita is completing her master's in educational administration at the University of Saskatchewan and hopes eventually to get a Ph.D. in environmental studies.

For more than a decade, she and others have taken on the reserves' powerful and sometimes corrupt leadership. Reserve residents, and taxpayers outside, have long winced at stories of financial mismanagement. Governments give huge sums to band leaders who may or may not spend it for the good of all. Band accounts are closely guarded but scandal stories creep out.

In the late eighties, the educated Rita was invited to be administrator of her band at a salary of seventy thousand dollars, tax-free. After she looked at the books, she said, "What you're doing here is not legal. If you want to go with me to the RCMP, we'll sort it out." That suggestion didn't go down well. In the end she left, taking some documents with her. Over time, sympathetic elders fed her more documents. The Pelican Lake Concerned Citizens group sprang up. CBC publicity gave them a powerful boost. From this grew the Accountability Coalition, which now reaches across the Western provinces. At last, aboriginal people were taking charge of their destiny.

But not without pain. Manitoba Coalition leader Leona Freed reported harassment by native youth gangs. Galloway was verbally abused – "I didn't mind when they swore at me, as long as they didn't hit me!" – and some of her relatives on reserve were beaten up.

Yet more and more people quietly offered encouragement. "Some of the elders say, 'Don't back down, don't be timid,' and, 'What you are doing, somebody has to do,'" Rita says. Some MPs and MLAs turned out for Coalition forums. "It's ironic that the Canadian Alliance, the party called racist by its opponents, was the first to come out and support us."

Noel Starblanket, a former chief of the National Indian Brotherhood (now the Assembly of First Nations), spoke out on CBC in 2002: "I come down on the side of the Canadian Alliance, the First Nations Coalition for Accountability, and against my fellow First Nations chiefs.... I have personal knowledge of chiefs and councillors who have collected two hundred thousand dollars in per diems above their salary annually."

Some band leaders have taken themselves or their favourites on junkets far and wide at taxpayers' and band members' expense. The RCMP has investigated fraud allegations.

"Conditions on some reserves are like the Third World," Rita Galloway concludes. "If money was properly used, the standard of living wouldn't be so devastating. We can't blame it all on the white man."

With more realists like Rita, and reciprocal goodwill from the white community, Canada's third solitude could melt away once and for all.

XIII

THOSE WHO WENT AWAY

Age eleven
I was a clumsy beanpole of a knobby-kneed kid
walking into walls in the sub-zero Canadian Prairies
looking for a way out-of-town . . .

"First Words"
from *Between Lovers*, 2000

SHERI–D WILSON
Calgary poet, playwright, and performance artist

"And Departs for Far-Off Places . . ."

"When a Saskatchewan man shakes the dust of the province from his person," wrote that passionate prairie advocate Edward A. McCourt, "and departs for far-off places where the air is warm and the wind is quiet and there are hills and trees and water on every side, he finds himself, more often than not, still bound in spirit to that great and strange and savage land that shaped him."

McCourt could as well have said "prairie" for "Saskatchewan." But *does* the prairie always cling to one's boots? If the place is so magnetic, why do people leave? Do they ever look back and wonder?

Expatriates are everywhere. The Guess Who and Burton Cummings came from Winnipeg. So did veteran parliamentarian Mitchell Sharp, champion speed skater Susan Auch, former Canadian ambassador to the U.S. Allan Gottlieb and his writer wife, Sondra, and political scientist Thomas Axworthy. Lloyd Axworthy, his brother, is from North Battleford. Michael Barnett, general manager of the NHL's Phoenix Coyotes and formerly sports agent to the stars (his clients included Wayne Gretzky, Brett Hull, Jaromir Jagr, Mats Sundin, Kurt Browning, Alexander Mogilny), was born in Olds, Alberta. The glorious voice of k.d. lang belongs to the world, but Kathy Dawn was born in Edmonton and grew up in Consort (although Alberta cattlemen have never felt the same about her since, in support of animal rights, she proclaimed that "meat stinks").

I put the questions to a few other former prairie chickens. Nearly all left for better jobs and money, but for nearly all, the prairie still lies gentle on their minds.

Like Re-Frozen Peas

Singer Connie Kaldor, with a string of albums ranging from *One of These Days* to *Love Is a Truck*, reflects, "I live in the East now, something I thought I never would do, and although my home is here, there is a sense of being an immigrant. [This] landscape hasn't made its mark deep enough."

One of her favourite places is the view from her husband's family farm near Willow Bunch, Saskatchewan. It's a high point overlooking a coulee and a long stretch of fields, sometimes dotted with grazing deer.

"The prairie landscape is so unique and powerful you would have to be a stone to not have it influence you. There are so few places in the world where the sense of space and pervading wilderness are in your consciousness." Kaldor says her songs – such as "Skies Are Bigger," "Wood River," "Whistle Gone," "Harsh and Unforgiving"– express her feelings more eloquently than any prose.

She was born in Regina, where her father was choirmaster at the local Lutheran church. She and her four siblings sang in the choir every Sunday. When other choir members didn't show up, Connie sang their parts, from bass to soprano.

She worked in theatre in Toronto but gravitated back to music. Before long she was singing her own material, headlining folk festivals, and releasing albums on her independent label, Coyote Entertainment. In live performances, she often takes her audiences on an audio trip to the legion hall, a prairie wedding, or a bonspiel. She always gets a laugh with "Prairie people are like peas that are thawed and re-frozen; we're freezing and we stick together in clumps."

"I get great pleasure when playing on the prairies to see people laugh and recognize just what is their culture," Kaldor says. "I have a true prairie sense of humour about the whole thing, a kind of dry-crop-failure sense of humour."

A Fascinating Microcosm

Humour, agrees sculptor Robert Murray of Pennsylvania, is integral to prairie life.

"Maybe more for my parents' generation," he says (born in 1936, he grew up in Saskatoon), "but we all inherited a terrible tendency to tell bad puns, which has my children driving their nails through their palms. And I am totally unrehabilitated."

Murray was tempted to stay in the West. He taught school, went to art school, had a chance for a job in a Regina art gallery, but there weren't enough galleries or museums at the time to sate his appetite. So New York it was.

"When you're growing up in Saskatchewan, it's kind of unappreciated on certain levels. . . . New York was such an exciting place, and at my particular point in life I couldn't have timed it better. One thing led to another and I forgot to go home."

Like nearly every prairie person, the lanky Murray grew up with a love for landscape: "Saskatchewan is a fascinating microcosm of geology or geography." He was a painter before turning to sculpture (and still picks up a brush for a change of pace), and his heroes were the Group of Seven. Now he is known for huge welded steel sculptures, painted in vivid colours.

Friends still see the prairie in his work. "It's probably got to do with certain qualities that some pieces have where people kind of imagine being out in wide-open spaces."

The Reverend Is Hooked

Strictly speaking, Reverend Neil Earle doesn't qualify. Now the pastor of two Californian congregations of the evangelistic Worldwide Church of God, he was born in Newfoundland, graduated from Memorial University, studied theology in England, and didn't reach the prairie until 1972. But how can you deny a man who – during a twelve-year stint as minister in Regina, Moosomin, Brandon, and Calgary – became an utter convert? If he preaches the gospel the way he celebrates the prairie, Reverend Earle surely sets the church on fire.

"Prairie people are wonderfully warm and hospitable," he enthuses. "When you make a friend there it is for life. I feel wonderfully privileged to have lived and worked among the honest, hard-working, unpretentious prairie folk. That changes a bit when you factor in Calgary" – presumably he's referring to unpretentiousness, of which Calgary has never been accused – "but compared to Tinseltown, Calgarians are true believers.

"There's no blue like prairie blue and no green like Manitoba in harvest time. The freshest air in the world, and when you live in L.A., that counts! I'm hooked. I always look for an excuse to go back."

"My Roots Are There"

Can a man remember his place of birth after sixty-two years, having lived there only four years? David Silcox, vice-president and managing director of the fine-art auction house Sotheby's Canada, does. He distinctly recalls climbing a hill in Moose Jaw (hills aren't very high there, but neither was Silcox at age four).

He was born the son of a United Church minister at the end of the Depression. "It was a period very important to my father and mother, so it became vivid in the family. The hard times were part of what we all grew up with, a kind of a baseline that carried through our lives."

During part of that time they lived in a Briercrest manse, the only brick house in that part of Saskatchewan. A family memoir records that "it was covered with wooden shingles and a heart-breaking mortgage of $4,000. . . . The furnishings were comfortable, mostly purchased from Edna Jaques [famous poet and family friend]. . . . Water was scarce. David's bath water served also to wash his clothes, then the floor, and finally to water what there was of hope for the garden."

After his father was transferred east, Silcox went on to earn an M.A. in English, then studied art history. He worked variously as visual-arts officer for the Canada Council, associate dean of fine arts for York University, director of cultural affairs for the City of Toronto, federal deputy minister of communications, Ontario's deputy minister of culture and communications, and chairman of the Canadian Film Development Corporation.

Despite his *crème de la crème* career, Silcox is totally charming and approachable as befits a prairie denizen.

"When I'm travelling, as soon as I get west of the Ontario-Manitoba border and mention I was born in Moose Jaw, you see the defences melt away," he says. "I still feel a wonderful connection when I go back there, even though my recollections are zilch. My roots are there."

The Man Who Walks Like a Farmer

His prairie roots couldn't have been farther behind – so he thought – that day in the 1970s when Peter Hendry, once of McAuley, Manitoba, flew from Rome into Tunis.

At the airport a stranger hailed him, "Mr. Hendry, Mr. Hendry, over here!" She was a secretary from the Food and Agriculture Organization (FAO).

"How did you know who I was?"

"Easy," she said. "Mr. Fraser [an FAO colleague who had gone ahead] told me, 'Just look for someone who walks like a farmer.'"

Hendry ruefully guesses it was true. During the Second World War, as a twelve-year-old helping his father on the family farm, he developed a lasting and distinctive gait from shuffling behind teams of horses pulling harrows across ploughed fields. Even in Tunis, thirty-odd years later, you couldn't take the country out of the boy.

He might have stayed on the farm had it not been for one of those inspired teachers who sometimes crop up in a lucky student's life. This one urged Hendry to stay in school and try for a scholarship, which got him into university and a new direction.

He newspapered around Canada, freelanced with writer wife Jean in Europe, and ultimately became editor of the *Family Herald* before it closed in 1968. He joined the FAO, first in Washington, then Rome, where he edited its flagship magazine, *Ceres*, for ten years.

His prairie background surfaced often. "Whenever I had the opportunity to meet with peasant smallholders almost anywhere in the world, I did feel a sense of identity with their hardscrabble existence."

As once in a minuscule mountain orchard in Pakistan's Azad Kashmir, where the proprietor insisted on giving Hendry's party a jug of dubious-looking water, along with directions because they were lost. Or the imposing peasant woman in Peru, who, initially highly suspicious of a corn-seed collection mission from Lima that came to her doorstep, finally relented, served coffee, and gave a fascinating description of each of about ten different varieties of indigenous corn she cultivated.

"Here were attitudes to the outside world I could recognize and be comfortable with," says Hendry, who now lives in Guelph, Ontario. "Simple hospitality, rugged independence, and healthy skepticism."

"No Free Lunch"

Neil Wood relates to those attitudes. So does Robert Peterson. Perhaps that, in part, is why both soared to the pinnacle of their professions.

Wood's father was a Barnardo boy, one of thirty thousand British children plucked from poverty and shipped to Canada by the Thomas Barnardo organization. Most often they ended up as indentured servants to farmers. Not surprisingly the son, born in Winnipeg in 1931, "grew up with the attitude that we had to look after ourselves. I delivered newspapers, delivered groceries for stores, whatever. There was no free lunch."

Wood graduated from the University of Manitoba in commerce, worked a year with the Great-West Life insurance company, got an M.B.A. from Harvard, and took a Toronto job in Great-West's mortgage department. Still imbued with his father's maxim ("Life is not a free ride"), he rose to head the real-estate giant Cadillac Fairview. Now retired, he retains several directorships, including the International Council of Shopping Centres, of which he was president in 1981. He lives in Ontario, winters in Florida, but "I still think of Winnipeg as home."

Robert Peterson, son of a banker, grew up "a nomad." Born in Regina, he lived variously in Lloydminster, Wiseton, and Estevan in the forties and fifties. "In the prairie in those days there was always someone in the community who came from somewhere else." His own father was born on a boat coming to Canada from Iceland. "They brought a lot of experience of adverse times."

Couple that with the still-raw memory of the Depression among his elders and "one tended to be frugal. It was a society not rich in material goods but in social life." It was also a place that you left if you wanted to prosper. His teachers, recognizing his potential, advised him to get out in the world.

After earning an M.A. in chemical engineering from Queen's, he worked for Imperial Oil in Alberta and with its parent in the United States. The West, he thinks, affected his view "of what is success and what shapes success." With that outlook on life he rose to become chairman, president, and CEO of Imperial in Canada, until his retirement in 2002.

Still a Little Prairie Flower

"I still think of myself as my father used to describe me," says Jeannine Locke of Toronto. "Just a little prairie flower growing wilder by the hour."

She grew up in two Saskatchewan towns: Star City and Shellbrook. Her father was a dentist, her mother was a dedicated church worker, and she "was the smartest kid in school. Because I was smart the principal brought in books for a class that he called Modern Problems, and he tested me regularly. I don't recall the other kids considering this favouritism. I think they pitied me."

She became the thirteen-year-old rural correspondent for the Prince Albert *Daily Herald*. Later she got a job at the *Saskatoon StarPhoenix* for twenty-six dollars a week, which, said the managing editor, made her "the most overpaid woman in Saskatchewan."

That aside, she liked the job. "At the *StarPhoenix* I was treated like all the guys, no playfulness or rancour. I think that was a Western thing – women were so important to their communities that they couldn't be treated as inferiors. I'm grateful to have been born, raised, educated, and introduced to employment in the West. I was always treated better than well, and that's the way I always expected to be treated."

She left Saskatoon in 1950 to seek her fortune in the East, as so many have done. She worked at the *Ottawa Citizen*, *Chatelaine*, the *Toronto Star* as London bureau chief, then the *Toronto Star Weekly*, and finally put in twenty-one years with the CBC.

Prairie prudence is imbedded in her bones.

"My father had graduated from the University of Toronto into the Depression and I can remember that once, when we were planning a holiday with relatives (of course), Mum made us kids understand that it wasn't a certainty – it depended on Dad being paid money instead of a side of beef. To this day I consider it immoral to spend a lot of money on a restaurant meal, for example."

Locke believes there's an egalitarianism "in the marrow of Western bones in the long wake of the Depression. If no one has any money, there's no effective hierarchy.

"I wouldn't go back. There's a narrowness there that cancels out some of the virtues of the West. I could *not* live in a place that had an Alliance MP. And yet I still get homesick for Saskatchewan people, who, though they tend to hypocrisy, have a sweetness that I've met nowhere else."

The Bullshit Detector

"In truth, I am a stranger in a strange land when I visit the West now," writes Clellen W. Bryant, once of Lousana, Alberta. "A couple of years ago, there was a reunion of fifty Bryant cousins and second cousins in Rocky Mountain House. It was congenial and all that, but what was I doing among all these Stockwell Day enthusiasts and Mormon missionaries?"

Bryant worked his way through newspapers and magazines to the East and eventually to the United States, where he was on the editorial staff of *Time* and *Reader's Digest*. He now lives in Katonah, New York, with a thumb in many pies, including some editing for Time Inc. Custom Publishing.

"But hark," he adds, "there is at least one value that I hold high, not exclusively prairie, perhaps, but I did learn it there: the importance of keeping one's word, and of not making a promise unless one intends to keep it (items that too often have the life-span of a proton in New York and don't even count as intentions in Los Angeles).

"And yes, I think there is something about the prairie air that imbues one with a keen and active bullshit detector, which I have found has served me well, if not diplomatically. It is that bullshit detector, of course, that has made me an atheist and a leftist, that rings like a fire alarm every time the names Ronald Reagan or George W. Bush come up. . . . But then if the bullshit detector is prairie-grown, what's with all those Mormon missionaries and Stockwell Day supporters? The contradiction overwhelms."

Where Mosquitoes Dined Out

Richard Thomson, retired chairman and CEO of the Toronto-Dominion Bank, was born in Winnipeg and lived there and in Brandon until his banker father was promoted to Toronto head office in 1950. Thomson was only sixteen, just out of grade eleven, but he left the West with lasting memories.

One was of being shipped to the farm of relatives in Arcola, Saskatchewan, every summer during the polio scares that ran through Canada before the Salk vaccine was discovered. Another was in the dying days of the Depression when his father took Richard and a younger brother along on a weekend to take possession of a farm on behalf of the bank. The abandoned buildings with their broken windows and piles of dirt from dust storms were "frightening to a little kid."

Other memories, from those gentler times, are almost Norman Rockwell classics, shared by many of us of a certain age: walking to school in all weathers, playing hockey every winter night, even admiring one's teachers. "We had terrific teachers, because teaching was one of the better jobs in Winnipeg."

When Thomson's family moved east, he marvelled at the sights: paved highways and, especially, people sitting outdoors of an evening, dining in their backyards. It wouldn't have happened in the Winnipeg of his day: the mosquitoes would have eaten them alive.

"A Distinct Culture"

Broadcaster Larry Zolf, forty-odd years a CBC man, left Winnipeg in 1956. Now a sprightly sixty-eight, still with his trademark heavy-framed spectacles and generous proboscis (his latest book is called *Nose for News*), Zolf is part of a self-styled Winnipeg mafia, including writer Martin O'Malley and Peter Herrndorf, president and CEO of the National Arts Centre. "We all talk about Winnipeg a lot."

Zolf (like many of us) regularly mines his prairie upbringing for editorial gold. His column on the CBC Web site is rich in such Winnipeg nostalgia as: "We played road hockey because our parents couldn't afford to give us skates or even a real puck. It was a big childhood thrill when a Buick stopped in front of our road hockey game. Stanley Z, the king of illegal gambling in Winnipeg, stepped out of the car and yelled at us: 'Kids, here's a five-dollar bill. Buy yourself a real puck.' We used Stanley Z's puck until we lost it playing road hockey in a snowstorm."

Zolf – like Mel Manishen, another witty Winnipegger of my acquaintance – is master of the one-liner: "I like living in Toronto, 'cause it has no character. Winnipeg shoves itself in your face," and, "I'm a claustrophobic in Toronto. I'm used to walking across Portage Avenue [widest street in Canada]," and, "The rich in Winnipeg were more tolerant, they would marry the poor," which, Zolf suggests, improved the genetic pool in that city's higher society.

"I miss that racial mix," he sums up. "Winnipeg's not the finest place on earth. I miss it because it was my youth. It was a distinct culture, no bullshit."

"Being Open of Heart and Mind"

"I am a diehard Albertan," says author and former Edmontonian Katherine Govier. "The values, my parents' in particular, which are Western in many ways – to do with working hard and being a patriot and loving to be out-of-doors and being open of heart and mind – are still with me. It seemed to me when I was growing up that most things were possible, and, when the time came, that included my being a writer."

She left in 1971 to attend graduate school in Ontario, believing that to be a writer (she has written ten books), she "needed to live here, wanting to experience the Big Smoke." She and others like her regularly hold Alberta-mafia parties.

One, in Govier's Toronto home, drew three fire engines when the smoke alarm went off. "Other than watch the firemen run in with hoses, we talked and ate roast beef."

Good thing k.d. lang wasn't invited.

The down-to-earth prairie people who stayed behind are proud of their distinguished expatriates but not awed by them. Quite the contrary. Consider Jim and Vern Alcock, once from the Saskatchewan town of Central Butte. In the 1960s both won scholarships to McGill University and went on to considerable achievement. Vern became a senior manager with IBM. Jim Alcock obtained his Ph.D., teaches psychology at Toronto's York University, and has a private practice.

In 2001 Jim and his wife, Karen Hanley, attended a Central Butte reunion. Karen, in conversation with one of Jim's former classmates, asked if her husband and Vern had been resented in school, as the kind of brainers that everyone else loves to hate. The ex-classmate denied it.

"We knew they were smart," she said, "but we thought they just couldn't help it."

XIV

HOW DO WE HATE THE EAST?
LET US COUNT THE WAYS

*As far as Ottawa is concerned we're a flea
on a fly on a gnat's ass standing on coon shit.*

TERRY LAUDER
Calgary businessman

An Everlasting State of Mind

Let's be fair: not everyone on the prairie hates everyone in the east. Rarely is an Easterner hung in effigy from a prairie hydro pole (just the occasional member of parliament, nothing serious). Individual tourists from east of the Manitoba-Ontario border are greeted with warmth and courtesy (and the generous Eastern farmers who gave hay to the parched prairies in 2002 can expect cheering throngs and garlands of wild roses).

But beneath this civility and goodwill lurks a pervasive distrust. Robert Mummery, editor of the award-winning Minnedosa, Manitoba, *Tribune*, says flatly, "There's tremendous animosity between Western Canada and Eastern Canada. But we're not talking about people in Thunder Bay or North Bay. We're talking Toronto and Ottawa."

"East" in the prairie lexicon means the Centre.

In his last address to a Western audience as prime minister, Lester B. Pearson said, "I feel I have never succeeded in getting through to the people of the West." He was by no means the only prime minister to have failed, but was the only one honest enough to admit it.

In "Looking West 2003," 62 per cent of prairie residents overall said their provinces don't get the respect they deserve. Saskatchewanites felt it most keenly at 70.7 per cent. Albertans were next at 60.2 per cent, and even 56 per cent of Manitobans were aggrieved. When asked (in a 2001 survey) if their province lacked influence in national affairs, the respondents were more emphatic: 75 per cent of Saskatchewanites, 64 per cent of Albertans, and 57.8 per cent of Manitobans said it did.

"Canada has never really come to terms with the West," says Dr. John Conway of the University of Regina, "nor has the West ever really come to terms with Canada."

The reason, from the prairie viewpoint, is a massive accumulation of slights, injustices, and federal arrogance reaching back more than a century.

"Most of those issues are long gone and nobody knows about them any more," acknowledges political-science professor Tom Flanagan of the University of Calgary, "but they've created a state of mind that persists."

Precisely: a state of mind that is ingrained in the prairie soul. Ask prairie people how they feel about the East, and their disenchantment pours out in varying degrees of sorrow or outrage.

"Whenever prairie men gather for their morning coffee," says John Archer, a former president of the University of Regina and lifelong chronicler of prairie history, "their very first comment is, 'What've those stupid bastards down east done today?'"

"It's painfully obvious that we're just here to serve the East," says Stacy Wilson, an even-tempered, university-educated young farmer from Tugaske, Saskatchewan. "Politically we have no power. We're nothing. Government has no reason to do anything for us, and they don't."

Government would dispute that, but in the Western view no amount of loans, grants, or flying visits from myopic federal cabinet ministers can outweigh the wrongs.

"Less and less it is grievances that the federal system doesn't respond to, and more and more it is frustrated aspirations, particularly in Alberta," Preston Manning points out. "People with ideas on health care, how to make federalism work better, how to stimulate economic development – when those ideas are not taken seriously by the federal government, you offend ambitious people, people with clout, in a pretty dramatic way. Particularly when they find their ideas are better received in Texas or California."

Most federal politicians, Robert Mummery contends, have no knowledge of the West. "As an example," he said, in the summer of 2002, "Chrétien has been golfing in Florida more times since he was elected than he's been to Western Canada. And that's noticed by the people."

"I honestly think that I could stand on the street in Assiniboia, and of the first hundred people that went by me, I could replace the goddam cabinet in Ottawa with equally competent people," says Frank Hamilton of Mazenod. "I know I could, I *know* I could!" Hamilton is a former Tory MP, but Westerners of many political stripes agree with him.

A common Eastern reaction to such complaints is that prairie people are whining malcontents. Pierre Trudeau, with his famous insolence, said as much in a conversation with *Toronto Telegram* journalists in the late 1960s: "Some of my reading of the west is that it is always disenchanted. In the years when wheat is good and selling, it is disenchanted; if there is too much sun it is disenchanted; if there is too much rain it is disenchanted. . . ."

It isn't that simple. Calgarian Terry Lauder, whose pithy comment ("flea on a fly on a gnat's ass . . .") adorns the beginning of this chapter, runs a communications business with his wife, Anne McNamara, and another native Westerner, Ralph Hedlin. The stocky Lauder, fifty-seven, is Alberta-raised, can still ride a horse and swing a rope, and every year helps a rancher friend brand calves just for the hell of it. That, along with his language, might mark him as an archetypal redneck. Lauder wouldn't care if it were true, but it isn't.

He and Anne are gourmet cooks and wine connoisseurs (a dinner at their home can run: smoked goose-breast canapés; salad with grilled scallops; venison medallions with saskatoonberry sauce, asparagus, squash, onions, and Brussels sprouts; Pouilly Fume, port, cheese, and fruit). They own fine paintings and sculpture, and have travelled France in a houseboat. For many years they celebrated July 1 by camping in the Cypress Hills, with ringing renditions of "O Canada." Lauder doesn't clean his ears with a matchstick or blow his nose on his mittens. He is simply a prairie person – albeit more volatile than some – who is fed up to the teeth with Ottawa. In that he is fairly typical.

Although Ottawa and Toronto are the main targets of prairie outrage, some Westerners have doubts about the entire Eastern mindset.

"I think they are as a whole ignorant of anything outside their little pocket of the world," says Jocelyn Hainsworth of Redvers, Saskatchewan. "I had a conversation with a woman from North Bay during a flight home from Toronto. She couldn't see a problem with charges of federal patronage in the news at the time. She said, 'If I was in government and had a chance to help out my friends, that's what I'd do! Wouldn't you?' It's still hard for me to get my mind around it."

The Dispossessed

When Sigrid Eyre of Saskatoon tells her University of Saskatchewan agricultural students about the programs that Quebec gives its farmers, "they are green with envy. I think it's important that we know what happens in the various regions, so we know how dispossessed we are."

"Dispossessed" is a fitting description of the West since the founding of Manitoba. Before settlement, the sprawling plains west of Ontario were simply a fur reserve for the Hudson's Bay Company. After Confederation, the new Dominion of Canada bought the HBC lands. From then on central Canada regarded the West as its fiefdom.

"The Canadian expansionist movement was essentially an attempt to increase the hinterland of such centres as Toronto," writes Western historian Douglas Owram, "and, more generally, to provide an extension for the great trade artery of the St. Lawrence." (The word *hinterland* – sometimes defined as "backwater" – haunts Westerners to this day.) Clifford Sifton's celebrated quest for new prairie immigrants had a prime objective: *not* the well-being of the West but the enrichment of the East.

"The idea of a vast agricultural region buying from the East while pouring its produce through the Great Lakes system became a dominant theme of Canadian development for the next century," Owram adds.

Manitoba, the only prairie province in existence when Sifton launched his immigrant search, had already felt Ottawa's pique. Manitoba was founded in 1870, but the federal government – having had to make concessions to the new province (French-language rights, control of education, and settlement of Métis land claims) – got even by granting it a mere ten thousand square miles. It was known as the "postage-stamp province," to the merriment of Easterners. Alexander Mackenzie, leader of the Liberal opposition, jeered, "The whole thing has such a ludicrous look that it only puts one in mind of some incidents in *Gulliver's Travels.* . . ." He set the standard for a long line of Liberal jibes.

Not until 1912 did Manitoba attain its present size and boundaries. Earlier, despite foot-dragging from the Wilfrid Laurier government, plans went ahead to carve a province or three from the swath of North-West Territories between Manitoba and B.C. One of six proposals would have had Manitoba swallow up much of what was is now Saskatchewan. Another called for a single large province named Buffalo. It was the brainchild of Frederick Haultain, premier of the North-West Territories from 1896 to 1905. It made sense, he said, because the area was already administered as a single unit, one provincial government would be more efficient than two, and one big province would help counter the power of the East.

That last item was precisely what the East did not want. Prime Minister Laurier feared "one large province would assert a preponderant influence" in parliament. Ontario and Quebec wouldn't let those uppity Westerners gain any real control. So Alberta and Saskatchewan were born in 1905, not big enough to be threatening. (The single large province would certainly have exerted some badly needed political influence. On the other hand, a Westerner announcing in Toronto that he came from the city of Moose Jaw in the province of Buffalo would never have lived it down.)

Neither of the new provinces, nor Manitoba before them, was given jurisdiction over its mineral resources. Ontario, Quebec, Nova Scotia, and New Brunswick were immediately granted those rights upon entering Confederation. So were British Columbia, formed in 1871, and Prince Edward Island, in 1873.

"The plain fact," write Calgarians Don Braid and Sydney Sharpe in *Breakup: Why the West Feels Left Out of Canada*, "is that seven provinces entered Confederation as legal equals, but Manitoba, Saskatchewan, and Alberta did not." Theirs was second-class membership.

After twenty-five years of cajoling and complaining, the three provinces received their due in 1930. The Laurier Liberals had withheld the mineral rights on the premise that they were part of the Dominion's purchase from the Hudson's Bay Company. In the late 1920s Regina lawyer Bram Thompson proved Ottawa had never had that right: only *administrative* control had been transferred to the Dominion.

Little wonder that the prairie West has kept its guard up ever since. Or that it has continually experimented with new political parties: Provincial Rights Party, Non-Partisan League, United Farmers, Co-operative Commonwealth Federation (now the NDP), Social Credit, Reform (now the Canadian Alliance), Western Canada Concept, Western Canada Federation, Confederation of Regions, National Party, Saskatchewan Party. All were efforts to find a strong standard-bearer for the West. None has formed a federal government.

Let Us Count the Ways

Mineral rights didn't end the malaise. The West continued to endure a succession of perceived indignities. In the perilous Depression years, "bankruptcy became a way of life for western farmers," writes Tom Flanagan. Farmers "had to sell their grain on world markets while the protective tariff, legislated for the benefit of eastern manufacturers and workers, prevented them from taking full advantage of cheaper American farm machinery and consumer goods."

The Canadian Pacific Railway, with its near-monopoly on rail transport, was for generations a favourite target for prairie wrath. "My paternal grandfather was a rancher south of here," says political-science professor Barry Cooper of the University of Calgary. "He talked about the 'goddam CPR.' For the longest time I thought that was the first name of the railroad."

Alberta claims to be the biggest contributor to the cost of Confederation. It's estimated that, in 2000, every living Albertan paid a net $2,905 for the privilege of being Canadian. Over the last thirty years, the province says, it has poured about $200 billion into the federal government.

National elections are always a burr under the Western saddle. With the prairies heavily outnumbered in electoral seats (a total of 54 in the three provinces versus 75 in Quebec and 103 in Ontario) elections are nearly always settled before the polls close in Manitoba, Saskatchewan, and Alberta. In effect, they are disenfranchised.

Gordon Gibson, a senior fellow with the Fraser Institute, writes in *Memos to the Prime Minister*, "Canada has a primitive, even pathological version of the British parliamentary system. It amounts to a four year elected dictatorship by a prime minister with a majority (which our equally primitive electoral system regularly delivers – last time, for example on the basis of the support of only 41 per cent of those actually voting).

"This system locks whole regions out of effective representation in the government. Any region . . . that has the temerity to vote for the losing party has little clout."

"The House of Commons under our current first-past-the-post electoral system has proven unable to provide fair and balanced representation to Canada's regions," agrees John Conway of the University of Regina.

Within the House of Commons the Atlantic provinces are quite overrepresented, Tom Flanagan points out. An "arcane provision" in the constitution, going back to the days of Robert Borden, stipulates that a province cannot have fewer MPs than members of the Senate. This ensures representation in Nova Scotia and New Brunswick does not fall below ten because each has ten senators. P.E.I. has four senators so must always have four MPs.

"Quebec is the balance wheel," Flanagan says. "The system starts by giving Quebec seventy-five and adjusts the other provinces in proportion to Quebec. The fixed points in the system are all in the East, so the West is always behind in number of seats. If you're playing a political game, you get more votes per dollar by creating policies that target Quebec and east. You've got a bigger number of seats at play there for a smaller expenditure. The system is inherently sluggish and will probably remain that way."

Writers Braid and Sharpe call the introduction of the Canada Pension Plan in 1966 a classic example of Eastern paternalism: "Ottawa struck a separate deal with Quebec, made sure Ontario had no objection, and then revealed the details to the rest of the provinces. There were really three senior partners in the country – Ottawa, Ontario, and Quebec – and eight junior ones."

In 1986 the federal Tories yanked the CF18 aircraft-maintenance project away from Winnipeg – which had the lowest and, experts say, technically superior bid – and gave it to Canadair in Montreal. Yet another example of Quebec's favoured position at the federal trough. Westerners were not surprised to read in a 2000 edition of the *Globe and Mail* that the Chrétien Liberals had handed out millions more in grants to Quebec than to all the Western provinces combined.

Along with those larger issues comes a steady dribble of petty insults, each in itself a mere mosquito bite but aggravating in total. Such as the time in 1989 when then Ontario Tory MP Don Blenkarn had an attack of foot-in-mouth disease during a meeting in Edmonton over the proposed GST. As Braid and Sharpe report it, Blenkarn said, "I fail to understand how the level of education can be so low in the community. I guess what we ought to do is send a bunch of grade five school teachers out here. I've never seen such stupidity in all my life. I wonder what they are, out to lunch or what." They hanged Blenkarn in effigy the next time he ventured west.

In 2001 Will Chabun of the *Regina Leader-Post* sent me an e-mail with a covering note: "For some insights on why the West is pissed off, see this." It was a column from Toronto-based *Now*, a free weekly tabloid. *Now* had sent a writer to Red Deer to interview a lawyer who was suing Stockwell Day.

His lead set the tone. As he drove into central Alberta, "My year took a turn into the hick dimension. . . ." He avoided a formal dinner for Ralph Klein (was he invited?) because "I don't want to tip off the Alliance types that a pinko reporter from 'gawd damn Toronaw!' is snooping around town."

In fact, his presence if known would have drawn only glazed looks in the West. Although *Now* runs some solid news stories, it is best read for its pop-culture coverage and its many pages of adult classifieds displaying semi-clad bodies of all sexes.

Now's correspondent exulted at finding an actual bookstore in Red Deer (as of 2002 there were nine new or second-hand stores). In a small Vietnamese restaurant, he wanted to "hug the owner but content myself with telling him his soup is the best thing I've eaten since I got to town." He said he was "not ashamed to admit that I believe Toronto is the centre of Canada's universe" (he *must* have been joking).

Maybe the entire screed was just a clumsy send-up. Is the West too quick to take offense? In 2002, when Izzy Asper & Sons fired publisher Russell Mills of the *Ottawa Citizen*, the resultant outcry rang across the land. But Reginan Alan Beasley in a letter to the editor noted, "Most of the commentators in the *Globe and Mail* could not refrain from pointing out repeatedly that the Aspers are from 'the West' and used Winnipeg as a near pejorative term in their analysis. Jean Pigott, former chairwoman of Ottawa's National Capital Commission, appeared to encapsulate the tone of the reaction best: 'I'm indignant. . . . We are the fourth-largest community in Canada and someone from the West does this to us.'"

This, Beasley concluded, revealed the East's true attitude. Overly sensitive? If so, count me in; I found the same thinly veiled sneer in much of the Eastern coverage.

Although some of the sins, errors, and omissions over the years were attributable to federal Tories, the Liberals have surpassed themselves. As David Smith wrote in *The Regional Decline of a National Party: Liberals on the Prairies*, "The Liberal party has been the author of its own demise in western Canada." He cited a list of unpopular policies over several decades, from federal minister of trade and commerce C.D. Howe's refusal in the 1950s to make cash advances on farm-stored wheat, to the bilingualism campaign in the 1970s. "Each action revealed an insensitivity to western opinion which apologists found difficult to explain and which others interpreted as further cause for distrust."

Some parties would have adjusted their policies accordingly. The Liberals know they don't need the West to get elected.

OTHER VOICES

As Westerners never tire of repeating, the Canadian fact is not *a simple matter of English or French. Jim Carr, president and CEO of the Business Council of Manitoba, remembers once when the message got through.*

In 1998 Daniel Johnson, who had just announced his retirement as leader of the Quebec Liberal Party, went to Winnipeg to make a speech. Carr snagged him for a breakfast meeting of the council.

On short notice, twelve or fifteen CEOs gathered around the table. Johnson spoke at length on the importance of Western Canadians understanding the basic bargain of Canadian federalism: that it was between the English and the French. And until Westerners recognized that basic fact of Canadian history, Canada would not be whole as a nation.

"So Art DeFehr, president of Palliser Furniture, and I looked around the room and winked at each other. Not a single person around the table that morning was either English or French."

DeFehr responded to the guest speaker with a reminder of the third component of Canadian life – those who came from neither England nor France: Italians, Jews, Ukrainians, Mennonites, Irish, Icelanders.

Johnson got the message, Carr says. "He wrote me a note afterward, thanking us for introducing him to reality of the rest of Canada that he hadn't appreciated."

"Let the Eastern Bastards Freeze in the Dark!"
All the aforementioned affronts, large and small, pale beside the Trudeau government's introduction of the National Energy

Program (NEP) in October 1980. After twenty-three years it rankles still.

The NEP came on the heels of a 160 per cent increase in world oil prices in 1979-80 and a long standoff between Ottawa and Alberta over energy pricing and revenue-sharing. The program was Ottawa's three-pronged attempt to achieve energy security (meaning oil self-sufficiency), to redistribute energy wealth in favour of the federal government and consumers, and to ensure greater Canadian ownership of the oil industry.

To accomplish this, Ottawa – without consulting the affected provinces or industries – established grants to encourage oil drilling in remote areas; grants to consumers to convert to gas or electric heating; new taxes on the oil industry (pouring billions into the federal treasury, supposedly to be shared with other Canadians); a 25 per cent government share of all oil and gas discoveries offshore in the north; and a bigger role for the Crown corporation Petro-Canada. Petro-Can was soon intensely hated in Alberta. Its red-brick building in downtown Calgary was dubbed the Kremlin.

The Progressive Conservatives dismantled the NEP after their 1984 election victory, but the West didn't forget. If the oil and natural gas had been in Ontario or Quebec, Westerners are convinced, the NEP would never have happened. In Minnedosa, Manitoba, where you wouldn't expect much outrage over that long-ago event, I struck a geyser of passion in publisher Robert Mummery.

"I happened to live in Alberta when the NEP came down." He was for ten years a staff photographer with the Edmonton Oilers and other NHL hockey teams. "The day that announcement was made, business died. Alberta shut down on that day. I had friends who were millionaires and were broke the next day. The highway was jammed with oil rigs heading to Texas. The entire oil industry just stopped and said, 'We will not deal under these circumstances.' Thousands of people employed in the oil-service industry and all the peripheral industries were instantly out of work. It was a crushing blow to them. Entire communities emptied overnight. Banks took back hundreds of brand-new houses whose value suddenly dropped below the mortgage rate."

Mummery himself lost a camera store in Edmonton "directly because of the NEP. I don't think Ontario realizes how deeply that knife cut. People out here will never forget. It will last for generations. It was a huge, huge turning point in the relations between East and West. Remember that slogan, 'Let the eastern bastards freeze in the dark'? Don't think we were kidding! We fucking well meant it!"

Peter Lougheed, then premier of Alberta, became the West's champion leading the fight against the NEP.

"It wasn't an East-West issue," Lougheed says now. "It was an Ottawa-Alberta issue. Ottawa wanted to control Alberta. The bureaucrats in Ottawa didn't like the fact that Alberta was becoming a very strong province."

Others don't dispute that, but it does not diminish their rage.

"What was really irritating about it was not the transfer of money – that was bad enough – but that we were fed a line of bullshit that this was in our interest because we were part of Canada," says Barry Cooper, political-science professor at the University of Calgary. "The lie, and the expectation that Westerners were too stupid to figure out that it was a lie, was insulting. That's why Trudeau and Lalonde and those other assholes have never been forgiven – because they were so damned insulting. And that's what irritates people. That's why we use these four-letter words to describe Trudeau or Lalonde. It's not just because they stole a bunch of our assets."

Not surprisingly, the West did not indulge in mass mourning at Trudeau's death in 2000. Along with the NEP they remembered his infamous one-liner "Why should I sell your wheat?" and the time he flashed a one-finger salute to a Western audience.

"Out here his death was a non-event," says Mummery. "Nobody liked him in the first place." Ted Byfield of *The Report* called the "national wallow of grief, mourning and lamentation" over Trudeau's death the "most mystifying Canadian event of the year."

"I grew up believing he was a hero," says Nicky Brink, a young writer in Canmore, Alberta. During her Toronto childhood her parents regarded Trudeau as a visionary and always voted for him. "When he died, I'm out here, still the kid mourning the dead hero, but radio callers and my extended family [her partner's] were saying, 'This is what he did to us!' I wanted to mourn, even in the slightest way, but had to keep it secret."

Holding Ottawa's Feet to a Firewall

In December 2000 Stephen Harper, then president of the National Citizens' Coalition (now leader of the Canadian Alliance), wrote a letter to the *National Post* that caused Eastern politicians to gag on their morning toast.

Not long before, Jean Chrétien was asked why in the 2000 federal election he had won only seventeen seats west of the Manitoba-Ontario border. He indicated in his circumlocutory fashion that Albertans could thank Ottawa for their prosperity and that maybe Albertans, like Quebecers, needed an emissary from Ottawa to correct their bad attitude. Maybe the West needed some "tough love" (of the sort the prime minister had allegedly meted out to bring a recalcitrant Quebec to heel).

Given that tough love is commonly applied to unruly teenagers, Westerners didn't take to it kindly. Also, the West had a nagging suspicion that the Liberals were spinning a new version of the NEP to suck money out of Alberta.

"We must not ignore the implied threat: If Ottawa giveth, then Ottawa can taketh away," Harper wrote. "Albertans should decide that it is time to seek a new relationship with Canada."

His statement became the basis for the Alberta Agenda, a hard-hitting open letter co-signed by Harper, political-science professors Tom Flanagan, Ted Morton, and Rainer Knopff, chairman of the Canadian Taxpayers Federation Andrew Crooks, and former Alberta treasurer Ken Boessenkool (to be dubbed the Gang of Six).

Although addressed to Alberta premier Ralph Klein, it was really aimed at Ottawa. The time has come, said the Gang of Six, for Albertans to take greater charge of their future. "This means resuming control of the powers that we possess under the Constitution of Canada but that we have allowed the federal government to exercise."

They suggested Alberta should:

1. Withdraw from the Canada Pension Plan and create an Alberta plan;
2. Collect its own revenue from personal income tax;
3. Prepare to let its RCMP contract expire in 2012, to be replaced by an Alberta provincial force (as Alberta once had and as Ontario and Quebec already have);
4. Resume provincial responsibility for health-care policy;
5. Force Senate reform back on the national agenda.

"All these steps can be taken using the constitutional powers Alberta possesses," wrote the Gang of Six.

The Gang did not advocate secession. In his *National Post* letter, Harper stated, "We should not mimic Quebec by lunging from rejection into the arms of an argument about separation. . . . Separation will become a real issue the day the federal government decides to make it one."

The passage that set the Eastern media clucking and flapping its tail feathers was buried on page three: "It is imperative to take the initiative, to build firewalls around Alberta, to limit the extent to which an aggressive and hostile federal government can encroach upon legitimate provincial jurisdiction."

Firewalls! It left Eastern journalists and bureaucrats breathless (but not speechless). Those damn Western rednecks were stepping out of line again.

In Calgary I discussed the letter with Barry Cooper.

"I agree with everything in it," he said. "I found it really interesting that to both the prime minister and Stéphane Dion this was evidence of Western separatism. I thought, in no other country in the world would an argument that says that there should be a restoration of constitutional responsibility be seen as a threat to the constitution."

It was further evidence, Cooper said, of what Northrop Frye, scholar and critic, called the "garrison mentality" of the St. Lawrence Valley. "Anything that seems to be changing the status quo is seen as a threat. But there's nothing unconstitutional in that document. Nothing demands greater powers than the provinces are accorded under the Constitution Act of 1867. So why was it attacked rather than embraced? I don't know. Except that they [the East] have this kind of mentality."

"We think the ideas in the Alberta Agenda are of important substance," Tom Flanagan agrees. "We're hoping that over a period of time we can drive it forward."

Did it have any immediate impact? "It probably contributed to the Liberal charm offensive," Flanagan grins. "In the last few weeks [this in 2001] every time you looked around there's another federal minister passing through town." And for a change, he says, they were trying to be less insulting.

Ottawa probably realized, Flanagan says, that there are several ways in which Alberta could, if it chose, upset the federal apple cart. Setting up an Alberta pension plan is probably the biggest one; it would be well within Alberta's capacity to undertake. "If we did this, we would pull out of the Canada Pension Plan the very considerable subsidy that we are paying into it for everybody else."

The Alberta Agenda was tough love, just not the sort Jean Chrétien had in mind.

XV

TOMORROW

Canada needs the West – but does the West need Canada?

JOHN CONWAY,
The West: The History of a Region in Confederation

The Republic of Alberta?

They've been thinking about it for years. Now, they're fed up and ready to move. They're planning to take Alberta out of Confederation (maybe take British Columbia and Yukon with them, Saskatchewan and Manitoba too, if they wish to follow).

They are five (four men, one woman) – academics and top-ranking business people – plus two major investors. They have earmarked five hundred thousand dollars (there is more in the wings, if needed) to study the feasibility of breakaway, to write their own constitution, and to mount a massive information campaign that, they hope, will enlist support throughout Alberta.

By now they may be out of the closet, but as of early 2003 the Alberta Five were choosing to remain incognito. They wanted to get the movement on firm ground before facing federal retaliation. Paranoid? Maybe, but they cite other Western organizations that have openly opposed the federal government and were rewarded with subtle harassment, such as a siege of tax audits. If nothing else, the group's suspicion demonstrates its depth of loathing for the Ottawa political establishment.

Western separation is not a new idea. Ted Byfield launched 2003 with an editorial in *The Report* titled: "Irrefutable Lesson from Kyoto: The West Is Doomed Unless It's Ready to Get Out." The Alberta Independence Party and the Western Canada Concept call for autonomy. The Alberta First Party promotes "a new vision for Alberta" (although "separation" does not loom in its language).

None of the three parties has created great waves. The Alberta Five may have no better luck, but not for lack of planning or commitment. For them, the last straw was the revelation in autumn 2002 of the massive waste in the federal gun-registration program. Add to that the everlasting Western grievances: the unseemly power of the Prime Minister's Office;

disgust at continuous federal waste and scandal; lack of equal Senate representation and of any real Western influence in federal elections; and, in Alberta's case, the bad deal it gets financially from Confederation. Finally, Chrétien's decision to stay out of Iraq; polls showed that Alberta was the province least supportive of the prime minister's position.

The Five hope the Alberta Conservative Party will be their vehicle to power (they have lost patience with Reform/ Alliance). It would depend upon Ralph Klein stepping down from office, perhaps after the 2005 centennial. "Ralph has lost the fire in his belly," one of them told me. They would seek a young successor aged thirty-five to forty-five to head the party and the new republic, if that's what Albertans choose in a referendum. There would be no attempt to negotiate with the federal government; the group feels that day is long past.

Their new republic would levy a flat income tax of 24 per cent and offer a personal deduction of $12,000 per taxpayer (as opposed to $7,634, the deduction in 2002). They would foster a warm relationship with the United States, which they consider Canada's best friend.

Separation or Disengagement?

Could breakaway happen? Polls show that close to 50 per cent of Albertans are unsatisfied with the Canadian constitutional arrangement and would explore separation, but less than 10 per cent are ready to separate.

"Canada needs the West, but does the West need Canada?" wrote the University of Regina's John Conway. On good days – when the East is not shafting the West in some new exquisitely devised manner – most prairie people would say yes. They are optimists, by nature and of necessity.

"Westerners still love the idea of Canada," wrote Don Braid and Sydney Sharpe in *Breakup: Why the West Feels Left Out of*

Canada, "and hope the country can some day work to everyone's full benefit."

"Separatism represents a very minute part of the population," Peter Lougheed told me in autumn 2002. From his forty-seventh-floor office in Calgary with a spectacular view of the Rockies, Lougheed sits high atop Alberta as he has for much of his political life. He is still one of the West's champions, as in the eighties when doing battle with Pierre Trudeau.

"I'm concerned about separation because it is absolutely the wrong way," he went on. "It's not a Western characteristic. When things don't go our way, we try to stick it out and improve it. That's the nature of the West. That word, 'alienation,' has been overused in my opinion and become an excuse. We've had our problems, but realistically they are going to happen in a federation where the votes are with the population centres. In the years I've been involved it's been more severe than other times. It's going to be with us as long as we have a federalist state."

Preston Manning, founder and former leader of Reform, now a visiting lecturer at several universities, shares Lougheed's view.

"I don't think it will ever come to separation," he told me last winter. "The West is now achieving economic and demographic clout to the point where it can't be ignored. It would be a mistake to turn inward upon itself."

Roger Gibbins, president and CEO of the respected Canada West Foundation in Calgary, is also a moderate voice, keenly attuned to the Western mood. "I don't think there's a conscious withdrawal from the country," he says, "but there seems to be a sense of disengagement and it is probably strengthening."

And Regina's John Conway, after posing the provocative question at the top of this chapter, thinks the West will hang in. "It has never accepted its place in Confederation," he says. "But I don't see separation as a likely alternative. You maybe could get 6 or 7 per cent of the people to vote for it if you had a well-run party."

Nevertheless, Professor Faron Ellis of the University of Lethbridge thinks conditions are more auspicious for separatism now than in the 1980s. Then, it was easy to blame everything on the federal Liberals and Trudeau in particular. "Once the Tories get to power, the thinking went, Alberta and the West will get its due. In the 1980s we also still believed that our provincial governments could protect us."

But they couldn't, and even a Tory federal government had limited effect. Clearly the West needed a new federal party. Reform/Alliance came and faltered.

"It is within this vacuum of alternatives that the independence option has a great deal more currency now than it did before," Ellis told me. "However, political organization takes much more than a receptive segment of the electorate. It takes leadership, professional organization, an army of human resources, and money. All of these latter variables have yet to come into play. But if they were to surface, it is my contention that they would be able to provide a powerful historical argument that would be meaningful for a large number of electors, especially the Gen X and echo boomers, who are more continentalist and internationalist than are the older generations."

Calgary businessman Jim Gray, no separatist himself, admits to unease.

"There's a delicate relationship out here," he says. "They [the feds] got away with messing it up in 1980 with the National Energy Program because we were still children. If they mess it up today, even fractionally, I'm fearful for the results. Separation is a very strong word but there would be lines drawn in the sand. I don't know if we can survive all this. I worry that we are not going to."

The Stars and Stripes Whenever?

Even more far-fetched than separation, you might think, would be the West joining the United States. But not to publisher Ted Byfield.

"We're American now in everything except politics," he says. "In twenty-five years we'll be part of the United States. B.C. and Alberta will go first. Then Saskatchewan and Manitoba. Then the Maritime provinces, to New England and maybe Newfoundland to Iceland." In a poll in late 2002, 6 per cent of Albertans favoured joining the United States.

"Certainly in economic terms the West is becoming more and more linked to American markets, although we're still behind Ontario," says Roger Gibbins. "Secondly, the U.S. is a slightly more abstract being in the prairie West because the bulk of our population is not up against the American border. You can go a long way into the States before actually running into anyone. We don't have the same immediate negative images of American society.

"Third, a lot of the fear about integration is linked to fear about the survival of Canadian culture. The cultural engines of Canada tend to be elsewhere. The need to defend the distinctive Canadian culture doesn't strike the same resonance on the prairies.

"So I think Western Canadians look upon the evolving economic relationship with the United States in a somewhat more impartial and neutral way because they don't see the same risk and cultural loss."

"Will the West join the States?" says Barry Cooper. "A lot of that will depend on how stupid Easterners are. I don't fear being part of the United States. A lot will depend not on interests but on how insulting, how injurious to the pride of Westerners, policies are."

A Western Parliament

What about a semi-autonomous West within Canada? Saskatoon writer Wayne Eyre proposes a Western parliament, similar to Scotland's fledgling Holyrood parliament.

Eyre suggests that any party seeking election to the Western parliament could create East-West factions or operate only in the West, as it wished. Contending parties would choose their Western leader, who would become first minister (Western counterpart to the prime minister) of the Western parliament upon the election of his or her party. Members would meet in assembly to legislate made-in-the-West laws to reflect Western sensibilities and priorities.

It's intriguing, but Eyre, who in 2001 launched a Web site dedicated to the proposal, hasn't found strong support. "I've had about ten thousand hits, but I can't honestly say that I've ignited a prairie fire," he reports. "I wish I could say that I'm flooded with feedback but, alas, I cannot."

"It's hard to see at this point much enthusiasm for what would be seen as another level of government," says Roger Gibbins. "I think Eyre put his finger on some real problems, but it's not quite clear to me what issue would draw the three prairie provinces together."

Still, Eyre is by no means alone. In 2001 Saskatoon business leader Hugh Arscott (shortly before his death) sent an angry column to the *StarPhoenix*. "We are being asked to celebrate the creation of Alberta and Saskatchewan in 1905 as a glorious achievement," he wrote. "I say it is an infamous tragedy and a major catastrophe, which should be mourned with sackcloth, ashes and black armbands. The Prairies should never have been divided. It's time to put them back together again."

He urged all Saskatchewan political parties to call for a referendum or at least a plebiscite on the union of Saskatchewan and Alberta. The former, he wrote, "has become the East Germany of the Prairies."

Saving Saskatchewan

Long ago Dr. C.M. "Red" Williams and I were playmates in Shamrock, Saskatchewan. Now he's professor emeritus at the University of Saskatchewan's animal and poultry science department, and president of Agrivision Corporation. I turned to him for some crystal-ball gazing on the most troubled of the three provinces.

"Saskatchewan can't maintain its infrastructure," he said. "We don't have the money. There aren't enough taxpayers. Answer: more people. We have one million. If we could induce up to two million we'd solve our problem."

He's on the right track. Elwin Hermanson, leader of the new Saskatchewan Party, which took twenty-six of the province's fifty-eight seats in the last election and, some think, will topple the NDP next time, says his party could expand the provincial population by a hundred thousand in ten years. Like Williams, Hermanson believes a larger tax base is essential.

Regina economist Graham Parsons opens his intriguing study *This Year Country: Creating Wealth in Saskatchewan* with a statement that will startle most Canadians. "In the first half of the 20th century, Saskatchewan was the third-largest province in confederation by population after Ontario and Quebec," Parsons writes. It held that position until 1941. Now it has slipped to sixth place among provinces. Between 1996 and 2001 it lost nearly twenty-five thousand people. Yet it is loaded with potential, as noted by Parsons and the architects of another Saskatchewan study by Vancouver's Fraser Institute. It is the second-largest petroleum producer in Canada and has major potash and uranium deposits, plus diamonds, copper, gold, coal, sodium sulphite.

"Saskatchewan has all the ingredients to become a growing 'have' province and leader in Canada and the world," Parsons concludes. It need not be forever doomed as "next year country."

The current NDP premier, United Church minister Lorne Calvert, agrees (as one would expect). "I truly believe the great things going on in our province are the best-kept secret in Canada," Calvert told me. "And I truly believe we have a wonderful future."

What went wrong? Answers come from Parsons's study and the Fraser Institute's *Saskatchewan Prosperity: Taking the Next Step*, both published in 2002. Both blame a succession of Saskatchewan governments:

1. The province has the second-worst job-creation record in Canada and the lowest labour-force growth. Many of its economic problems "lie in its near complete lack of business development and investment," wrote the Fraser Institute analysts.

2. One reason for poor business development has been Saskatchewan's heavy reliance on Crown corporations. Their spending, as a percentage of the provincial GDP, far exceeds that of any other province. Their employment, as a percentage of total employment in the province, is also far higher than others.

   "The phone company, liquor stores, even a bus line are owned by government in Saskatchewan," wrote Barry Cooper in a foreword to the Fraser study. "Crown corporations have sopped up a great deal of scarce investment capital in the province that could be employed much more effectively and efficiently in the private sector. . . . Far from being a source of pride, the plethora of Crown corporations is properly Saskatchewan's shame."

3. "The Saskatchewan provincial tax system clearly works against the development of entrepreneurs when compared against other provinces," Parsons reports. Cooper added, "Risk taking, business development, and

innovation, if the tax-system guides your decision, are all unwelcome in Saskatchewan."

4. Consequently, over the last two decades, Saskatchewan's population grew only 4.7 per cent (compared to Manitoba's 10.7 per cent, Alberta's 31.2 per cent, and the nation's 24 per cent).

Parsons cites a personal example. His daughter, a University of Saskatchewan graduate, married a fellow grad in Calgary, where both worked. Most of the wedding guests were also Saskatchewan refugees. "The foregone income from the Saskatchewan graduates attending would have exceeded $200 million," Parsons notes. "At a more fundamental level the loss is larger, since a whole generation of leaders moves away."

Parsons concluded his study with a Utopian vision of Saskatchewan in, say, 2050. Fanciful, perhaps, but optimistic. "Positive attitudes matter," he wrote. "Without vision there is no path."

His vision includes the two million people, half of them in Saskatoon and Regina. Another ten cities of fifty thousand would concentrate on food processing, energy, forest products, mining, and tourism. Saskatchewan would be the "food processing centre for North America and much of Asia. Very few crops or animals would leave the province unprocessed."

Governments would be smaller and more efficient. Technology would expand. (Premier Calvert reminded me that the "biggest science project in Canada in three decades" is the Canadian Light Source synchrotron in Saskatoon. A synchrotron produces light – principally X-rays – with extreme brightness and short wavelengths. With an intense beam about the width of a human hair, scientists can analyze materials with more accuracy and precision than ever before.)

Saskatchewan would become a producer of clean energy, including nuclear and ethanol. The province is rich in raw materials for ethanol: wheat, feed grains, and straw. Manufacturers would fractionate wheat, remove the protein for human and animal food, and use the starch for ethanol.

Aboriginal people would have taxable jobs, own successful businesses, and turn their reserves into "models of community economic and social development." With the demise of the Canadian Football League, the Saskatchewan Roughriders would enter the NFL. In Parsons's 2050 dreamscape they "last year hosted and played in the Super Bowl beating the Miami Dolphins."

All of us who love the province hope most of this comes true (maybe the Super Bowl is a stretch). There could be at least one fly in the ointment. Both Parsons and Williams call for expanded prairie irrigation – but will the water be there?

Dust Bowl

The windblown dried-out prairies of my childhood were Canada's dust bowl. Afterward, we hoped that label was gone forever. Not so. It could get worse.

The warning comes from Dr. David Schindler, world-famous ecologist at the University of Alberta, winner of the Stockholm Water Prize (considered by some to be the Nobel Prize of water science); winner of the million-dollar Gerhard Herzberg Canada Gold Medal for Science and Engineering; member of the prestigious Royal Society – and sometimes a thorn in the side of the Alberta government.

Water levels in many prairie lakes and rivers are down, Schindler says. Wells are running dry or are contaminated by effluent from increased oil drilling and livestock operations. Is "dust bowl" too extravagant a threat?

"I think not," he said. "Our past four years have been exceptionally dry, with 2001 and 2002 the driest two years on record.

Some will argue that we have had such droughts in the past and indeed the evidence shows that this is true."

But this drought was different. "We have several million head of livestock," Schindler explains, "and many demands from agriculture and industry for water that is scarce at the best of times. Also, the temperature now is two to three degrees warmer at most sites than in the Dirty Thirties, probably due to increased greenhouse gases. Even if we get lucky and this drought ends soon, we can expect two to three additional drought cycles by 2100, each with more people, industry and livestock, and warmer temperatures."

Will the Kyoto Accord help the prairies? (Schindler was speaking in late 2002, when the Alberta government was bitterly opposing Kyoto, fearing its effect on the province's energy industries.)

"Kyoto offers no short-term relief because of the long residence time of greenhouse gases in the atmosphere," Schindler says. "But rapid reductions of greenhouse gases are necessary if we are not to have extreme temperature increases in the late twenty-first century." The longer we delay, the heavier the burden we place on our grandchildren. "While I am not a total Kyoto fan, at least it has the promise of making us get serious about greenhouse problems. We have known of their potential for over twenty years, and politicians and industries have done little."

The West should quickly implement wide-ranging water conservation, Schindler urges: less water for irrigation, more efficient irrigation systems, no more draining or filling of the wetlands that recharge our aquifers; recycling "grey" water in urban areas; water-saving methods of livestock culture; better protection of our remaining waters from chemical pollutants.

In "Looking West 2003," 80 per cent or more respondents in all provinces favoured charging industries the full cost of the water they use, to promote conservation. Sixty per cent or more were also open to the same treatment for private citizens.

"The sooner we start, the better off we'll be," Schindler concludes. "Water shortage may be the ultimate demise of the 'Alberta Advantage.'"

The reasonable Roger Gibbins told me, "The issue in my mind is whether the federal government comes up with a implementation strategy [to comply with the Kyoto Accord] that pulls the country together or drives it apart. If the implementation strategy is aimed at producers of oil and gas, Alberta will take a very heavy hit. If the strategy is aimed at all Canadians and that was the price of our commitment to global warming, that's very different." He felt Albertans wouldn't hesitate to be part of a national strategy to combat global warming. But could the feds forge a global-warming strategy that would unify all Canadians? "I don't think it's beyond their capacity to do so, but I'm not sure it's within their political will to do so."

Early in January 2003, the Chrétien government showed where its political will lay by letting the Ontario auto industry off the hook with Kyoto concessions.

"Westerners want only one small thing from Canada – equality," wrote Don Braid and Sydney Sharpe. "They long to be equal partners in a truly united land."

At this writing, no such equality was in sight.

Getting to Know Ourselves

"You might be interested in this," Peter Lougheed says as I am about to leave. "I'm concerned at the way we teach history. One of my current projects, one of my *major* activities, is working with a group called Historica, business people, historians, academics across the country, to get more Canadians interested in their own history.

"Social studies should be dismantled. We should teach history and geography and throw social studies in the ashcan."

"They didn't have social studies when I went to school," I tell him.

"You were lucky," Lougheed grins. Then he adds seriously, "It's *so* important that Canadians get to know each other better."

And that, of course, is really what it is all about. Understanding the West's feelings of distrust. Addressing the East's fundamental ignorance of the West (which is what this book is all about).

Ah, my homeland – will they ever come to know you?

Nearly twenty-five years ago I wrote a magazine article about Alberta and Saskatchewan on the seventy-fifth jubilee. Not much has changed. Then, as now, they were demanding a better deal within Confederation. Then, as now, there was serious talk of separation.

All three provinces, although markedly different as always, are, in varying degrees, running out of patience. Manitoba, calm and comfortable, will never separate but is tired of Ottawa's indifference. Saskatchewan, hurting badly, will survive because it always has. It will not separate either, but deeply resents federal apathy that is eroding the farming heritage so fundamental to Canada's character. Alberta, ebullient, prosperous, in a frequent state of outrage, probably won't leave Confederation, but *could*.

Much depends on whether the Centre of Canada wakes up to realize its prairie people are slipping away, in their hearts if not in fact, and understands that, without those prairie hearts, this country would lose much of its soul.

EPILOGUE

This book is, I now realize, a kind of love story.

Anyone who has lived away from the prairies for forty-five years is surely more tourist than native. Yet I feel I still belong. I left the West for studies and stayed for jobs. A much-loved family holds me in the East, but every trip back is a benediction.

From the vantage point of age I realize that much of what I am, for better or worse, is rooted in the prairie. My love of space. My tendency to self-effacement, a Saskatchewan trait. My aversion to government handouts (still fairly prevalent in the West). My delight in characters, of whom I maintain the most eccentric and endearing are in the West.

There's also my stubbornness – some would say orneriness – coupled with a relentless optimism that refuses to give up on a problem when common sense dictates otherwise: that's pure prairie. So is my distaste for an obdurate Ottawa and an arrogant Central Canada. (When one of my closest friends, Bob Riddell, an Edmonton cameraman with a shelf-full of awards from all over North America, was told by a denizen of Hogtown, "You can't be very good or you'd be here in Toronto," I felt as affronted as Bob did.)

The prairie of my childhood has changed profoundly, but on these recent journeys its fundamentals seemed intact: straightforward tough-spirited people, tremendous pride of place, blessed space, mostly-clean air, the land. It is full of sites and scenes I cherish. The long drive west over the ancient glacial lake bed south of Winnipeg into that endless flatland where my father and all those other immigrants gazed from their chuffing trains with hope and awe and trepidation a century ago. The glittering view of Calgary from the east in early morning when a rising sun lights up the distant backdrop of white-capped Rockies, marking the end of "prairie." The dirt road south of Shamrock where at a certain place a thicket of hand-planted poplar and Manitoba maple springs into sight between small hills – last remnants of the farm where I was born.

Always, when in southern Saskatchewan, I return to that farm. It was sold a half-century ago, its buildings are gone, but its trees remain because a sign at the gate proclaims this a Heritage Homestead. Successive owners, with a nudge from the Saskatchewan government and me, have generously agreed to leave the tangled trees for wildlife. I walk among them – rabbits or a small deer darting away in surprise, crows and kingbirds rising with a hammer of wings – and listen for ghosts: the creak and jingle of horses' harness, the hiss of cows' milk into a tin pail, a woman's near-forgotten voice calling "Supper!"

A lifetime ago, this and all the prairie rippling wide around it was home. It still is.

SOURCES

Books

Adams, Howard. *Prison of Grass: Canada from a Native Point of View.* Saskatoon: Fifth House, 1989.

Allen, Richard (ed.). *A Region of the Mind: Interpreting the Western Canadian Plains.* Regina: Canadian Plains Research Centre, 1973.

Archer, John A. *Saskatchewan: A History.* Saskatoon: Western Producer Prairie Books, 1980.

Bagnell, Kenneth. *The Little Immigrants.* Toronto: Macmillan, 1980.

Barnard, Jayne. *Booze Games: The Bush Leagues 1882-1912.* Moose Jaw: Bootleg Booklets, 1998.

Barnard, Jayne. *Buicks and Boxcars: Prohibition in Saskatchewan 1915-1925.* Moose Jaw: Bootleg Booklets, 1998.

Barr, John, and Owen Anderson. *The Unfinished Revolt: Some Views on Western Independence.* Toronto: McClelland & Stewart, 1971.

Barr, John J. "The Impact of Oil on Alberta: Retrospect and Prospect." From *The Making of the Modern West: Western Canada Since 1945*, A.W. Rasporich (ed.). Calgary: University of Calgary Press, 1984.

Barss, Beulah M. *Come 'n Get It: Cowboys and Chuckwagons.* Calgary: Rocky Mountain Books, 1996.

———. *Come 'n Get It: At the Ranch House.* Calgary: Rocky Mountain Books, 1996.

———. *The Pioneer Cook: A Historical View of Canadian Prairie Food.* Calgary: Detselig Enterprises Limited, 1980.

Barss, Beulah M., and Sheila Kerr. *Canadian Prairie Homesteaders.* Calgary: Barss & Kerr, 1979.

Berton, Pierre. *The Promised Land*. Toronto: McClelland & Stewart, 1984.

Bibby, Reginald W. *Restless Gods: The Renaissance of Religion in Canada*. Toronto: Stoddart, 2002.

Bickersteth, J. Burgon. *The Land of Open Doors*. Toronto: University of Toronto Press, 1976.

Bokamyer, Arlene. *Let's Rodeo*. Moose Jaw: Grand Valley Press, 1994.

Bott, Robert. *Our Petroleum Challenge: Into the 21st Century*. Calgary: Petroleum Communication Foundation, 1993.

———. *Our Petroleum Challenge: Exploring Canada's Oil and Gas Industry*. Calgary: Petroleum Communication Foundation, 1999.

Bouchard, David, and Henry Ripplinger. *If you're not from the prairie. . . .* Vancouver: Raincoast Books, 1993.

Boyens, Ingeborg. *Another Season's Promise: Hope and Despair in Canada's Farm Country*. Toronto: Penguin Books Canada, 2001.

Brack, Joyce, and Robert Collins. *One Thing for Tomorrow: A Woman's Personal Struggle with Multiple Sclerosis*. Saskatoon: Western Producer Prairie Books, 1981.

Braid, Don, and Sydney Sharpe. *Breakup: Why the West Feels Left Out of Canada*. Toronto: Key Porter Books, 1990.

Breen, David H. *The Canadian Prairie West and the Ranching Frontier 1874-1924*. Toronto: University of Toronto Press, 1983.

Brennan, Brian. *Alberta Originals*. Calgary: Fifth House, 2001.

Byfield, Ted (ed.). *Alberta in the 20th Century*, vols. 2, 3, 5, 9. Edmonton: United Western Communications, 1992-2002.

Carpenter, David. *Courting Saskatchewan*. Vancouver: Greystone Books, 1996.

Calderwood, William. *The Rise and Fall of the Ku Klux Klan in Saskatchewan*. Regina: University of Regina, 1971.

Chavich, Cinda. *The Wild West Cookbook*. Toronto: Robert Rose Inc., 1998.

Coates, Ken, and Fred McGuinness. *Manitoba: The Province & The People*. Edmonton: Hurtig, 1987.

Collins, Robert. *The Age of Innocence: 1870-1880*. Toronto: Natural Science of Canada Ltd., 1977.

Conway, J.F. *The West: The History of a Region in Confederation*. Toronto: James Lorimer & Company, 1983, 1994.

Copping, Arthur E. *Canada: The Golden Land*. New York: Hodder & Stoughton, 1911.

Czumer, William A. *Recollections About the Life of the First Ukrainian Settlers in Canada*. Edmonton: Canadian Institute of Ukrainian Studies, 1981.

Davidiuk, Mykola. *My Memoirs as a Pioneer*. William Philipovich (trans.). Edmonton: privately printed, 1982.

Dempsey, Hugh A. *The Golden Age of the Canadian Cowboy*. Calgary: Fifth House, 1995.

Dempsey, Hugh A. (ed.). *The Best from Alberta History*. Saskatoon: Western Producer Prairie Books, 1981.

Denham, Robert D. (ed.). *The Correspondence of Northrop Frye and Helen Kemp 1932-1939*. Toronto: University of Toronto Press, 1996.

Dubeta, Ann and John C. *Harvests of Dreams*. Kelowna, B.C.: Jon-N-Publishers, 1992.

Dunae, Patrick A. *Gentleman Emigrants: From the British Public Schools to the Canadian Frontier*. Vancouver: Douglas & McIntyre, 1981.

Eagle Valley Book Club. *Wagon Trails Plowed Under*. Sundre, Alta.: Eagle Valley Book Club, 1977.

Ebert, Myrtle V. *Wir Sind Frei! We Are Free! A Mennonite Experience: From the Ukraine to Canada*. Scarborough, Ont.: Lochleven Publishers, 1995.

Elton, David. *One Prairie Province: A Question for Canadians; proceedings of a national conference to study the feasibility of one Prairie Province*. Lethbridge: Lethbridge Herald, 1970.

Empress Historical Society. *Echoes of Empress Through 75 Years*. Empress, Alta., 1990.

Fairbairn, Brett. *Prairie Connections & Reflections: The History, Present and Future of Co-operative Education*. Saskatoon: Centre for the Study of

Co-operatives, University of Saskatchewan and Association of Co-operative Education, 1999.

Friesen, Gerald. *The Canadian Prairies: A History*. Toronto: University of Toronto Press, 1984.

———. *River Road: Essays on Manitoba and Prairie History*. Winnipeg: University of Manitoba Press, 1996.

———. *The West: Regional Ambitions, National Debates, Global Age*. Toronto: Penguin-McGill Institute, 1999.

Gagan, David P. (ed.). *Prairie Perspectives: Papers of the Western Studies Conference*. Toronto: Holt, Rinehart and Winston, 1970.

Garreau, Joel. *The Nine Nations of North America*. Boston: Houghton Mifflin, 1981.

Gayton, Don. *The Wheatgrass Mechanism*. Calgary: Fifth House, 1990.

Gray, James H. *Booze*. Toronto: Macmillan, 1972.

———. *Men Against the Desert*. Saskatoon: Western Producer Prairie Books, 1967.

———. *Red Lights on the Prairies*. Toronto: Macmillan, 1971.

———. *The Roar of the Twenties*. Toronto, Macmillan, 1975.

Gruending, Dennis (ed.). *The Middle of Nowhere: Rediscovering Saskatchewan*. Calgary and Saskatoon: Fifth House, 1996.

Hall, D.J. *Clifford Sifton*, vols. 1, 2. Vancouver: University of British Columbia Press, 1981–85.

Heat-Moon, William Least. *PrairyErth*. Boston: Houghton Mifflin Company, 1991.

Hendrickson, James E. (ed.). *Pioneering in Alberta: Maurice Destrub's Story*. Calgary: Historical Society of Alberta, 1981.

Herriot, Trevor. *River in a Dry Land*. Toronto: Stoddart, 2000.

Humeniuk, Peter. *Hardships & Progress of Ukrainian Pioneers*. Winnipeg and Steinbach, Man.: Peter Humeniuk, publisher; Dirken Printers, printer, 1977.

Kates, Jack. *Don't You Know It's 40 Below?* Cypress, Calif.: Seal Press, 2000.

Kerr, Aubrey. *Leduc*. Calgary: S.A. Kerr, 1991.

Kerr, Donald C. (ed.). *Western Canadian Politics: The Radical Tradition*. Edmonton: NeWest Institute for Western Canadian Studies, 1981.

Knight, Leith. *All the moose . . . all the jaw.* Moose Jaw: Moose Jaw 100, 1982.

Kyba, Patrick. "Ballots and Burning Crosses – The Election of 1929." From *Politics in Saskatchewan,* Norman Ward and Duff Spafford (eds.). Don Mills, Ont.: Longmans Canada Limited, 1968.

Lalonde, Meika, and Elton La Clare. *Discover Saskatchewan.* Regina: Canadian Plains Research Centre, 1998.

Lehr, John. *Homesteading on the Prairies: Iwan Mihaychuk.* Toronto: Grolier Limited, 1990.

Liddell, Ken E. *This Is Alberta.* Toronto: Ryerson Press, 1952.

———. *Alberta Revisited.* Toronto: Ryerson Press, 1960.

Lindal, W.J. *The Icelanders in Canada.* Winnipeg: National Publishers, 1967.

Livesay, Dorothy. *The Documentaries.* Toronto: Ryerson Press, 1968.

Lysenko, Vera. *Men in Sheepskin Coats.* Toronto: Ryerson Press, 1947.

Macdonald, Max. *The Dam the Drought Built.* Regina: Canadian Plains Research Center, 1999.

MacGregor, James G. *A History of Alberta.* Edmonton: Hurtig, 1981.

———. *Vilni Zemli (Free Lands).* Toronto: McClelland & Stewart, 1969.

Mavor, James. *My Windows on the Street of the World,* vols. 1, 2. London: J.M. Dent & Sons, 1923.

McCourt, Edward A. *Saskatchewan.* Toronto: Macmillan, 1968.

McKenzie, Glenn A. *More Pothole Philosophy: Cowboy Poetry.* Medicine Hat: self-published, 1996.

McGowan, Don C. *Grassland Settlers.* Regina: Canadian Plains Research Center, 1975

McGuinness, Fred. *Friesens – A Unique Company.* Altona, Man.: Friesens Corporation, 2001.

———. *Letters from Section 17.* Winnipeg: Great Plains Publications, 1999.

Meadows, Anne. *Digging Up Butch and Sundance.* New York: St. Martin's Press, 1994.

Melnyk, George. *Beyond Alienation.* Calgary: Detselig Enterprises, 1993.

———. *Radical Regionalism.* Edmonton: NeWest, 1981.

Momatiuk, Eva, and John Eastcott. *In a Sea of Wind: Images of the Prairies*. Camden East, Ont.: Camden House, 1991.

Morris, Alexander. *The Treaties of Canada with the Indians of Manitoba and the North-West Territories*. Toronto: Bedfords, Clarke & Co., 1880.

Nordegg, Martin. *The Possibilities of Canada Are Truly Great: Memoirs 1906-1924*. Toronto: Macmillan, 1971.

O'Brien, Mike. *Calling the Prairies Home*. Vancouver: Raincoast Books, 1999.

Owram, Doug. *Promise of Eden: The Canadian Expansionist Movement and the Idea of the West 1856-1900*. Toronto: University of Toronto Press, 1980.

———. "Reluctant Hinterland." From *Western Separatism: The Myths, Realities & Dangers*, Larry Pratt and Garth Stevenson (eds.). Edmonton: Hurtig, 1981.

Palmer, Howard (ed.). *The Settlement of the West*. Calgary: University of Calgary, Comprint Publishing, 1977.

Palmer, Howard and Tamara (eds.). *Peoples of Alberta*. Saskatoon: Western Producer Prairie Books, 1985.

Petryshyn, Jaroslav, with L. Dzubak. *Peasants in the Promised Land*. Toronto: James Lorimer & Company, 1985.

Phillips, Alan. *Into the 20th Century 1900-1910*. Toronto: Natural Science of Canada Ltd., 1977.

Phillips, David. *The Climates of Canada*. Ottawa: Ministry of Supply and Services Canada, 1990.

———. *The Day Niagara Falls Ran Dry!* Toronto: Key Porter Books, 1993.

Pickel, Vesta A. *Under the Prairie Sky*. Regina: self-published, 1993.

Piniuta, Harry. *Land of Pain Land of Promise: First Person Accounts by Ukrainian Pioneers 1891-1914*. Saskatoon: Western Producer Prairie Books, 1978.

Potrebenko, Helen. *No Streets of Gold: A Social History of Ukrainians in Alberta*. Vancouver: New Star Books, 1977.

Pratt, Larry, and Garth Stevenson (eds.). *Western Separatism: The Myths, Realities & Dangers*. Edmonton: Hurtig, 1981.

Rees, Ronald. *New and Naked Land: Making the Prairies Home*. Saskatoon: Western Producer Prairie Books, 1988.

Reineberg Holt, Faye. *Settling In: First Homes on the Prairies*. Calgary: Fifth House, 1999.

Ring, Dan, Guy Vanderhaeghe, and George Melnyk. *The Urban Prairie*. Saskatoon: Mendel Gallery and Fifth House Publishers, 1993.

Roberts, Sarah Ellen. *Alberta Homestead: Chronicle of a Pioneer Family*. Austin: University of Texas Press, 1971.

Robertson, Heather. *Salt of the Earth*. Toronto: James Lorimer & Company, 1974.

Romaniuk, Gus. *Taking Root in Canada*. Winnipeg: Columbia Press Limited, 1954.

Ross, Lois L. *Prairie Lives*. Toronto: Between the Lines, 1984.

Schachter, Harvey (ed.). *Memos to the Prime Minister – What Canada Could Be in the 21st Century*. Toronto: John Wiley & Sons, 2001.

Scholz, Al. *Don't Turn Out the Lights: Entrepreneurship in Rural Saskatchewan*. Saskatoon: Saskatchewan Council for Community Development, 2000.

Shamrock History Book Society. *Harvest of Memories*. Shamrock, Sask.: 1990.

Silverman, Eliane Leslau. *The Last Best West: Women on the Alberta Frontier 1880-1930*. Montreal: Eden Press, 1984.

Silversides, Brock V. *Prairie Sentinel*. Calgary: Fifth House, 1997.

Smith, David E. *The Regional Decline of a National Party: Liberals on the Prairies*. Toronto: University of Toronto Press, 1981.

Stanley, George F.G. *The Birth of Western Canada*. Toronto: University of Toronto Press, 1961.

———. "French and English in Western Canada." From *Canadian Dualism: Studies of French-English Relations*, Mason Wade (ed.). Toronto: University of Toronto Press, 1960.

———. "The Western Canadian Mystique." From *Prairie Perspectives*, D.P. Gagan (ed.). Toronto: Holt, Rinehart and Winston, 1970.

Stebner, Eleanor J. *Gem – The Life of Sister Mac, Geraldine MacNamara*. Ottawa: Novalis, Saint Paul University, 2001.

Stegner, Wallace. *Wolf Willow*. New York: Viking, 1962.

Stensrud, Mary McConville. *Quimper S.D. #3254 – A Saskatchewan Potpourri*. Yakima, Wash.: Abbott's Printing, 1996

The Telegram Canada 70 Team. *The Prairie Provinces: Alienation and Anger*. Toronto: McClelland & Stewart, 1969.

Trofimenkoff, S.M. (ed.). *The Twenties in Western Canada*. Ottawa: History Division, National Museum of Man, National Museums of Canada, 1972.

Troper, Harold. *Only Farmers Need Apply*. Toronto: Griffin House, 1972.

van Herk, Aritha. *Mavericks: An Incorrigible History of Alberta*. Toronto: Penguin Viking, 2001.

Tupper, Allan. "Mr. Trudeau & the West." From *Western Separatism: The Myths, Realities & Dangers*, Larry Pratt and Garth Stevenson (eds.). Edmonton: Hurtig, 1981.

Ward, Norman, and Duff Spafford (eds.). *Politics in Saskatchewan*. Don Mills: Longman's Canada, 1968.

Wheaton, Elaine. *But It's a Dry Cold! Weathering the Canadian Prairies*. Calgary: Fifth House, 1998

Wilson, Sheri-D. *Between Lovers*. Vancouver: Arsenal Pulp Press, 2002.

Woodsworth, James S. *Strangers Within Our Gates*. Toronto: Missionary Society of the Methodist Church, 1909.

Studies, Documents

Anielski, Mark, Mary Griffiths, David Pollock, Amy Taylor, Jeff Wilson, and Sara Wilson. *Alberta Sustainability Trends 2000 – The Genuine Progress Indicators Report 1961-1999*. Drayton Valley, Alta.: The Pembina Institute, 2001.

Berdahl, Loleen. "Looking West: A Survey of Western Canadians." Calgary: Canada West Foundation, 2001, 2003.

Bidwell, Julie, and Brenda Pilkey (with photographs by Mark Ballantyne, Paula Reban, and Naomi Friesen). *OffGuard: Farmers and Machinery Injuries*. Saskatoon: Centre for Agricultural Medicine & Kenderdine Art Gallery, 2001.

Canadian Grain Commission. *Grain Elevators in Canada*. Winnipeg: 2002.

Clemens, Jason, Joel Emes, and Nadeem Esmail. *Saskatchewan Prosperity: Taking the Next Step*. Vancouver: The Fraser Institute, 2002.

Gerrard, Dr. Nikki. *What Doesn't Kill You Makes You Stronger: Determinants of Stress Resiliency in Rural People in Saskatchewan*. Unpublished, 2000.

Lawrence, Patricia. *Advantage for Whom? Declining Family Incomes in a Growing Alberta Economy*. Calgary: Parkland Institute, 2001.

Lehr, John C., and Julie Kentner Hidalgo. *The Art of Survival: Murals and Tourism in Boissevain, Manitoba*. Brandon: Brandon Geographical Studies No. 2, 1997.

Martin, David, and Chris Adams. "Canadian Public Opinion Regarding Aboriginal Self-Government." *The American Review of Canadian Studies*, Spring 2000.

Moore, Dr. Robert J., and Wendee Kubik. *Women's Diverse Roles in the Farm Economy and the Consequences for Their Health, Well-Being and Quality of Life*. Regina: Canadian Plains Research Centre, 2001.

Reed, Paul B., and Kevin Selbee (with assistance of Tanya Levesque). *Formal and Informal Volunteering and Giving: Regional and Community Patterns Across Canada*. Ottawa: Statistics Canada and Carleton University, 2000.

Reed, Paul B., and Kevin Selbee. *Volunteering in Canada in the 1990s: Change and Stasis*. Ottawa: Statistics Canada, 2000.

Regina Police Service. *A Perspective on Western Canadian Crime Rates, Incarceration Rates, Aboriginal Issues and Youth at Risk*. 2001.

Roach, Robert, and Loleen Berdahl. *State of the West: Western Canadian Demographic and Economic Trends*. Calgary: The Canada West Foundation, 2001.

Welsted, John, and John Everitt. *The Yorkton Papers: Research by Prairie Geographers*. Brandon: Brandon University, 1997.

ACKNOWLEDGEMENTS

Hundreds of old and new friends (see also pp 340–42) helped with leads, information, and hospitality. I'm particularly indebted to Patricia McLaughlin, Janice Sanderson, Laura Morton, Allison Molgat, and the late Gildas Molgat, all of Winnipeg; Fred McGuinness, Brandon; Maurice and Lil Falloon, Foxwarren; Paul and Julie Bidwell, Wayne and Sigrid Eyre, and Dr. C.M. "Red" Williams, Saskatoon; Max and Hedi Gossweiler, Herbert; Will Chabun, Regina; Larry and Karen Bonesky and Kevin and Donna Beach, Morse; Edwin Henry, Moose Jaw; Sam Hawkins and Paulette Pinsonneault-Hawkins and Paul Boisvert, Gravelbourg; Bonnie and Norris Currie, Swift Current; Loleen Berdahl, Barry Cooper, Evelyn de Mille, Tom Flanagan, James K. Gray, Anne and Terry Lauder, and Mike and Marilyn McGarry, Calgary; Bob and Marilyn Riddell and Cora Taylor, Edmonton.

I'm grateful to Paul Bunner and Ted and Link Byfield, editors of the superb *Alberta in the 20th Century* history series, for permission to use excerpts from material I originally wrote for them: portions of "The Sweet Siren Song of Clifford Sifton," " 'Beeda' Meant Misery," and "No English Need Apply" in Chapter III and "White Faces Preferred" in Chapter IV.

Parts of "The Last Great Train Robbery" in Chapter IV, "Pilgrim" and "And They Need No Candle . . ." from Chapter X, and "From Hobbema to Hollywood" in Chapter XII are excerpted, with permission, from my original articles in *Maclean's* magazine. The epigraph for Chapter VIII, from *The Urban Prairie* by George Melnyk, is used with the publisher's permission. Portions of "Unsinkable Ted,"

Chapter VIII, are adapted with permission from my article in *Reader's Digest*, © 1988 by the Reader's Digest Canada Magazines Limited.

The epigraph for Chapter XIII, from Sheri-D Wilson's "First Words" from *Between Lovers*, Arsenal Pulp Press, is used with the author's permission, as is the epigraph for Chapter II, from Vesta Pickel's "Under the Prairie Sky." Excerpts in Chapter IX from "All the Outs are in FREE!" by Dale Hayes and from "Masculinity" by Lee Bellows are also with author's permission.

Thanks to Carolynne Doucette, friend and technological wizard, who intervened when my computer sulked. Thanks also to my agent, Frances Hanna, for her friendship and wise counsel. Deep gratitude to copy editor Peter Buck, whose keen eye and Western background spared me from many an embarrassing gaffe. Special thanks to my editor, Alex Schultz, whose skilled and sensitive hand, and the editorial equivalent of perfect pitch, lifted the final manuscript to a whole new level.

Above all, I thank my daughters for their love and everlasting support: Lesley for transcribing thousands of words of taped interviews, and for providing cookies, tea, sympathy, and laughter when sorely needed; Catherine, professional editor and my first reader, whose insights, encouragement, and impeccable editorial eye frequently saved me from myself and made this a better book.

MORE PRAIRIE PEOPLE

Along with those listed in Acknowledgements, I thank the following, who gave valuable information and support:

Ian Adnams, Don Adolf, Pam Albert, Jim Alcock, Jeanne Allard, Elaine and Richard Allden, Elsie Anaka, Patricia Andrews, Earl Andrusiak, Mark Anielski, Paul Antrobus, Judy Applegarth, John Archer, Douglas Armstrong, Joe Ashfield;

Don Baron, Beulah "Bunny" Barss, Laurence Beckie, Camille Bell, Lee Bellows, Brian and Beverly Bennett, Janet Blackstock, Michael Blanar, Marie Boivin, Paul Bonneau, Trudy Bosch, John Bourne, Gail and Ted Bowen, Jim Bowman, Steve Bown, Margaret Boyd, Bob and Joyce Brack, Nicky Brink, Ann and Fred Brown, Clellen Bryant, Tracey Bryksa, Nik Burton;

Lorne Calvert, James Carr, Graham Chandler, Susan Chase, David Chatters, Solange Chevrier, Colin Chisholm, Jean Marie Clemenger, Christie Cockwill, Chris Coffey, Blaine Coleman, Sarah Constible, John Conway;

Joan Dawkins, Jason and Lorie Dean, Sister Amanda Desharnais, Charlene Dobmeier, Mike Dolinski, Helga Downey;

Reverend Neil Earle, Donna Easto, Dr. Faron Ellis, Herb Emery, Roger Epp, Marvin and Marilyn Evans, Ross Evans;

Brad Faraquhar, Nona and Bill Finnbogason, Lillian and Cyril Flint, Reg Forbes, Louis Fournier, Margaret Fraser, David Freeman, David Friesen;

Rita Galloway, Reverend Betty Garrett, Don Gayton, Eric Geddes, Pauline Gedge, Nikki Gerrard, Dr. Roger Gibbins, Janine

Gibson, Dr. James Gomes, Linda Goodman, Katherine Govier, Kelly Green, Malcolm Green, Dennis Gruending, Lorrie Guillame;

Jocelyn Hainsworth, Bep Hamer, Frank Hamilton, Mickey and Jim Hamilton, Karen Hanley, Jim and Olive Hannah, Bill Harrison, Lynne Hawrelak, Darlene Hay, Dale "Doc" Hayes, Ralph Hedlin, Wayne Helgason, Peter and Jean Hendry, Elwin Hermanson, Peter Herrndorf, Jacob Hofer, Stan Hoffman, Rose and Art Hopfner, Nathan Hudye;

Cary Isaak;

Police Chief Cal Johnston, Robert Jolly, Warren and Paula Jolly, Wes Jones, Mary and Bob Juby;

Connie Kaldor, Natalie Kallio, Mike and Violet Kasper, Karen Kiddey, Candis Kirkpatrick, Gary Kowalchuk, Mary Krieger, Helen and Larry Kristjanson, Wendee Kubik, Allison Kydd, Joyce Kydd;

Elmer Laird, Jean Lazar, Gerald Legault, Jock Lehr, Joanne Lemke, Maria and Henri Lepage, Dan Letourneau, the Honourable Peter Liba, Jeannine Locke, Peter Lougheed;

Michelle Mabon, Alex MacDonald, Max Macdonald, Joe Madero, Violet Mailman, Mel Manishen, Preston Manning, David Martin, Dawn Martin, Conni Massing, Glenn McKenzie, Joe McLaughlin, Rob McLaughlin, Sgt. Iain McLean, Ed McNally, Christie McNeill, Ninian Mellamphy, George Melnyk, Ken Mitchell, Sylvia Mitchell, Anne Molgat, Lee Morrison, Robert Mummery, Sharon Munger-Osborne, Carol Munro, Daniel Murphy, Robert Murray, Judge Rodney Mykle;

David Newman, Art Newton, Tim Novak;

Sean O'Hara, Kathy Odegard, Victor Olivier, Carol Osborne, Michael Owen;

Graham Parsons, Deb Pedlar, Robert Peterson, Miles Phillips, Claude Piché, Patricia Piché, Vesta Pickel, Mark Pickup, Walter Pinsonneault, Bella Pomer, Marilyn Pomeroy;

Fred Quigley;

Diane Redsky, Jean Reinhardt, Shahna Rice, George Richardson, Brenda Riddell, Ken Romaniuk, Liliana Romanowski, Carol Ross, Reverend Dwight Rutherford;

Sister Lesley Sacouman, Michelle Sauvé, Wilma Schafer, Gina Schall, Inger Schnerch, Dr. David Schindler, Patti Scott, Fraser Seely, Wayne Shaw, Maggie Siggins, Stuart Slayen, Dr. Josephine Smart, Tony Smith, Larry and Melinda Stewart, Mike Stork, Murray Straker, Catherine Strempler, Jennifer Strilchuk, Joselle Stringer, Louis Stringer, Monique Sundlie, Jamie and Laurie Syer;

Mike Tatarynovich, Messeret Tessera, Verona Thibault, Nik Thomson, Ted Turner;

Barbara Vennard, Alesa Verrault, Michel Vézina;

Cheryl Wallach, Reverend Kenn Ward, Mary Weimer, Joyce Wells, Florence and Jack Widdicombe, George Willard, Shirley Willner, Wayne and Anne Willner, Stacy Wilson, Neil Wood;

Lisa Young;

Larry Zolf.

INDEX